Janusz Piekalkiewicz **ROMMEL**
AND THE SECRET WAR IN NORTH AFRICA • 1941-1943

Janusz Piekalkiewicz
ROMMEL

AND THE SECRET WAR
IN NORTH AFRICA • 1941-1943
Secret Intelligence in the North African Campaign

SCHIFFER MILITARY HISTORY
West Chester, PA

Translated from the German by Edward Force.

Copyright © 1992 by Schiffer Publishing Ltd.
Library of Congress Catalog Number: 91-62740.

Printed in the United States of America.
ISBN: 0-88740-340-9

This title was originally published under the title,
Rommel und die Geheimdienste in Nordafrika 1941-1943,
by F.A. Herbig Verlagsbuchhandlung, Munich.

We are interested in hearing from authors with book ideas on related topics. We are also looking for good photographs in the military history area. We will copy your photos and credit you should your materials be used in a future Schiffer project.

Published by Schiffer Publishing, Ltd.
1469 Morstein Road
West Chester, Pennsylvania 19380
Please write for a free catalog.
This book may be purchased from the publisher.
Please include $2.00 postage.
Try your bookstore first.

Contents

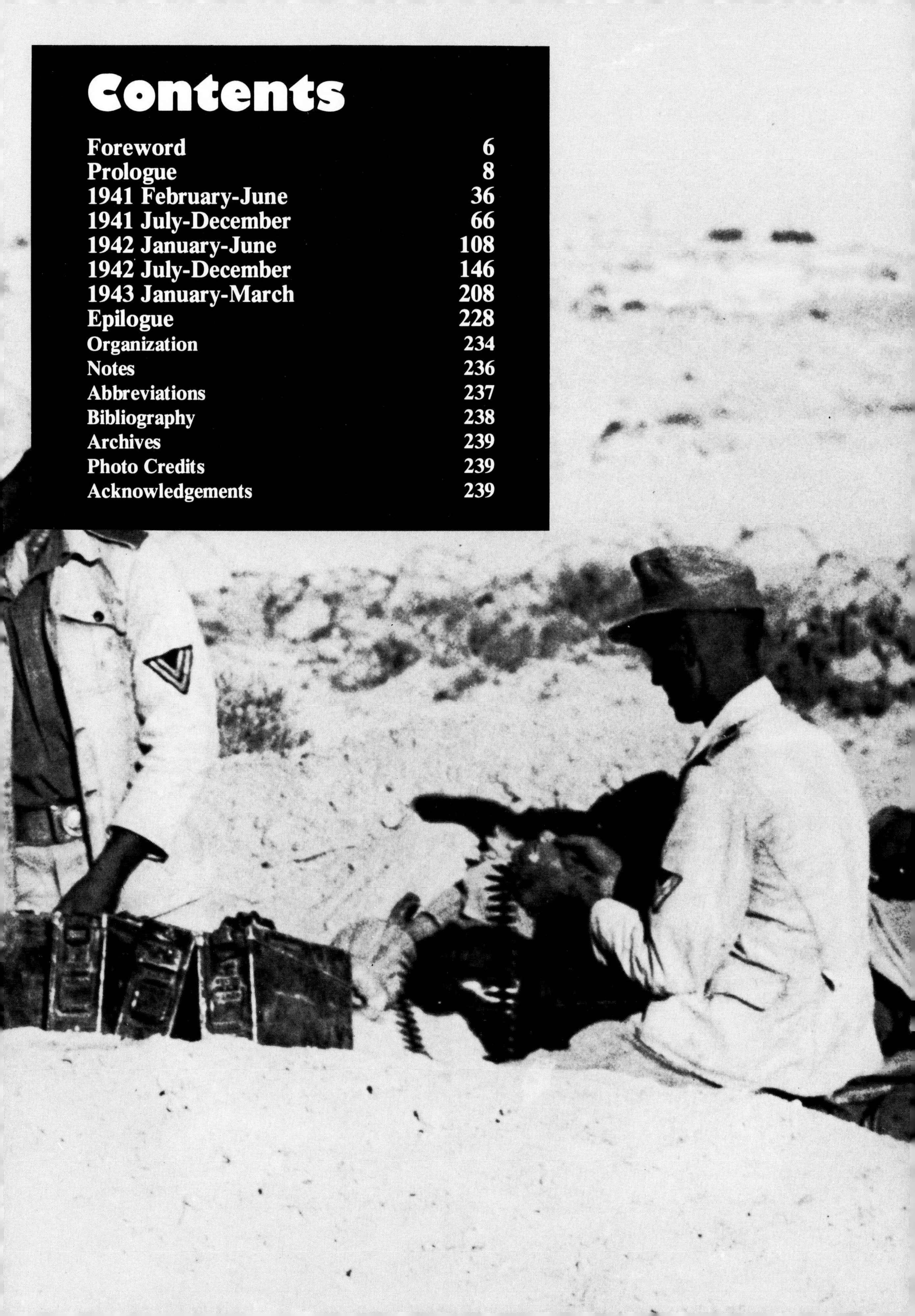

Foreword

"Gentlemen, using the radio is betraying your country!", the chief of the German intelligence, *General der Nachrichtentruppe* (General of the Intelligence Troops) Fellgiebel, warned his colleagues at the beginning of the war.

This oversimplified formula was meant as a warning not to use this convenient means of long-range communication too carelessly. But not only *General* Fellgiebel, but also the entire German leadership was under an illusion: They were firmly convinced that decoding the message transmitted by the "Enigma" code machine was impossible.

In theory, their assurance was justified; but in practice the situation was completely different. As of the spring of 1940, the British Secret Service was reading the German code messages. This most clandestine of all secret operations of World War II was designated "Ultra Secret", meaning the highest level of secrecy. "Ultra" became the pivotal element of the Western Allies' intelligence and formed the basis of numerous tactical and operational decisions.

Its value was increased by the ability of the individual commanders to recognize the significance of the decoded messages and put this advantage to use in the course of the combat. Many of them did not think much of the "Ultra" reports: They seemed to be a too mysterious source and had no parallel with their long years of previous experience.

The most important significance of the "Ultra" messages was their often-decisive role in forming a precise picture of the enemy's position, composed of countless brief individual reports. "Ultra" information offered the Western Allies both unexpected possibilities of seeing through the German deceptive maneuvers and, in many cases, also confirming the validity of information from other sources.

"Ultra" offered not only background material important to the Western Allies' strategic planning, but even more, the knowledge thus gained not only indicated alternatives but also showed their advantages and disadvantages.

In spite of everything, the "Ultra" reports have their limits: the time needed to decode them. From the moment when an enemy radio message was intercepted by Allied surveillance posts to the usability of the decoded, translated and analyzed materials at the appropriate operational command posts took one to two days as a rule, and at first even several weeks. Thus the "Ultra" information often had more to do with confirming the existing picture of the enemy's position than with completely vital new information.

Even when "Ultra" began to provide an unmistakably clear picture of the enemy, the "Intelligence" picture was presented only in conjunction with additional information from other sources. These included primarily the results of air reconnaissance as well as of radio traffic in the lower tactical area, which was decoded by simpler means.

Breaking and interpreting the material to utilize movement analysis and orientational values under field conditions was particularly beneficial in North Africa. The advantage: Radio reconnaissance in the lower tactical area provided "Intelligence" news on enemy movements and their tactical combat positions with practically no delay.

Often the information from the "lower" radio reconnaissance, in combination with air and ground reconnaissance and information from prisoners, provided an extremely valuable basis for the identification of enemy units and made the terse "Ultra" broadcasts comprehensible on many occasions.

At the very beginning of the campaign in North Africa in autumn of 1940, Churchill knew, thanks to "Ultra", that Hitler had broken off Operation "Sealion", the preparations for a landing in England. This news allowed him to throw parts of the British forces spared by the fall of France into the balance in North Africa at the right moment. And since Rommel set foot in Africa, "Ultra" followed him like a shadow.

Even so, Rommel's first two offensives were a surprise for Churchill. The cause of this, though, was not the questionable reliability of "Ultra" information, but the stubbornness of the "Desert Fox", who even ignored Hitler's orders. On the other hand, the British commanders simply did not have the ways and means to evaluate properly the knowledge that "Ultra" gave them.

Then too, Rommel was also a master of making use of intercepted enemy radio messages, as the British became aware of only too late and after great sacrifices.

The fact that many of Rommel's operations, which went down in military history as strokes of genius, were only possible thanks to the information gained by his surveillance company, was learned by the British leadership only on 10 June 1942; during previous night, parts of the Australian 9th Division had taken the German Intelligence — Long-Range Reconnaissance Company 621 (*Hauptmann* Seebohm) in a bold move at Tel el Eisa.

It had been Rommel's ear in the enemy's camp. Its elimination can be seen as the actual turning point of the North African campaign. For there at Tel el Eisa the battle of El Alamein had already been decided.

Seen dispassionately, "Ultra" was the superior force that defeated Rommel, and no one understood better than Montgomery how to incorporate this information into his planning. The battles of Alam el Halfa, El Alamein and Medine prove this.

But there was one thing that "Ultra" certainly was not: the sole deciding factor in the North African campaign.

Janusz Piekalkiewicz

Prologue

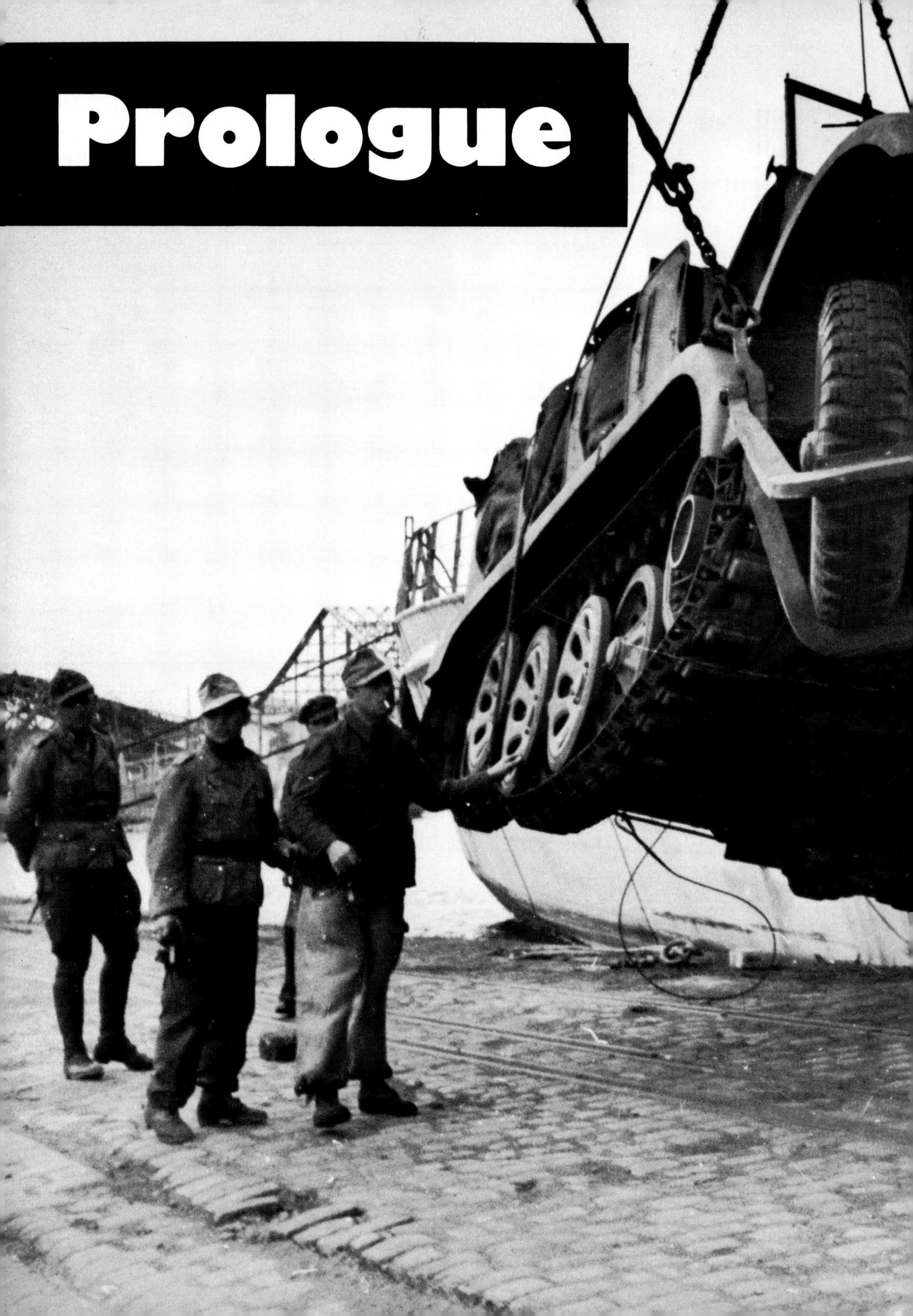

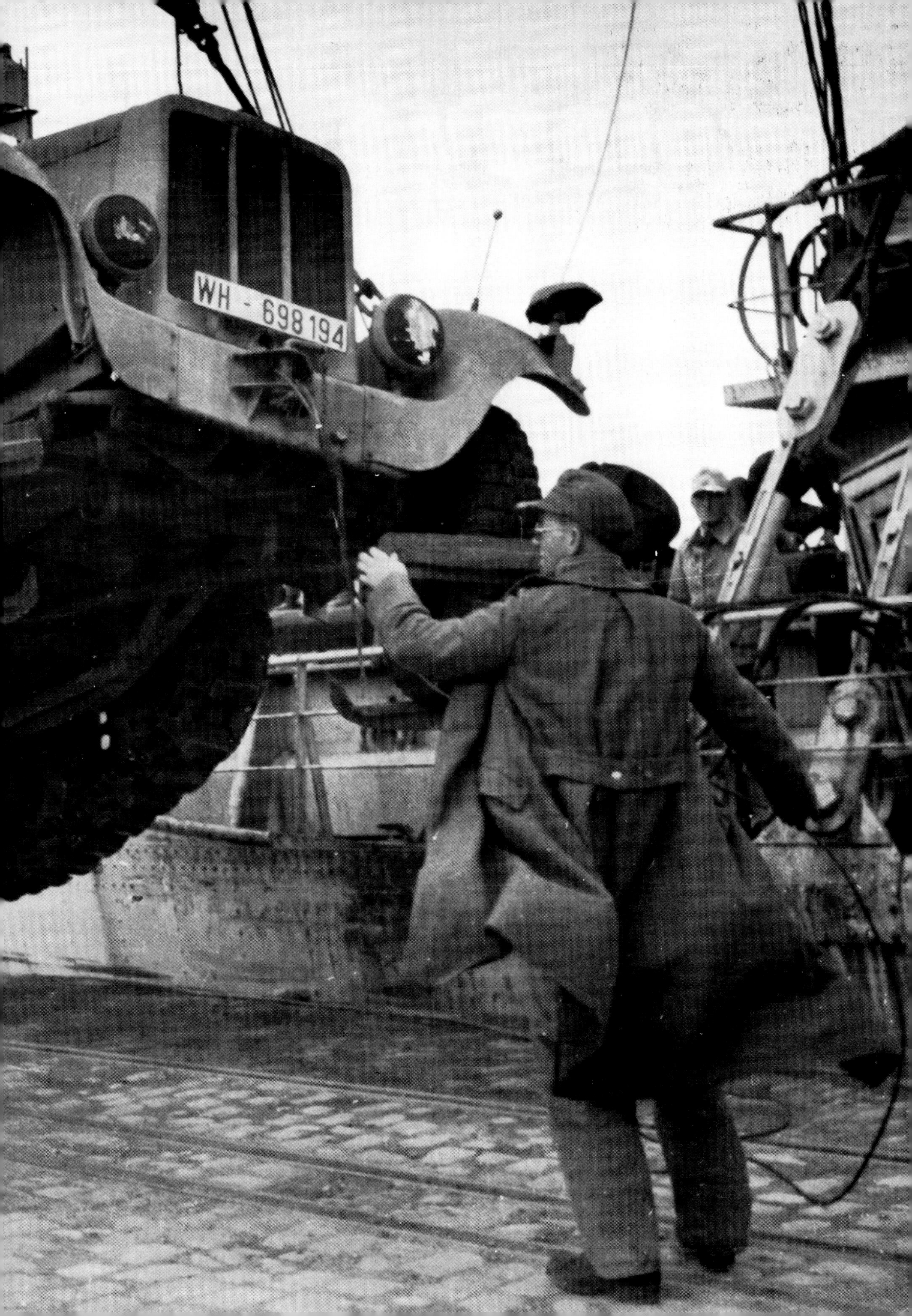
WH - 698194

24 August 1941. It was exactly 4:00 A.M. when the howling of sirens interrupted the nightly stillness in the North African city of Bardia. Almost immediately the Italian Flak guns opened fire, and in the heavy thunder of the countless enemy planes that circled the harbor area in the dark skies, the first bombs were heard to explode. The whole area was flooded with bright light from the flares that were slowly falling to the ground.

For weeks the officers of *Panzergruppe Afrika* (*Generalleutnant* Rommel) had observed the same game: With clockwork precision, English air raids were being made on Bardia, this harbor so important for supplying the Axis troops fighting in Africa, and always just when the Italian navy had announced, by radio, the arrival of a supply ship or U-boat with fuel and ammunition on board. The freighter "Bellona", with important supplies aboard, was also announced, to arrive to 3:00 A.M.

Among those closest to Rommel it was suspected that there was a traitor at the Supermarina in Rome, the supreme staff of the Italian navy. More than once the Germans had found out during a battle that the enemy was astoundingly well informed about the intentions and personnel of the *Afrika-Korps*. Captured documents and information from prisoners attested to this clearly, and even the British had an explanation ready: It was the words of a captured Italian officer to which they owed their knowledge of the enemy.

In reality, it was quite different and much more fantastic than Rommel or anyone from his staff ever could have imagined.

In 1919, a few months after the end of World War I, the Hollander Hugo Alexander Koch of Delft applied for a patent for the construction of a "secret writing machine" (Patent No.10700). Unfortunately, his code machine turned out to be barely functional. The engineer Dr. Alexander Scherbius of Berlin bought Koch's patent in 1923 and, in the same year, developed from it his first really usable code machine, which he appropriately named "Enigma" (Greek for "riddle").

In June 1923, the "Chiffriermaschinen AG" founded by Scherbius began to produce the Enigma at Steglitzer Strasse 2, Berlin W 35. This device, resembling a ponderous electric typewriter at first glance, was somewhat complicated for a layman: The keyboard transmitted electric impulses which were released by impact to the wired rollers. Twenty-six electric contacts, located on the inner surface of each code roller, represented the letters of the alphabet.

Besides the keyboard, each of the contacts was also connected with a contact in the other code roller. The linking cable ran to an indicator light. It made the coded letters that the electromagnetic system created light up. The first enigma model,

". . . particularly striking": from Panzergruppe Afrika's files, August 1941.

equipped with three rollers and battery-powered, could already create some 22 million code combinations.

The idea of an unauthorized person decoding the text encoded by the Enigma seemed absurd. Dr Scherbius said: "If one single man worked non-stop day and night and tried a different key to the code every minute, he would need 42,000 years to find all the possible combinations."

The Enigma Model A and B made their premiere appearance in Bern in 1923, then appeared at the Leipzig Fair and at the World Postal Congress in Stockholm in August 1924. The German postal system cabled a code greeting to the congress, and Enigma decoded it before a gathering of participants. It was portrayed as a dependable device for the transmission of business information and telegrams. It was also expensive: The first model cost 350 Reichsmark.

The greatest interest was not shown by the business world, though, but by the military, more precisely the code department of the Reichswehr. This 100,000-man army which Germany was allowed under the terms of the Treaty of Versailles, with *Generaloberst* von Seeckt at its head, had plenty to hide in its efforts to increase its potential for war secretly, and put a particularly high value on the security of its long-range communication connections. In addition, the chief of the "Chi" (Chiffre = code) unit, *Oberst* Fellgiebel, later (in World War II) became — after being promoted to General of Intelligence Troops — chief of German military intelligence.

On 9 February 1926 the Reich Navy introduced a considerably smaller version of "Enigma C", about the size of a portable typewriter, as electric encoder "C" for its highest-ranking radio traffic, and this "Funkschlüssel C" remained in use until

Enigma Model B (with writing apparatus)
2. *Carriage attaching screw*
4. *Line shift bar*
5. *Paper release*
6. *Roller release*
7. *Margin set*
8. *Controls for "coding", "decoding", and "clear text"*
9. *Electric plug*
10. *Carriage release screw*
11. *Carriage removal handles*
14. *Roller removal lever*
16. *Keyboard*
17. *Space bar*
19. *SS key*
20. *U.S. key*
22. *Counter*
23. *Counter knob*
26. *Crank*
35. *Number shift key*
36. *Letter shift key*

October 1934. It consisted of three code rollers which were chosen from a supply of five rollers, plus the usual keyboard with 26 letters and the field of indicator lights above them.

On 15 July 1928, the Reich Army produced an improved version, the Enigma G, which remained in use until 1932. It was also supposed to be more dependable: In addition to the three code rollers there was also a field of 26 two-pronged contacts installed, linked in pairs by small cables with plugs. This provided an additional overcoding of the text already encoded by the rollers. To avoid confusion, the Umlaut was omitted.

The "Schlüsselmaschine AG" also tried to sell its business version of the Enigma in other countries. Single examples were exported to Great Britain, the USA, Japan, Switzerland, Sweden and Poland or registered for patents.

After the death of Dr. Scherbius, who had gained no commercial success, two Berlin firms, Konski & Kröger and Heimsoeth & Rinke, obtained his patent rights.

Geheim!

H.Dv.g.7

Die Heeresschlüssel

Vom 27. 6. 1935

Berlin 1935

Gedruckt in der Reichsdruckerei

Cover of secret Army instructions for use of Enigma I

H.Dv.g. 16   Nr. 2215

Geheim!

Schlüsselanleitung
für das Heftschlüsselverfahren

vom 1. 11. 1937

Berlin 1937

Gedruckt in der Reichsdruckerei

Cover of secret Army instructions for German Wehrmacht radio stations.

When Hitler came to power in 1933, a new strategy of warfare, the "Blitzkrieg" (lightning war), was developed. Because the successful mass action of armored units supported by air forces could be carried out only with reliable radio communications, the Enigma finally came into its own.

On 27 July 1935, Enigma I was introduced as the Wehrmacht code machine. Since then, the secret intelligence broadcasts between the army, navy and air force and other agencies were transmitted by it. Enigma I had 26 letters, one panel of plugs and one code roller part for five changeable rollers. The last two rollers, IV and V, were still banned for the time being. On the other hand, the "Funkschlüssel M", a variation of Enigma I introduced by the navy a year before, was already using all five rollers.

Thus the Enigma code machine handled by far the greatest part of operative German radio communications, above the divisional level in the Army, the squadron level in the Luftwaffe and the ship and U-boat level in the Navy. It was also used by the SS and other Party and government offices, such as the Reich railroads. The Enigma was also put to work immediately in the tactical area of the Army, as well as in aircraft radio communications by the Luftwaffe, and by the Navy primarily as a reserve process and a method of communication between rescue ships and merchant vessels.

The Enigma I, with which the Army and the Luftwaffe encoded and decoded their radio messages, weighed 12 kilos and was built into a portable wooden box. It was powered by electricity of only 4.5 volts. The Navy's radio code machine M was even more complicated than the devices of the other two Wehrmacht arms: It had 336 roller bearings as compared to "only" 120 for the Enigma I, and could not be decoded by it.

The code machine required a two-man crew: While the radioman typed the text that was to be sent onto the Enigma, a letter lit up on the indicator panel over the keyboard, and the second man noted them down. Thus the text that the radioman could finally send by Morse code was composed of a meaningless mass of letters.

As of 1938, the "inner" and "outer settings" of Enigma I were changed every 24 hours (code of the day), while during World War II they were changed every eight hours in especially highly frequented code areas. At first the "inner setting" of radio code machines C and M were changed once a week at irregular intervals.

From the outbreak of the war to about the end of 1941, the "inner setting" was changed every 48 hours. As of 1942 the "inner" and "outer settings" were changed every 24 hours, and every radio post received only the key to be used on that one day. An exception was made for U-boats and ships that were supplied with daily codes on water-soluble paper for the duration of their action.

Before a radioman began encoding, he always had to make sure the correct daily code was installed. Then he checked four different settings on the device, two of which formed the "outer" and the other two the "inner setting."

The "outer setting" was changed daily. This included the setting of letters in three hatch windows, which fixed a new "basic setting" of the three to five code rollers each time. Only then were the electric lines plugged in according to a prescribed pattern.

To set the "inner setting", the device had to be opened: The radioman took the available code rollers (three to five) and put them into the machine's roller housing in a precribed order. He then set the inner letter ring on each of the inserted code rollers (ring setting).

To be doubly safe, every radio message was enriched with constantly changing code words, thus overcoded with a word code. The receiver first had to decode this word code, and could only then begin the decoding of the radio message. In this process, everything was the reverse of the encoding. The encoded text was typed in by the radioman, and the correct letter that lit up was noted down by the second man sitting beside him. The possibility of simultaneous encoding and decoding was made possible by the reverse roller, which made the electric power reverse and run back after it had run through the other rollers. Whatever word code was chosen for the code rollers of the Enigma served only to increase secrecy. No enemy intelligence service could find out what three letters any given radioman would choose. He, on the other hand, had strict orders never to use the same three letters a second time, and the coded text generally was not allowed to go beyond eighty groups of five.

Only wireless broadcasts were encoded by the Enigma. During the war, only a fragment of any transmitted message was accessible to enemy surveillance, and wire connections were used — on account of the constant danger inherent in radio communications — as much as possible: The messages were transmitted by wire, via tele-type or telephone.

Only in exceptional cases was radio reconnaissance the only means used by the intelligance services. It was almost always read and evaluated only in connection with the information gained from other sources.

The commercial Enigma and the versions used by the Wehrmacht shared several design features at first glance, but their chief difference invloved the plug connections: Only the Wehrmacht models, as opposed to the commercial Enigma, had these plug connections, and the inner connections of the code rollers were also different.

The German leadership was firmly convinced that the Enigma was guaranteed to be absolutely foolproof in operational and tactical communications alike. This meant that even if the enemy captured an Enigma machine in a war, a possible decoding would cost so much time that any message would be decoded too late to be of any use.

The use of the Enigma was an extremely complicated procedure. A radioman who received a message encoded by Enigma needed a machine of the exact same type with identically wired rollers to decode it. The radioman also had to know in what order and what positions which rollers had been inserted. Both the sender and the receiver had to have a list of the code settings available.

If an unauthorized person were to try to decode a message encoded by the Enigma by knowing the code settings, it would take him a great deal of time: Even today, with the help of computers, it could take up to fifty years before he had tried all the rollers and settings.

So one can well imagine that even the eventuality of one or more Enigma machines being captured — of the 200,000 that were used in the war — could not shake the boundless confidence that the German leadership placed in the safety of their numerous secret codes.

Around 1927, Polish listening posts on their western border, whether at Posen, Stargard or Krzeslawice near Krakow, frequently reported hearing puzzling radio messages. The Polish intelligence service then ordered the code and cypher bureau BS-4 (Biuro Szyfrow) of the "German Department" of their military secret service to investigate. And their renowned cryptologists, to whom Poland essentially owed the defeat of the Red Army in the Warsaw area in 1920, slowly began to develop an interest in their western neighbors' mysterious radio messages.

The cryptologists of BS-4 were able to break the code of the German Reichswehr, which used a manual encoding process, but when the code was changed in 1928, they were lost. They suspected, and quite correctly, that the new code operated mechanically. To be sure, they possessed the text of Dr. Scherbius' patent application and even a normally obtained example of the commercial Enigma, but this was scarcely any help in deciphering military radio messages.

In the same year, a course for cryptologists was offered in collaboration with the University of Posen, with support from the BS-4. Some twenty students, who were already studying mathematics there, took part in this secret special training. Three of them soon stood out: Marian Rejewski, Jerzy Rózycki and Henryk Zygalski. They were not only remarkably talented mathematicians,

but also spoke fluent Germans, as did numerous Poles in the Posen area. Rejewski was even sent to the University of Göttingen for further study, paid for by the Polish secret service.

Then chance came to the assistance of the BS-4. Early in January 1929 — according to unconfirmed reports — the Polish secret service had possession of a military Enigma for a good 48 hours: An Enigma code machine, sent by the Foreign Office in Berlin to the German embassy in Warsaw and "carefully packed in straw" — as Colonel Lisicki, the Polish radio expert and intelligence officer, now living in Britain, recalls — was taken from the parcel section of the Warsaw railway customs office by BS-4 experts one Friday and kept over the weekend. After thorough study, it was returned to the customs authorities before dawn on Monday.

Still it was hardly possible that the Foreign Office would have disobeyed all security regulations and sent such an extremely secret device to its embassy in Warsaw by ordinary railway freight, especially as German diplomatic couriers traveled between Berlin and Warsaw several times a week.

According to Colonel Lisicki, the examination of this Enigma gave BS-4 information on the switch connections of the three code rollers as well as the additional plug connections for double encoding. As of 1 September 1932 the three colleagues worked as a team in BS-4 of the "German Department" of the cryptology section of the Polish general staff. According to Polish reports, they succeeded by the end of December 1932 — in the remarkably short time of less than three months — in breaking the Enigma code.

At the same time, in October 1932, an officer of the code section of the German Reichswehr, by the name of Hans-Thilo Schmidt, made efforts to make contact with Capitaine Gustave Bertrand, the chief of the code office of the Service de Renseignement, the secret service of the French general staff.

Under the code name of "Asche" (Ash), H.T. Schmidt provided the French with strictly confidential documents from the higher staffs of the Reichswehr, including code settings for a certain period of time and copies of radio logs consisting of clear texts and coded texts side by side. Over a period of time, a total of 303 important documents changed hands.

In December 1932, Capitaine Bertrand made personal contact with the BS-4. In addition to exchanging intercepted radio messages and other intelligence material, Bertrand offered the Polish

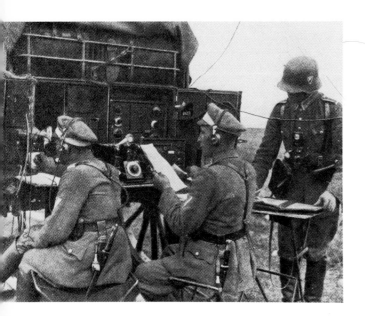

A mobile radio transmitter used by the German Reichswehr in the late 1920s.

Oberst Fellgiebel (center) and the chief ideologist of the Nazi Party, Alfred Rosenberg (second from left), during the Reich Postal Minister's speech at the opening of radio-telephone connections between Berlin and Tokyo, 12 March 1935.

military secret service something of incalculable value: a complete list of all Enigma code settings for two months in the autumn 1932, plus secret German army instructions for operating the code machine and much more. This made it easier for the three young Polish cryptologists to solve the extremely complicated series of equations.

In 1934, BS-4 contracted with the communications firm of AVA Wytwornia Teletechniczna, located at ul. Stepinska 25 in Warsaw, to build, in complete secrecy, a copy of the reconstructed military Enigma. At first the devices were quite primitive, but as of 1938 they differed from the original Enigma only in certain arrangements of parts. By September 1939, fifteen such machines had been built by AVA.

In January 1935 the Poles were able to break the code of the German Navy's Code Machine C. To determine the daily settings of the code machine quickly, they originally used a chart on which the numbers and cycle lengths of all possible roller

positions were shown. Because this procedure was still much too time-consuming for manual operation, the Polish mathematicians developed a series of cryptological assistance devices.

One of these devices, the so-called "cyclometer", consisted of two sets of Enigma rollers linked by switchable inner linkages, but without a keyboard. When the periods that corresponded to each other were determined, lights lit up, giving the basic setting of the daily code.

But in October 1936 the Germans began to make changes: For example, the double-coding switchboard was enlarged considerably, and as of 1937 the wiring of the code rollers was changed. The polish cryptologists worked out a method of determining the code on the basis of the first words of the text, and as of January 1938 they were able — according to their own statements — to decode about 75% of the intercepted German code messages with the "cyclometer" in a test. But the time needed for any possible operational use of the decoded messages was still too great.

On 15 September 1938, at the peak of the Munich crisis, the German Army and Luftwaffe unexpectedly introduced a new code system: the fourth and fifth code rollers for the code ranges of these two service arms, banned until then, were released. From now on the three usable Enigma code rollers could be chosen out of five available ones. This greatly increased the security of the Enigma code. This fact was interpreted in both Paris and Warsaw as a step toward mobilization.

To decipher the encoded Enigma messages, Rejewski designed an electromagnetic machine known as "Bomba." In November 1938 the first "Bomba" was finished. The code rollers in it ran through all the possible combinations for the three rollers until the correct setting was found with which a message could be decoded on the Polish copies of the Enigma. Since the Enigma, using three rollers, could have six possible roller positions, six "Bombas" were needed. With them it was possible to determine the roller positions and ring settings of the day in less than two hours, utilizing three pairs of message codes including one-letter cycles. With the introduction of rollers 4 and 5, the need for "Bombas" rose from six to sixty, which also required a far greater number of specially trained personnel to operate them. But BS-4 had neither the time nor the means to carry this out.

On the initiative of the energetic Capitaine Bertrand, a top-secret conference of the leading French, Polish and British cryptologists and representatives of their secret services was held in Paris on 7-9 January 1939. From Great Britain there came, among others, Commander Denniston, leader of the Government Code and Cipher School, from Poland Colonels Langer and Ciezki, while France was represented by Capitaine Bertrand and a cryptology expert. Colonel Mayer, chief of the Polish intelligence service, said: "No positive result was achieved at this conference. Langer and Ciezki got the impression that their partners, though frank and honest, knew practically nothing about the enigma."

Toward the end of 1938 the Polish cryptologists were able to come one step further in deciphering the Enigma code: Zygalski developed a system with 26 perforated cards — one for each of Enigma's 26 letters — with some 1000 holes, that could be placed on top of each other. When they were arranged correctly, the one-letter cycles could be determined, which in turn indicated the right roller positions and ring settings. This in turn indirectly made possible the determination of the Enigma's plug linkages. In theory, this process offered a solution, but it was too laborious and time-consuming to allow any operational use of the decoding.

Today it can no longer be determined exactly from what point in time and to what extent the Polish cryptologists could really read the Enigma code, and which solutions were used.

On 1 July 1939 the Germans again changed the settings of Enigma. And while the political situation grew more ominous, Colonel Mayer decided to turn to Poland's allies, France and Britain. At his and Colonel Langer's invitation, a meeting was held at the "Wicher", Poland's secret decoding center, in the woods near Pyry, some twenty kilometers southeast of Warsaw, from 24-27 July, 1939; Major Bertrand and Commander Denniston, chief of the Government Code and Cipher School in Britain, his chief cryptologist Knox, and a professor from Oxford were there.

Knox, one of the most brilliant of cryptologists, was already working in the legendary "Room 40" of the Admiralty during World War II. "Professor Sandwich of Oxford", according to Polish information, was actually the chief representative of the Secret Intelligence Service (SIS) and later leader of MI6, the "C", Colonel Menzies. But Bertrand, who knew him personally, denies this. The Polish representatives were Colonels Mayer and Langer and several cryptologists.

They made detailed reports on their work on Enigma and showed their colleagues an exact reproduction of the code machine, an AVA product. Bertrand exclaimed: "Ce fut un moment de stupeur!" — a moment of the greatest amazement! They arranged to work together to break the codes of the German machine from then on: The Poles were to concentrate from then on on solving the mathematical-theoretical problems, the French were to continue their extremely important contact with secret agents, and the British task was to work on developing improved techniques and machines for fast decoding of daily codes.

The Poles gave their two teams of visitors two Polish copies of the Enigma, blueprints of the "Bomba", and other cryptological materials. In the second week of August 1939, a Polish special courier brought them by air to Paris via Scandinavia and Belgium.

On 16 August 1939 Major Bertrand accompanied the official courier of the British embassy in Paris to London. In his diplomatic baggage was an AVA Enigma. At Victoria Station it was taken possession of personally by Colonel Menzies. Three weeks later, World War II began.

During the first week of September, while German armored spearheads moved toward Warsaw, the AVA factory was emptied inconspicuously, and the decoding center in the Pyry forest was destroyed without a trace along with the entire facility. Most of the Polish cryptologists were able to escape from both the Wehrmacht and the Red Army into Rumania, then still neutral, or

Hungary. The entire staff of BS-4, including the mathematicians Rejewski, Rozycki and Zugalski, checked into the French embassy in Bucharest at the end of September 1939, as already agreed on with Major Bertrand.

By 1 October 1939 fifteen Polish Enigma experts met with Colonel Langer in Paris, some coming by the Orient Express, others on a special train. In their luggage were two AVA copies of Enigma code machines.

After 3 September 1939 Denniston moved the Government Code and Cipher School (GC & CS), which was officially renamed "Government Communications Headquarters", out of the London secret service headquarters at 54 Broadway, near St. James' Park in Westminster, to the outskirts of a small town in Buckinghamshire, Bletchley Park (called B.P. for short — see notes pp. 236-237), some 80 kilometers north of London.

This move was made under the code name of "Captain Ridley's Hunting Party", and Ridley was in fact responsible for its administration. From the start, a regiment of the RAF was in charge of guarding B.P. and its surrounding area. Commander Denniston had sought out B.P. as a site for future GC & CS activity with very special circumstances in mind: B.P. is halfway between Oxford and Cambridge and was easy to reach by train. Thinking in terms of expansion, Denniston wanted to assure an influx of prominent scientists and mathematicians from England's two great

A copy of the Enigma built to Polish plans in France, 1939-40, with lid raised. Other than the keyboard and indicator lamps, the windows for the wheels on the code rollers also correspond to the German original.

Bletchley Park (B.P.), a country estate in Buckinghamshire, England, headquarters of the Government Code and Cipher School (GC & CS).

universities.

This lordly country estate in Victorian style with its extensive park offered plenty of room for improvised housing facilities for the fast-growing number of various special services within the parameters of the GC & CS. To the delight of the local building contractor, a certain Captain Faulkner, who built countless wooden cabins called "huts" using high-speed methods. The barracks were of varying sizes, most of them 20 meters long and 10 meters wide. In the middle was a corridor with three small rooms on each side and a large room at each end. Everything was quite Spartan, with block tables and folding wooden chairs.

The Women's Royal Naval Service (WRNS), women's auxiliary of the Royal Navy, who operated the cryptological machinery, the so-called "bombs", and other devices, named Bletchley Pary (B.P.) — in naval tradition — HMS Pembroke. "Bombs" bore the names of British cities and were serviced by RAF technicians.

The work was done in three shifts, day and night, without any holiday interruption. The shifts, known as "watches", had a fixed four-week schedule: 8:00 AM to 4:00 PM for the first seven days, 4:00 PM to midnight the second week, midnight to 8:00 AM the third week, and then three hectic days of alternatinging eight-hour

Bletchley Park (B.P.), one of the barrack-like wooden buildings, Hut 3, with the manor house in the background.

work and eight-hour free time, ending with four days of urgently needed vacation.

The constantly changing work times and the great responsibility caused lasting stress. Everyone who worked at B.P. had to sign the Official Secrets Act in advance, which obligated them, under threat of the severest penalties, to keep the secrets forever. For the nerve-wracking work that the WRNS had to do under conditions that any business would not have dared to demand of its employees they received thirty shillings per week. They wore no insignia of rank, and if their families or friends asked what they did, they had to answer that they were "scribes." Their discipline was strict. Their only free-time activity,

other than very rare trips to London, was going for walks or bicycle rides in the neighborhood.

In time, B.P. was decentralized because of the growing number of Enigma messages and because of the danger of air raids: Branch offices were founded, at first in nearby country houses, such as at Adstock Manor or Wavendorn Manor, Gayhurst Court, Stanmore, Eastcote, 15 kilometers from B.P., and later in a special center built for the purpose near London.

In November 1939 Colonel Menzies was appointed Director of Military Intelligence (MI6) of the Secret Intelligence Service (SIS). The Government Code and Cipher School at B.P. was also placed formally under his command. Menzies

Bletchley Park (B.P.): A look through the entry gate to the stables.

then entrusted RAF Group Captain Winterbotham with the organization of the so-called Hut 3 and the planning and division of decoded Enigma messages.

This marked the beginning of the Special Liaison Units (SLU), a special communications unit whose future task was to be transmitting the decoded Enigma messages to the commanders in the field over a separate communications network with appropriate personnel. The SLU was made an integral part of Operation "Ultra Secret."

This special communications unit (SLU) was under the command of Captain Winterbotham. The men of this unit, to whom the Empire's greatest secret during World War II was entrusted, were chosen personally by Winterbotham.

The SLU was staffed exclusively by RAF officers and men, with a small unit of non-commissioned officers and radiomen who had been trained in decoding. They were assigned to the headquarters of the army groups, armies and air fleets in the field. The radio broadcasts from B.P. (Hut 3) to

the SLU overseas were transmitted by the powerful British SIS transmitter at Whaddon Hall in the absolutely unbreakable "one-time-pad" code, a slow and very laborious process. Later, about 1943, SLU transmissions were made by the Type X machine, a coding system based on Enigma and developed in Britain.

After the texts transmitted by the Whaddon Hall transmitter had been changed into clear texts, the SLU officer turned them over to the appropriate and authorized general staff officer or commander. Every SLU man was obligated to make sure by constant observation that complete secrecy was maintained for Operation "Ultra Secret." They even had to disguise their own activities to their own troops. For this reason, they usually bore the ranks of RAF non-commissioned officers and functioned as "weather specialists."

The radio messages transmitted to the commanders by the SLU generally did not include any evaluation of the message, at best explanatory comments, explanations of technical details or indications of especially important contents. The actual Enigma messages, though, were strictly detached from these comments.

In addition, words such as "Enigma" or "Ultra" were never to be seen by outsiders during transmission of material. This information bore the headings "OFFICER ONLY" and "MOST SECRET", and the actual source was disguised by terms such as "from reliable sources" or "it was reported as reliable." Many years after World War II, Churchill used only the term "my most secret source" in reference to Ultra in his memoirs.

The leader of B.P. through almost the whole war was a high official in the Foreign Office. In the organization of B.P. there was a strict differentiation between Ultra and non-Ultra departments. Although the cryptologists at Bletchley Park worked with codes and messages of all kinds, Ultra was something special. It had an extraordinary level of security, and only a few of those who worked at B.P. actually knew about Ultra.

When using Ultra material, commanders were always involved and had to supply their operational commands with a plausible "cover story" to protect the secrecy of the "Ultra Secret" operation. The word "Ultra" was never to appear. Cited sources of information included air reconnaissance, reports from agents, visual reports and the like.

The extent of time between the reception of an Enigma message and the moment of operational use of knowledge gained through decoding the message was one of the biggest problems in any analysis and evaluation of its contents.

In six years of war, some 10,000 men and women worked at B.P. and its branches on the decoding of German military secrets. The code name of the GC & CS was "Foreign Office — Room No.47."

The activity at B.P. was the best-kept secret of World War II. The organization and work at B.P. were anything but simple: The network of listening posts (Y-stations), at which radio listeners, usually women, received the radio traffic of the Axis powers around the clock, was so extensive as early as 1940 that ultimately any possible frequencies could be monitored from geographically favorable positions.

The radio messages spotted by "X-stations" and intercepted by "Y-stations" were originally transmitted by teletype networks to the offices at B.P. responsible for radio traffic analysis. Then, according to their external features, they were sorted according to traffic and code areas, meaning according to whether they concerned the German Army, Navy or Luftwaffe. Here they were always given code ames such as "Chaffinch", "Red" or "Brown."

The five-place radio messages encoded by

Whaddon Hall: The transmitters of the British SIS.

Enigma, identifiable as Army or Luftwaffe messages, then went to the "Hut 6" department for deciphering, while the four-place naval messages went to "Hut 8." Here the attempt was made to find the appropriate daily code according to the priority assigned according to their individual code areas, by using the "Bomb." When this was done, the messages could be decoded with practically no trouble on the copied Enigma machines, using the same daily code.

As of spring 1940, "Hut 6" was suddenly put on 24-hour duty and constantly staffed on a three-shift schedule. The decoded material was sent from "Hut 6" to "Hut 3", the reconnaissance department, where the army and Luftwaffe messages were translated from German and evaluated by the intelligence service, or from "Hut 8" to "Hut 4", where the translation and evaluation of German naval messages took place.

After the messages were translated, they went to the technical advisors for the army or Luftwaffe, or to the naval advisors in "Hut 3", for examination. The contents were checked against registers of information and personnel lists, and also subjected to commentary and evaluation. After that, the message went back to the officer of the watch and was checked once again by the watch panel before it was sent out.

This concerned only the original text, for the radio messages were sent on only "raw", without notes or comments. The decoded and translated radio messages were now equipped with a paiority marking by the officer of the watch on duty at "Hut 3." The highest level of urgency was marked ZZZZZ, the normal level with only one Z. Only now was it decided who was to receive the completely processed Enigma radio message.

In 1940 the hierarchy was still as follows: The Prime Minister, the Chiefs of Staff, the directors of the intelligence departments of the services, the Fighter Command and the Commander of the Home Forces. To these superior officers there were sent by teletype all the intercepted and deciphered Enigma messages in original form.

Churchill, the most important receiver of the Enigma radio messages, was decisively involved in Operation "Ultra Secret"; without his approval the listening, decoding and processing of the Enigma messages at B.P. would never have attained the proportions that it did. Churchill always had the last word on all matters that concerned the "Ultra Secret."

Material from the German or Italian navies was separately sent directly to the Operational Intelligence Center (OIC). This was located in the Admiralty building in Whitehall. As of 1941, the OIC was housed in the large Citadel bunker nearby.

The transmission of the decoded Enigma radio messages overseas from B.P. led in the latter half of 1940 to a whole series of security problems. For example, the Navy's system differed from those of the Army and the RAF.

Since the Admiralty was an operative leadership position in addition to the government, it asked to receive the entire raw material of decoded messages translated but not processed. At the OIC, where all intelligence information from all sources came together, the messages were evaluated. Then they were turned into actions in closest cooperation with the operative command staffs.

The information from this "Special Intelligence" of importance to the individual naval commanders was then transmitted exclusively to the flag officers under the "Ultra" level of security, whether by teletype or by radio, encoded in a "one-time-pad" code.

One notweorthy disadvantage of the Enigma messages was that they were never complete, and information about the highest German leadership could hardly ever be gained from them, as this was transmitted almost exclusively via the unbreakable teletype network.

H. Dv. g. 14
M. Dv. Nr. 168
L. Dv. g. 14

Prüf=Nr. 9872

Geheim!

Schlüsselanleitung
zur
Schlüsselmaschine Enigma

Vom 13. 1. 40

Nachdruck mit eingearbeiteten Deckblättern Nr. 1—8

Berlin 1940
Gedruckt in der Reichsdruckerei

Cover of the secret Army instructions for using the Enigma.

A Royal Navy radio transmitter, subordinated to the Operational Intelligence Center (OIC) of the Admiralty.

When the war began, and while the general mobilization was still in progress, Major Bertrand moved the 5th Bureau, the intelligence department of the general staff, to the small town of Gretz-Armainvillers, some 60 kilometers northeast of Paris. Here, in the Chateau de Vignolles (code name P.C. Bruno), Bertrand housed his code department. Polish Enigma experts were quartered at P.C. Bruno and worked for Bertrand as Special Decoding Unit Z (Equipe Z).

The British Secret Intelligence Service (SIS) also sent its representative to P.C. Bruno. He was Captain McFarlan, known as Pinky, an experienced radio reconnaissance officer, who had a direct teletype link with the War Office in London and with Bletchley Park. Since Captain McFarlan was also in close contact with the headquarters of the British Expeditionary Corps in France (Lord Gort), P.C. Bruno actually became the first Allied Operational Intelligence Center (OIC).

Soon there were built, in several fine-mechanical workshops in Paris — and on orders from Major Bertrand — several dozen copies of the AVA Enigma, under the strictest secrecy.

Early in January 1940, the 28-year-old mathematician Dr. Alan M. Turing, who ranked among the brightest minds at Bletchley Park, visited P.C. Bruno. This brilliant and no less eccentric scientist had already been summoned to join the GC & CS in September of 1939. Turing brought along some sixty sets of 26 perforated cards, each with 1000 holes punched in it, to make breaking the Enigma code easier.

On 17 January 1940, P.C. Bruno was finally able to break the key of the Army Enigma (British code name "Green"): It involved radio broadcasts

At Château de Vignolles (P.C. Bruno), May 1940; left to right: Polish Intelligence Colonel Langer (Luc), Lieutenant Colonel Bertrand, and the representative of the British SIS, Captain McFarlan (Pinky).

Tobruk Harbor, with the 9232-ton Italian cruiser "San Giorgio" in flames.

of 28 October 1939, which now provided several Enigma settings for that day.

At the eginning of the Norwegian campaign early in April 1940, B.P. was able to decode about fifty, and "Section Z" about 25 daily codes, with an average of 30 to 40 messages per daily code. But their decoding took several weeks, so that there was no hope of any operational or tactical utilization.

On 15 April 1940, during the fighting in Norway, B.P. broke the new yellow Enigma code introduced in the five preceding days, used especially for the development of radio traffic between the Army and the Luftwaffe and also including operational-tactical material. By the time that code was removed from use, a total of 27 out of 52 daily codes had been broken and 768 messages decoded, but the use of this information came to grief because the countless German abbreviations and code names could not be interpreted. Before the Germans began their western attack on 10 May 1940, the coding procedure of Enigma was changed again. The result was that no Enigma radio message could be translated, even fragmentarily, in the decisive first ten days after the German offensive began.

But then, as Bertrand reported later, the Polish experts at P.C. Bruno succeeded in decoding and passing on to the Allied secret service a total of 3074 radio messages between 20 May 1939 and 14 June 1940. Yet their useful effect was absolutely nil: The transmission of intelligence material to the combat troops no longer functioned.

Even the transmission of information gained from Enigma radio messages to the British commanders in Norway proved to be fully impossible at that time.

When the German units moved into Paris, the Chateau de Vignolles had to be evacuated at top speed, along with all the important documents and holed cards, after the Enigma machines had been removed.

Meanwhile, Turing and his team at Bletchley Park worked on a machine that he called "Bomba." As big as a wall closet, full of electric relays, it was a forerunner of today's computers. It was to help decipher the Enigma messages mechanically in a short time. Since the greatest number of radio messages were sent in the Luftwaffe (red) code, the Turing machine was set up for them.

On 22 May 1940 the cryptologists at B.P., with the help of "Bomba", were able to break the first red code, which was only two days old. From this day on, the deciphering of almost all Luftwaffe Enigma code variations was done almost at once, and the delays became shorter and shorter until the war ended. Winterbotham said: "Soon we could read all the messages regularly; normally the code was broken by breakfast time of the same day."

On Monday, 10 June 1940, the Italian Navy and the Regia Aeronautica changed their code systems used in the Mediterranean area, and later those used in East Africa.

On Tuesday, 11 June 1940, Mussolini declared war on Britain and France.

Months before that, British cryptologists had been able to decipher the greatest part of the Italian radio traffic. On the other hand, the Italian radio reconnaissance had been able to make breakthroughs into the British radio traffic.

On Monday, 24 June 1940, Major Bertrand was able to requisition three French airplanes and fly to Algiers with the Polish and Spanish teams. McFarlan escaped to England via Bordeaux and was assigned to Bletchley Park.

On Saturday, 29 June 1940, the newest Italian code book with the overcoding guide was obtained when the Italian submarine "Uebi Scebeli" was boarded. After the British press published photos of the Italian submarine "Galileo Galilei", taken on 19 June 1940, the Italian Navy introduced a separate and very clever code system with new

overdoding charts for its submarines on 5 July 1940.

On Wednesday, 17 July 1940, new code systems and code books were put into use by the whole Italian fleet. After that, the activity of the Italian naval "Servizio Cifra" can be divided into two phases: In the first period, lasting from July 1940 to mid-1941, the "SM 19 S" code system was used, to be broken only rarely.

The second phase began in about June 1941. From then on the navy used several basically different systems for encoding their radio messages. One of them, for example, was based on the new variations of Code SM 91 S with doubled overcoding, and used for high-ranking operational radio communications, especially between land command posts and naval units.

At the same time, two different code machines were introduced in the Marina: The Model C 38 made by Hagelin and the Enigma Type D code machine, which Italy had had since the Spanish Civil War. Independently of these, various other codes with low levels of security were also used.

What was not known in Rome, though, was that in April 1937, during the Spanish Civil War, the SIS had been able to break the Enigma D code. It was a code machine that resembled the commercial Enigma and was used by both the German *Legion Condor* and the Italian troops fighting under General Franco.

In summer 1940 there was a fighting force of some 236,000 men, with 1811 guns, 339 tanks and 151 fighter planes, in the Italian possessions in North Africa. The defeat of France in June 1940 ruled out any danger from French North Africa. Thus Marshal Balbo's forces faced only the small British garrison in Egypt under General Wavell, including the 7th Armored Division and the Indian 4th Division, with a combined fighting force of 31,000 men.

In western Libya Marshal Balbo commanded the 5th Army (General Gariboldi) with the XXX. and XXIII. Corps, consisting of six infantry and two Black Shirt divisions; in the eastern area was the 10th Army (General Berti), with the XXL. and XXII. Corps, consisting of three infantry, one Black Shirt and two native divisions.

As early as Wednesday, 31 June 1940, *Generalfeldmarschall* von Brauchitsch, Commander of the Army, suggested while discussing the situation with Hitler that a German expeditionary force be sent to North Africa to support the Italian operation against Egypt.

In August 1940 the British War Ministry and the Joint Planners were of the opinion that there were certain indications that Hitler was ready "to

Adolf Hitler and Benito Mussolini: two who wanted to draw North Africa into their spheres of influence.

—by Illingworth.

support an Italian attack — perhaps on Egypt — with armored and motorized divisions." This supposition was based on reports from the Secret Intelligence Service (SIS), from British attaches and sources in the USA. This contributed to the decision to send a tank brigade from Great Britain to Egypt.

At this time the 3rd Mobile Section of the Army's Field Sigint Organisation (MSOAFSO), subordinated to the headquarters of the Western Desert Force (General Wavell), handled a particularly heavy flow of information, thanks to the decoding of the Italian tactical code and cipher. By listening to the Luftwaffe's Enigma radio messages, the British Secret Intelligence Service (SIS) was in a position to react to a sudden appearance of German warplanes over the North African theater of war immediately.

In addition, the viewpoint of the SIS was strengthened by the decoded radio reconnaissance reports that early in September 1940 a German delegation in three different kinds of airplane had landed in Libya. From Luftwaffe Enigma information on this delegation's activities, it was correctly concluded in London that no German intervention was on the verge of taking place, but that the Luftwaffe was interested in desert operations and was testing its planes under the particular climatic conditions.

On Friday, 13 September 1940, the Italian Army, under Marshal Graziani, began its offensive across the Libyan-Egyptian border. Mussolini had ordered Graziani to attack Egypt because he wanted his offensive to run parallel to Hitler's planned invasion of England.

On Saturday, 14 September 1940 Hitler decided, after conferring with the representatives of the Army High Command: "An armored corps must be prepared for action in Africa." Thereupon *Generaloberst* Halder, Chief of the General Staff of the Army, gave the Commander of the 3rd Panzer Division, *Generalmajor* Ritter von Thoma, the assignment of making a fact-finding trip to North Africa. He was to find out how German troops could be transported to North Africa and put in a position to support the Italian campaign in that area.

On Monday, 16 September 1940 Marshal Graziani reached Sidi Barrani, 80 kilometers away, which had been evacuated by British securing forces. Graziani stayed there, despite the Duce's exhortations, to "organize the supply

"Well, THAT'S not a mirage"

—by *Illingworth.*

This is how a London cartoonist saw the Italian offensive in North Africa.

the lack of harbor facilities, the great distances that had to be covered in Libya, and the effective British blockade.

In October 1940 the Italian military intelligence service, Servizio Informazione Militari (SIM), learned that General Wavell was planning an offensive. The Duce had been right when he suggested that the long inactive stay at Sidi Barrani would only help the British.

At this moment the crypto-analytical department of the British Army in Cairo was able to decode a series of encoded radio messages from Italian units up to the brigade level. They confirmed that at the end of October 1940 a German military mission had visited Marshal Graziani's headquarters. At the same time, a Luftwaffe Enigma report disclosed the beginning of the German advance into the Balkans and the arrival of Luftwaffe transport planes in southern Italy.

On Thursday, 31 October 1940 *Generaloberst* Halder learned that Hitler had changed his mind. The Libyan undertaking had been postponed.

On Monday, 11 November 1940 Hitler decided to order Luftwaffe units to Italy. They were to stop the Royal Air Force (RAF) from attacking Rumanian oil fields from bases in Greece and to weaken the British Mediterranean fleet before the next spring's planned Wehrmacht operations in the Balkans.

lines." Meanwhile the Royal Navy began to cause massive disturbances to the Italian supply lines over the sea.

The complicated encircling and outflanking maneuvers exhausted the Italian troops greatly. And the so-called "offensive" showed that the Italian Army was scarcely ready for operations in the desert, especially as it lacked the necessary means of transportation.

At the beginning of October 1940 Churchill was informed by the Foreign Office about "certain signs" that Hitler's next advance would be an attack from Libya, and not the expected operation against Gibraltar or the Balkans.

On Thursday, 3 October 1940 Hitler met with Mussolini at the Brenner Pass. During their conference, the Duce assured him that he would take up the Egyptian offensive again in the period from 12-15 October 1940. Hitler decided to support the operation by sending 100 tanks, amounting to about one tank brigade, and as many other vehicles as he could spare.

On Thursday, 17 October 1940 *Generaloberst* Halder received a report from *Generalmajor* Ritter von Thoma in North Africa. Thoma regarded supplying as the most urgent problem and stressed

On Monday, 9 December 1940 Operation "Compass", the offensive of the Western Desert Force (General Wavell) in Cyrenaica, began as a total of 31,000 men, 225 tanks and 120 guns moved against the totally surprised Italian 10th Army (General Gariboldi) in western Egypt and its fortified positions at Sofafi, Nibeiwa, East Tummar, West Tummar, Maktila and Sidi Barrani. The British 7th Armored Division (Major General Creagh) and the Indian 4th Division (Major General Beresford-Peirse) broke through between Nibeiwa and Sofafi. Despite the numerically weak British armored and motorized units under General O'Connor, the attack led to a catastrophe of unexpected dimensions.

The Italian defeat in North Africa forced Hitler — against his will — to help in the Mediterranean area.

On Tuesday, 10 December 1940 the X. *Flieger-korps (General der Flieger* Geisler) was transferred to Sicily and southern Italy. Its task: Knock out the RAF in Malta, fight against the British fleet and shipping traffic. The arrival of German Luftwaffe forces in the Mediterranean changed the strategic situation considerably. The X. *Fliegerkorps* was, to be sure, subordinated to the high command of the Italian Regia Aeronautica, but it received its commands directly from the Commander of the Luftwaffe.

Sicily, December 1940: A bomber unit of the X. Fliegerkorps takes off on a mission to Malta.

On Wednesday, 11 December 1940, the city of Sidi Barrani in Cyrenaica was taken by the British. Parts of the British 7th Armored Division turned off to the south and prevented the Italians from retreating to Sofafi. Four Italian divisions were annihilated, 38,300 men — including four generals — taken prisoner, 400 guns and 50 tanks captured. The British losses: 133 dead, 387 wounded, 8 MIA.

On Sunday, 15 December 1940 the British took the Halfaya border pass in a daring move. With that, the way into the interior of Cyrenaica stood open to the British tanks. What remained of the Italian 10th Army withdrew into the fortress of Bardia.

On Tuesday, 17 December 1940 British troops captured the heavily fortified town of Sollum. The Italian 10th Army (General Gariboldi) practically ceased to exist.

On Thursday, 19 December 1940 the Italian Comando Supremo turned to its German counterpart with the request to send a German armored division to North Africa as soon as possible.

In December 1940 the cryptologists at the Government Code and Cipher School (GC & CS) at Bletchley Park (B.P.) were able to decipher the code used for radio messages between the Italian

The British Lion and the two dictators.

command posts in North Africa and the upper leadership in Rome. They contained reports from the Italian army intelligence service, SIM, about Royal Navy movements in the eastern Mediterranean area. The information was astonishingly precise. For example, at 12:55 on 23 December 1940 Rome warned its subordinate command posts in North Africa that a British convoy with war materials and supplies was to arrive at the harbor of Marsa Matruh at 6:00 the next morning.

In spite of that, Bletchley Park (B.P.) was able by the end of 1940 to break into the communications of the Italian military forces in North Africa only infrequently and for very short times to any strategically or operationally significant extent. The reason was that both the Italian Army and the Regia Aeronautica changed their codes too often. As for the German radio traffic in Italy on the Mediterranean area at that

Encoding a radio message: a hitherto unknown photo of an Enigma being used by the Supermarina, the High Command of the Italian Navy.

ALWAYS EAT
WITH HP SAUCE

FOR KING AND EMPIRE

NO. 13,946   MONDAY, JANUARY 6, 1941   ONE PENNY

BRITISH FLAG OVER BARDIA

Italian Commander, 4 Generals Surrender

LONDON WAS READY

MEAT: THE SHORTAGE TO END

Stalin Sends for 4 Envoys

Balkans Tension

Stalin has ordered the Russian Ministers to Yugoslavia, Hungary, Rumania, and Bulgaria to return at once to Moscow "for consultations," state Balkan reports. Belgrade believes latest developments in South-East Europe are the cause of this summons to the Kremlin.

From CEDRIC SALTER, ally Mail Special Correspondent

25,000 PRISONERS IN OUR HANDS

From ALEXANDER CLIFFORD, Daily Mail Correspondent

CAIRO, Sunday.

BARDIA has fallen and the entire garrison of more than 25,000 men, including the Italian commander, General Berganzoli, are prisoners. This great victory, won in the amazing time of 55 hours, was announced in the following special communiqué issued from General Wavell's headquarters to-night:

"All resistance at Bardia ceased at 1.30 p.m. to-day. The town, with total forces defending it and all stores and equipment, is now in our hands.

'Woe, Woe!'
—Ansaldo

Rain of Fire by the Fleet

Eye-witness on Bombardment

From W. F. HARTIN
WITH THE MEDITERRANEAN FLEET, Sunday.

FIRE from sea, land, and air has rained down on Bardia with scriptural vengeance during the past three days.
On board the flagship of

No Fire Blitz THIS Time

By Daily Mail Raid Reporter

LONDON'S new fire watchers and the people—men, women, and boys even—were ready last night when hundreds of incendiaries showered down on three outer districts of the capital soon after the Alert sounded. There seemed to be many fire watchers as fire bombs.

In one district, after all the incendiaries dropped by two waves of raiders had been put out without a single fire starting, the watchers stood in doorways singing : "We want some more."

They had not long to wait. A third wave of raiders dropped more incendiaries. These, too, were quickly put out.

In another district, because of

Our Five New Battleships

THE meat shortage made yesterday Meatless Sunday for thousands of people, but there is better news now—

Home-killed meat is becoming more plentiful and within a week or two both the shortage and the temporary "extra rationing" many butchers have introduced will be ended.

Pork, which has been so rare and is rationed from to-day, will be more plentiful this week.

The reduced meat ration—1s 6d. per person instead of 1s. 10d. comes into force to-day, first day of the new couponless general rationing period.

".' Meatless Sunday — but supplies on the way — Page THREE.

6 January 1941: The Union Jack flies over Bardia.

time, B.P. was able to make particular use of the already broken "red" code of the Luftwaffe, though only occasionally, as the Luftwaffe bases generally used the safe, unbreakable teletype.

By the end of 1940, British ships and aircraft had sunk 28 ships with almost 190,000 tons of cargo heading for North Africa, a major contribution to the subsequent defeat.

On Saturday, 4 January 1941 General Wavell ordered further advances in Cyrenaica. While the British 7th Armored Division (Major General Creagh) went around Bardia and marched in the direction of Tobruk, the Australian 6th Infantry Division (Major General Mackey) advanced on Bardia.

On the same day, Hitler decided to put the German support in North Africa "into motion at once."

On Sunday, 5 January 1941 the Italian garrison at Bardia laid down their arms. 40,000 prisoners and 462 guns fell into British hands. Now the Italian Army Group Libya (Marshal Graziani) in Cyrenaica consisted of only five weak divisions.

On Thursday, 9 January 1941 Hitler decided, during a conference at the Berghof in Obersalzberg, so send a small German battle group to Libya within three weeks.

In the early days of January 1941 the War Office learned from diplomatic circles, Italian prisoners and SIS that German troop units were being transported singly through Italy and shipped to Sicily. In the reports it was even stated that the arrival of German troops in Libya was expected.

An SIS source reported of huge quantities of supplies and provisions being sent to Italy by the Germans. Interestingly, none of this information was sent on to the C-in-C Mediterranean or to Force H, which was operating at sea at that time.

On Sunday, 11 January 1941, as a result of Hitler's conference at the Obersalzberg Berghof, Hitler's Directive No.22 appeared, concerning the "cooperation of German forces in the combat in the Mediterranean area."

As early as Monday, 13 January 1941, Cairo knew from Luftwaffe Enigma messages that the Luftwaffe was arriving in North Africa.

On Wednesday, 15 January 1941 a German fact-finding mission set out for Libya.

On Saturday, 18 January 1941 Mussolini met with Hitler for two days of talks at Obersalzberg. The Duce approved the planned use of a German barrage unit in Libya, and it was agreed that the German transport could begin on 15 February 1941.

German troops were hastily equipped in the North African theater of war: pith helmets for the Afrika-Korps.

On Monday, 20 January 1941 — at the suggestion of the chief of the Wehrmacht staff — the use of German troops in North Africa was given the code name "Sonnenblume" (Sunflower).

On Tuesday, 21 January 1941 the Australian 6th Infantry Division, part of the British XIII. Corps (Lieutenant General O'Connor), began to storm the important Italian-Libyan port city and fortress of Tobruk.

In the early morning hours of 22 January 1941 Tobruk was surrendered by the Italian fortress commandant, General Pitassi-Manella, and Rear Admiral Vietina to the British XIII. Corps under Lieutenant General O'Connor. 25,000 men were

The Italian desert fort of El Mechili after being taken by the British 7th Armored Division.

taken prisoner, 208 guns and 87 tanks were captured. What remained of the Italian 10th Army drew back into the fortified El Mechili-Derna line.

As the Australian 6th Infantry Division rolled along the coast toward this line and the British 7th Armored Division circled around the Italian 10th Army from the south, Marshal Graziani gave the order to withdraw. But it was too late; the 7th Armored Division was already on the coast of the Great Syrte at Beda Fomm, cutting off the retreat of the 10th Army, which had to surrender after a short fight. 20,000 men were taken prisoner.

On Friday, 24 January the Australian 6th Infantry Division approached Derna, while the 7th Armored Division pushed forward into the desert to the southwest and attacked El Mechili. The Italians withdrew into the hills to the north, which made it possible for the British to cut off the entire salient of Cyrenaica.

On Thursday, 30 January Derna was captured by British units.

On Friday, 31 January the first railroad trans-

Naples roadstead, February 1941, before embarking for North Africa.

ports with parts of the 5th Light Division (*Generalmajor* Streich) left the Reich headed for Italy. When they arrived in Naples, the order not to take ship for Tripoli but to await further orders was waiting for them. Hitler had canceled his decision to send German troops to Libya.

On Saturday, 1 February *Generalmajor* von Funck returned to Berlin from his fact-finding mission. He reported to Hitler, in the presence of *Generalfeldmarschall* von Brauchitsch, *Generaloberst* Halder, *General* Jodl and *Generalfeldmarschall* Keitel on the critical situation of the Italian units in North Africa. Funck was of the opinion that a barrage unit was too weak to prevent the loss of Libya.

On Monday, 3 February Hitler changed his mind. Transportation of the barrage unit intended for North Africa was — reinforced by an armored regiment — to be continued at top speed, and at the same time an armored division was to be prepared to be sent after them.

Meanwhile, RAF air reconnaissance reported that almost half a million tons of Axis shipping,

mainly units of 6000 tons and more, was concentrated in the roadstead of Naples.

On Thursday, 6 February British troops marched into Benghazi, the capital city of Cyrenaica.

On the same day, a directive on action in North Africa (Operation "Sunflower") was sent by the Wehrmacht high command to the Army (OKH) and Luftwaffe (OKL) high commands: The German troops in Libya were to be tactically subordinated to the Italian commander, General Ambrosio. Otherwise they were under the command of the Army commander, who had constant contact with the Italian commander through liaison officers.

At the same time, *Generalleutnant* Rommel was ordered to the Führer's headquarters. Then the commander of the German 7th Panzer Division, he first reported to *Generalfeldmarschall* von Brauchitsch, who informed him

AFTER WAVELL'S "BRILLIANT STROKE":
PRISONERS AND WAR MATERIAL.

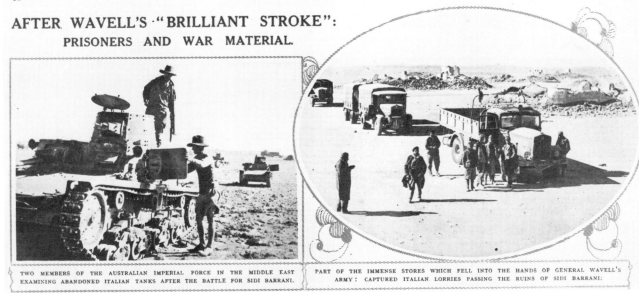

TWO MEMBERS OF THE AUSTRALIAN IMPERIAL FORCE IN THE MIDDLE EAST
EXAMINING ABANDONED ITALIAN TANKS AFTER THE BATTLE FOR SIDI BARRANI.

PART OF THE IMMENSE STORES WHICH FELL INTO THE HANDS OF GENERAL WAVELL'S
ARMY : CAPTURED ITALIAN LORRIES PASSING THE RUINS OF SIDI BARRANI:

For the Führer to see: the "Illustrated London News" is illustrated indeed.

that he had been named commander of the German troops in North Africa.

Meanwhile *Generalfeldmarschall* Keitel empowered the German general at the Italian headquarters in Rome, *Generalmajor* von Rintelen, to ask the Comando Supremo to subordinate all Italian motorized units and all German troops in North Africa to Rommel's headquarters for planned joint action.

That evening Rommel was invited to a private discussion with Hitler. The Führer showed him British and American magazines with reports on the British advance in Cyrenaica. Rommel said to *Generalmajor* von Rintelen later: "A damned hard job."

On the same day, Military Intelligence 6 (MI6) considered it to be not impossible that two or three German armored divisions would be located in southern Italy or Sicily, but MI6 was not in a position to determine for sure whether an operation against Malta, Tunisia or Libya was planned. Even the German radio broadcasts and newspaper articles about the coming transfer of German troops to Tripoli were evaluated by MI6

Naples, 8 February 1941: The first convoy with equipment for Operation "Sunflower" sets out for Tripoli.

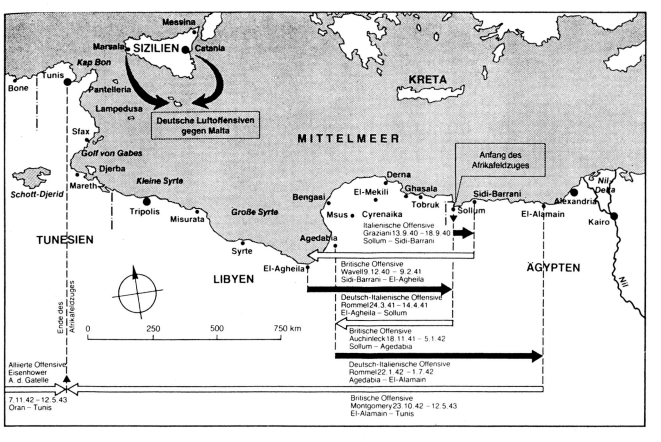

Map labels:

Messina
SIZILIEN
Marsala · Catania
Kap Bon
Tunis
Bone
Pantelleria
KRETA
Lampedusa
Deutsche Luftoffensiven gegen Malta
Sfax
MITTELMEER
Golf von Gabes
Anfang des Afrikafeldzuges
Djerba
Kleine Syrte
Mareth
Derna
El-Mekili
Ghasala
Sidi-Barrani
Nil-Delta
Schott-Djerid
Bengasi
Tobruk
Alexandria
Tripolis
Msus · Cyrenaika
Sollum
El-Alamain
Kairo
Misurata
Große Syrte
Italienische Offensive
Graziani 13.9.40 – 18.9.40
Sollum – Sidi-Barrani
TUNESIEN
Agedabia
Syrte
LIBYEN
Britische Offensive
Wavell 9.12.40 – 9.2.41
Sidi-Barrani – El-Agheila
ÄGYPTEN
El-Agheila
Nil
Deutsch-Italienische Offensive
Rommel 24.3.41 – 14.4.41
El-Agheila – Sollum
Britische Offensive
Auchinleck 18.11.41 – 5.1.42
Sollum – Agedabia
Ende des Afrikafeldzuges
0   250   500   750 km
Deutsch-Italienische Offensive
Rommel 22.1.42 – 1.7.42
Agedabia – El-Alamain
Alliierte Offensive
Eisenhower
A. d. Gatelle
7.11.42 – 12.5.43
Oran – Tunis
Britische Offensive
Montgomery 23.10.42 – 12.5.43
El-Alamain – Tunis

The North African theater, 1940-1943.

as purely a propaganda maneuver.

On Friday, 7 February the *Kampfgeschwader z.b.V.* No.1 with its Ju 52 transport planes was transferred to Comiso, Sicily. It was to amplify the sea traffic by sending in reinforcements, weapons and equipment to Africa by air and bringing back wounded men, unusable equipment and instructional material for troop training in Germany on its return flights.

On Saturday, 8 February the first convoy of German materials left Naples. It consisted of three transport ships and carried the back-line services of the 5th Light Division and supplies. That afternoon British aircraft, presumably carrier-based planes, were reported east of Sardinia. For safety reasons, the convoy ran into the harbor of Palermo.

On this day the X. *Fliegerkorps (General der Flieger* Geisler) began the first German air offensive against Malta. Its task was to make safe transport of the German troops to Tripoli possible. The suggestion of Vica Admiral Weichold, chief of the German naval command in Italy, to occupy the island immediately was ignored. Hitler also rejected the later advice of the Wehrmacht staff to conquer not Crete but the 26 times smaller but strategically incomparably more important Malta from the air.

On Sunday, 9 February a high-level coded message from the Italian air forces was intercepted; it included special instructions for Italian and German convoy-securing aircraft between Naples and Tripoli.

1941
February-June

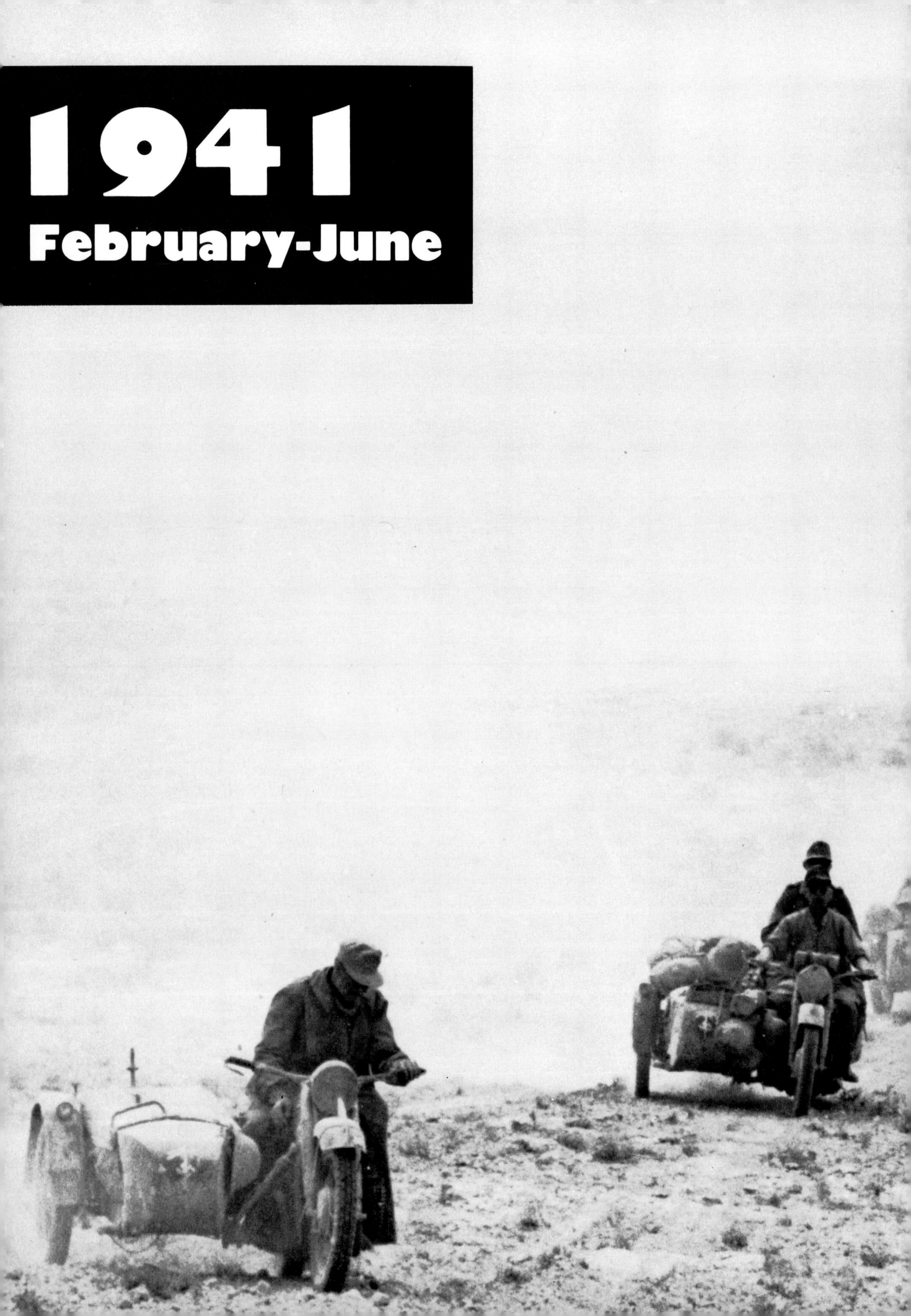

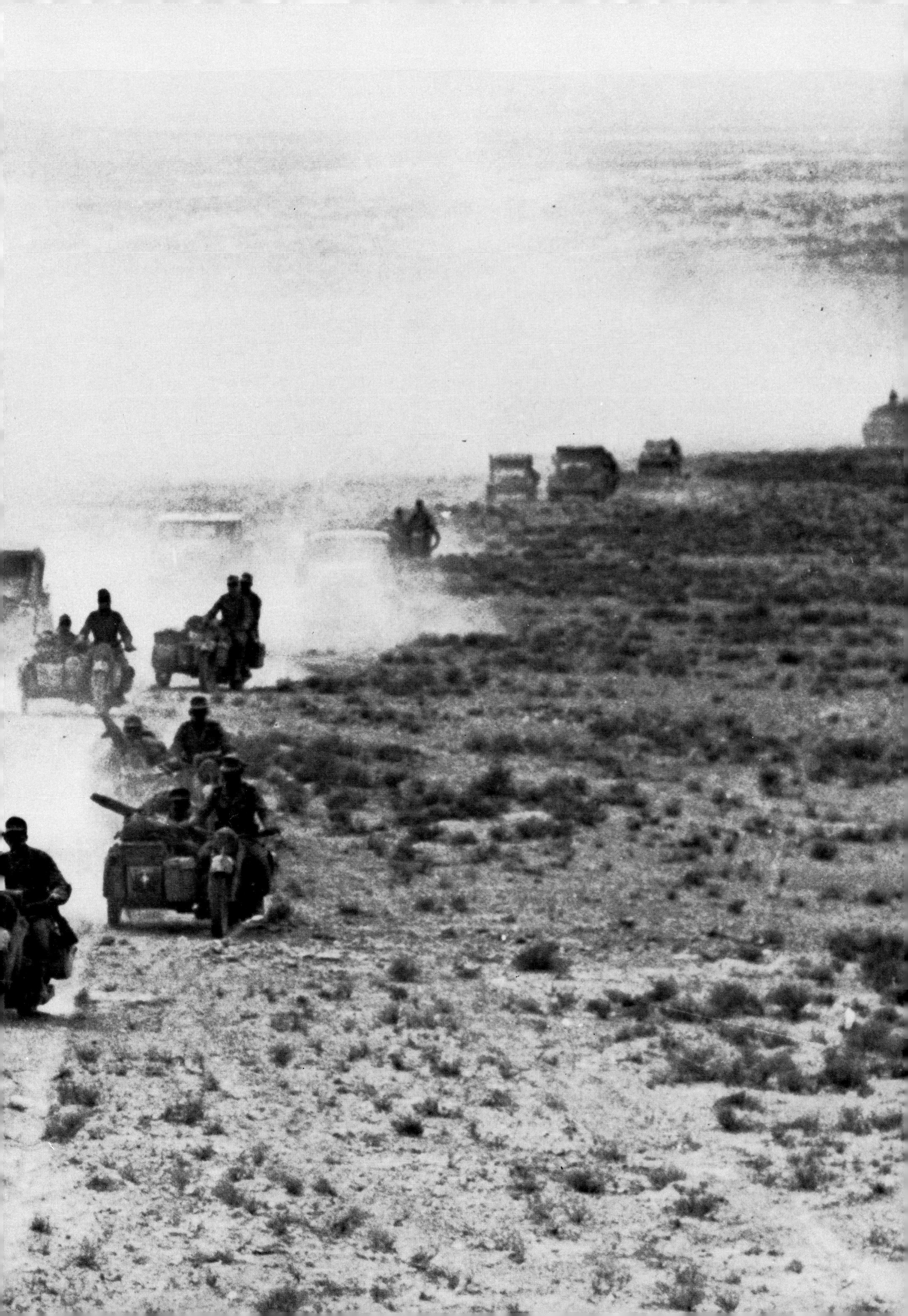

On Wednesday, 12 February Rommel landed early in the afternoon, accompanied by Hitler's chief adjutant, *Oberstleutnant* Schmundt, Rommel's chief of staff, *Oberstleutnant* von dem Borne, and several other officers, at Castel Benito, the Tripoli airport. In the Italian capital the OKH set up a "Special Staff Rome" under Major i.G. Count Klinckowstroem, associated with the staff of *Generalmajor* von Rintelen. This special staff was to coordinate all supply functions, present German requests to the appropriate Italian command posts, and provide for the transportation of supplies between the OKH and Rommel.

On the afternoon of 14 February Rommel went to the harbor of Tripoli to observe the debarkation of the first German combat troops, Panzer Reconnaissance Unit 3 (*Oberstleutnant* Baron von Wechmar) and Panzerjäger Unit 39. Rommel decided to order the two units to Syrte immediately to stop the British advance as far east of Tripoli as possible.

The coast road to El Agheila, site of the first battle between the Germans and British in North Africa.

On Saturday, 15 February the two German units had reached Misurata, and about 3:00 PM of the next day the head of Panzer Reconnaissance Unit 3 reached Syrte. Thus two days after their arrival in port, the German troops were already 450 kilometers east of Tripoli and ready to fight. "Armed reconnaissance" — that is all the German and Italian leadership told Rommel at first.

On Monday, 17 February, according to the situation report of the General Staffs Intelligence (GS Int), the department in charge of enemy position determination in the General Staff in London, first of all, the crossing from Italy to North Africa had been a problem for the German troops, and secondly, they had absolutely no experience in desert warfare. Thus "a considerable time will pass before a counteroffensive that needs to be taken seriously can be launched from Tripoli."

But Rommel's initiative in undertaking something with a comparatively small force without awaiting reinforcements was underestimated. In addition, of the total of 220,000 tons of Axis freight shipped from Italian ports to Libya in February and March 1941, only 20,000 tons had been sunk.

On Tuesday, 18 February the German units in Libya officially were given the name of "*Deutsches Afrika-Korps*" (*DAK*).

Only on that day did the British Admiralty inform the C-in-C Mediterranean that the convoys from Naples actually "seemed to be" German.

On Thursday, 20 February, at about 3:00 PM, the Germans first made contact with the British: A troop of Dragoon Guards with three scout cars under Lieutenant E.T. Williams, later the Senior Intelligence Staff Officer of the 8th Army, exchanged fire with parts of Panzer Reconnaissance Unit 3 on the coast road near El Agheila, but without observing any effect.

On Monday, 24 February the first combat between British and German forces took place. Parts of Panzer Reconnaissance Unit 3 (*Oberstleutnant* Baron von Wechmar) met two troops of the King's Dragoon Guards with tanks and one Australian antitank unit in the El Agheila area. The first British casualty, and the first prisoners, Lieutenant Rowley and two members of his tank crew, were reported.

On Tuesday, 25 February the first part of the 3rd Company (*Oberleutnant* Seebohm) of Intelligence Unit 56 of Surveillance Platoon "*Afrika*" landed in Tripoli under *Leutnant* Gerisch.

Tripoli, February 1941: Generals Gariboldi and Rommel » *review the DAK's first parade.*

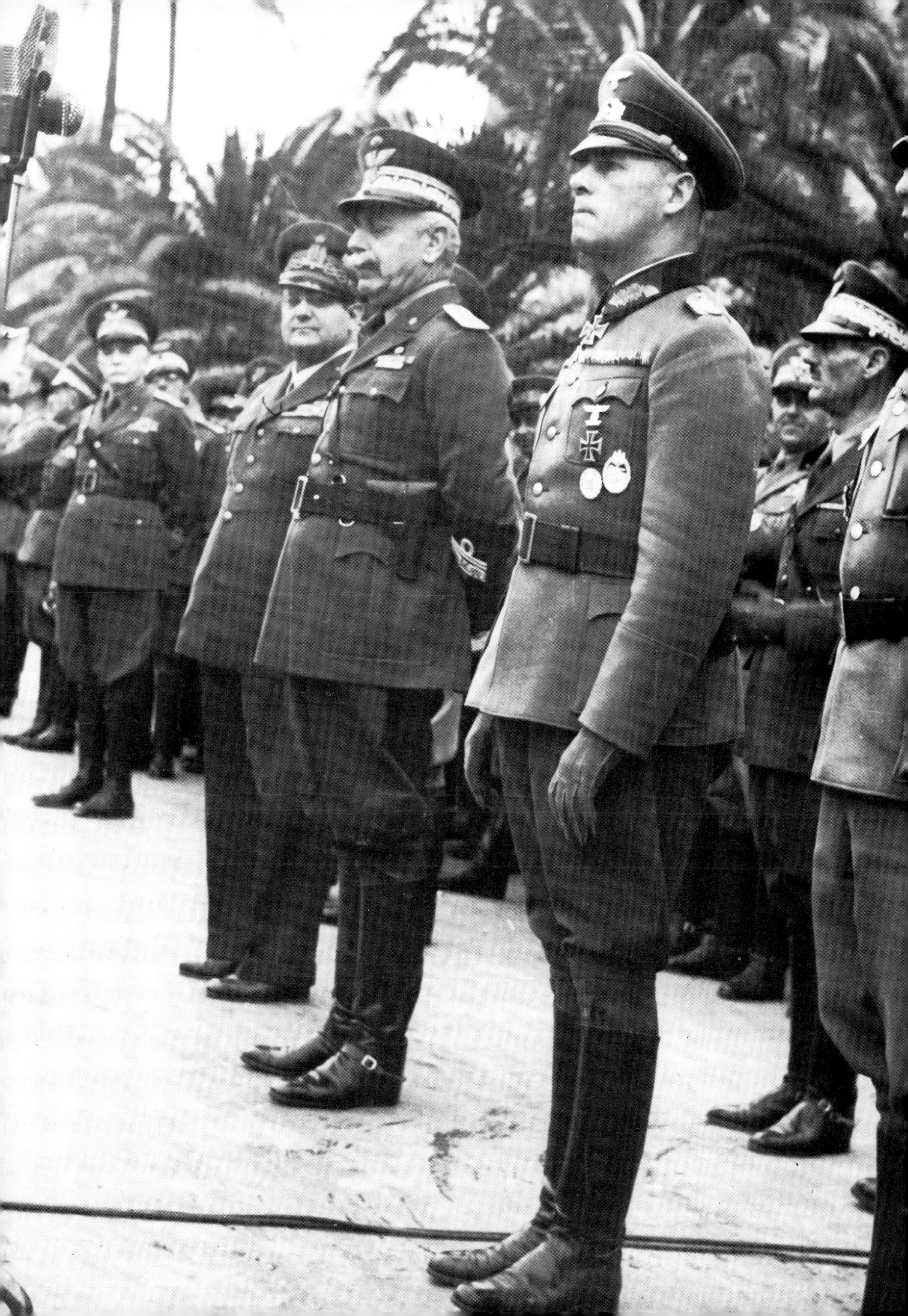

Friday, 28 February was an important date in the ensuing battle against Rommel. On that day GC & CS was able to break the new "Hellblau" Luftwaffe code (called "light blue" by the British). This Enigma code was used by the X. *Fliegerkorps* (*General der Flieger* Geisler) and *Fliegerführer Afrika* (*General der Flieger* Fröhlich), transferred from Sicily, for their radio messages.

Thus at one stroke the British Y Service, which was responsible for radio surveillance in the Mediterranean area, gained significance. From now until 31 December 1941, when the code was withdrawn from radio use, the British crypto-logists could solve the daily code and setting changes within 24 hours.

On Sunday, 2 March, according to the judgment of the C-in-C Middle East, the Germans could possibly advance to Agedabia without delay, but they absolutely would not try to reach Benghazi before additional armored forces were landed and

one infantry division and one or two tank brigades had been established. It was thought to be unlikely that the Germans could accomplish this before the summer. The Cabinet in London approved Churchill's decision to transfer troops from Egypt — notably one of the best units, the 1st Tank Brigade (Brigadier Charrington) of the 2nd Armored Division — to Greece. He presumed that the British flank in Cyrenaica was quite safe.

On Monday, 3 March Luftwaffe Enigma revealed the strength of the German army and Luftwaffe units in Libya. The position of the leading troop units was learned in the process, and Rommel was identified as the commanding general of the *Afrika-Korps*. Since the Enigma reports mentioned a 6th, 7th and 8th convoy, the extent of the troop reinforcements could be imagined.

On the very next day, MI6 had indications that Rommel's fighting forces could possibly be

increased to two armored divisions. Further information: Preparations for a surprise attack at an early date were being made. But the Joint Intelligence Committee (JIC), the committee in charge of evaluating enemy reports for the British chiefs of Staff, did not care to accept this estimation of the situation.

On Thursday, 6 March the Surveillance Platoon *Afrika* was transferred to its area of operations, the Syrte area east of Tripoli.

On Friday, 7 March the British captured Agedabia and advanced toward El Agheila. Here their offensive came to a stop. Within two months they had advanced a total of 900 kilometers, captured 130,000 Italians — including 22 generals — and 85 guns, as well as capturing or destroying 380 tanks. In the process, General O'Connor lost only some 500 dead, 1373 wounded and 56 missing. After the units of the Army of the Nile that had desert combat experience were transferred

to Greece, only the British XIII. Corps (Lieutenant General O'Connor), consisting of two divisions of not fully equipped troops, remained in Cyrenaica. Thus the front that faced Tripoli was now only weakly occupied.

Even in the first week of March 1941, when many of the British combat troops in North Africa had been transferred to Greece as a result of the JIC's misconception, the JIC continued to think the German troops would need a certain length of time to get used to Africa. Of even greater significance was their underestimation of the danger caused by Rommel's combat troops.

On Monday, 10 March General Staff Intelligence considered the possibility that Rommel might possibly venture an advance via El Agheila and Agedabia but would not be capable of making thorough preparations for it.

By Thursday, 13 March the most important information, along with that gained from

«

Tripoli, February 1941: German panzers on their way to the front.

Rome, March 1941: A coding group operating an Enigma machine in a Luftwaffe office.

The radio station of the 3rd Company (Oberleutnant Seebohm) of Intelligence Unit 56.

listening to high-level operative radio communications of the Regia Aeronautica, had been sent to Cairo by telex from the Air Ministry in London. Only on that day was a new type of communication put into service to send the decoded radio messages directly from B.P. to the Combined Bureau Middle East (CBME), the command of the united forces in the Near East. This was a valuable addition to the information that the C-in-C Middle East was receiving from air reconnaissance, all the more so as the Luftwaffe Enigma transmissions gave scarcely any information on the nature of the attack Rommel was planning. Aside from that, the commanders in Cairo continued to underestimate the value of the Enigma messages.

But on the same day, Luftwaffe Enigma revealed that Rommel was flying to Berlin, but neither the intention nor the result of his flight could be learned from the Enigma message. In reality, Rommel was trying to get permission from the OKH for an offensive in May of 1941.

On Wednesday, 19 March Rommel received, for the last time, strict orders from the OKH merely to strengthen the weakening Italian units and under no conditions to attack before the 15th Panzer Division (*Generalmajor* von Prittwitz) was ready for action, which was planned for the end of May 1941. Only then — Rommel was informed — was the OKH planning for limited operations by the *Afrika-Korps* in the Agedabia area, and under no circumstances was he to attack Marsa El Brega. Interestingly, Berlin's evaluation of Rommel's possibilities agreed with that of the C-in-C Middle East.

But Rommel had his own opinion of the matter. Thanks to excellent work by *Oberleutnant* Seebohm's listening company, verified by aerial

reconnaissance, he knew that the British were building extensive field fortifications in the Agedabia area and constantly bringing reinforcements there.

Around 20 March hints of a planned operation by the *DAK* increased; for example, the increasing numbers of Luftwaffe units under *Fliegerführer Afrika* and reconnaissance activity in the Agedabia area, as well as the cancellation of all furloughs as of 19 March. Only later was it realized that all of these pointed to Rommel's subsequent attack. But MI6 did not yet have the experience necessary to read these signs correctly.

On Monday, 24 March, despite strict orders from the OKH, Rommel undertook his first reconnaissance advance with only the 5th Light Division (*Generalmajor* Streich). Near the desert fort of El Agheila the first soldiers of the *Afrika-Korps* fell in action when one of their armored cars hit a mine. This operation shows that the British defense had been weakened considerably by the transfer of troops to Greece. Without stopping, Rommel moved forward toward Marsa Brega. He divided his unit into three columns that hurried along the coast road and spread out through the desert to advance on El Mechili. The taking of El Agheila was the first victory in Rommel's first offensive in North Africa. Until that time, the German and Italian forces had suffered scarcely any losses. They either used the route from the Tunisian coast or circumvented Malta so as not to come within range of the torpedo planes stationed there.

Tripoli: Unloading the first tanks of the 15th Panzer Division. At the right front is a cameraman for the German »weekly news.

Likewise on 24 March, General Staff Intelligence presumed that Rommel could be able to move against Cyrenaica, though to a limited extent and with one German light division and one Italian armored division, in about three weeks — thus in mid-April. At General Staff Intelligence it was still regarded as unlikely that Rommel would make an attempt to win back Benghazi before he had moved his armored and motorized units forward, which was not expected until about the middle of May at the earliest.

On Sunday, 30 March the Operational Instruction of the GOC Cyrenaica Command signaled: "Since the occupation of El Agheila, the enemy has shown no sign of making a further advance, and there is no clear assurance that he is planning a large-scale operation." The chiefs of staff, to be sure, reported active German troop movements east of Tripoli in their last report for the month of March, but they made no predictions for the future.

The chiefs of staff and the Chief of the Imperial General Staff (CIGS) agreed with General Wavell that the organizational difficulties of any attack that the enemy would make included great problems. For that reason, Rommel's possibilities of carrying out an offensive in Cyrenaica were underestimated. There were two reasons for this misjudgment. First, the British intelligence service in North Africa was not yet able to handle

its job thoroughly, and secondly, Rommel's units still represented a factor of unknown size.

At the same time, Rommel ordered the *DAK* to make a reconnaissance advance against Agedabia and Marsa Brega. Likewise on 30 March General Wavell radioed to General Neame, commander in Cyrenaica: "I do not believe that he can undertake anything big for at least another month." This grave error is attributable to Enigma reports from which General Wavell had concluded that Rommel merely had the task of stabilizing the Syrte front, and that his most important unit, the 15th Panzer Division, had not yet arrived in North Africa. In General Wavell's opinion, the Germans could attack in May at the earliest. Any earlier date for an attack would, in his eyes, involve a considerable risk, a military gamble.

The next day, 31 March, the first parts of the 15th Panzer Division were to arrive in the port of Tripoli to strengthen the *Afrika-Korps*. But instead of waiting for the arrival of this division, Rommel attacked the coastal town of Marsa Brega, the portal to Cyrenaica, with Panzer Regiment 5. To the amazement of the British and against the strict instructions from the OKH, the advance developed into a German-Italian counter-offensive: The Germans captured not only several tanks but also numerous trucks, and rolled on to the east.

In spring 1941, there was still no Special Liaison Unit (SLU) in Cairo that could supply the British command in the Middle East with Enigma reports from B.P. via its own means of communications. Yet Brigadier Shearer, the chief of the enemy intelligence service subordinated to General Wavell, got possession of them as "secret enemy information." But General Wavell's units were too weak to undertake anything against Rommel.

On Tuesday, 1 April the units of the Army of the Nile were already being overrun in their positions between the Mediterranean coast and several salt marshes in the south. Once again, Rommel divided his troops into three groups and pursued the enemy along the coast road and on the flank further to the south.

On Wednesday, 2 April the surprised British evacuated Agedabia. Rommel then received a radio message from General Gariboldi, who called the previous advance contrary to commands and ordered a halt to all further movements until a discussion had been held.

On this day it was particularly clear that the British intelligence service was still at a disadvantage: B.P. warned the C-in-C Middle East that parts of the 15th Panzer Division were in transit by rail between Trapani and Palermo, presumably on their way to Tripoli.

They neglected to mention, though, that information about an advanced command staff of this division located in Tripoli was at hand. The news that the time when the units would be shipped out of Palermo was unknown was also lacking. They also neglected to pass along the news that the reinforcements Hitler had promised Rommel would not materialize now that the German attack on the Balkans was beginning.

El Agheila area, 24 March 1941: The first interrogation of a British prisoner.

Marsa Brega area, March 1941: A Bf 110 reconnaissance plane surprises a British advance group.

Meanwhile the latest Luftwaffe Enigma reports revealed that reinforcements to *Fliegerführer Afrika* had been denied, as another operation had a higher priority.

On Thursday, 3 April a radio message from the OKW reached Rommel: Hitler had given clear orders to secure the attained positions and tie down as many British forces as possible — "The offensive operations with limited goals resulting from this may not be extended further than the limited forces allow before the arrival of the 15th Panzer Division. Above all, any risk to the open right flank that would result from a turn in a northerly direction toward Benghazi is to be avoided."

During the night of 3-4 April General Gariboldi tried in vain to find Rommel and place the responsibility for the unallowed operations on

Agedabia area, April 1941: An Italian division's radio station.

him. Meanwhile the mass of the 5th Light Division, followed by the "Ariete" Division, advanced further toward El Mechili.

On Friday, 4 April, German and Italian armored spearheads rolled toward Benghazi in a fast advance and took the city. The units of the German 5th Light Division now moved further through the desert in four columns in the direction of El Mekili. And the decimated units of the Army of the Nile began to retreat to Egypt, suffering heavy losses. On this day the British confusion grew into panic: The 2nd Armored Division (Major General Gambier-Parry) remained immobile near Msus without supplies, since the British crew had blown up all their fuel supplies out of fear of German tanks.

Oddly enough, Rommel could attribute the success of his offensive mainly to the fact that the British leadership was reading the OKW Enigma broadcasts intended for him. When Rommel received Hitler's strict orders to remain at the eastern boundary of Syrte before El Agheila, the C-in-C Middle East believed he could hold his attained positions with his weak forces. Thus Rommel's offensive, which completely disregarded the orders of his own leadership, also came as a complete surprise to the C-in-C Middle East.

On Saturday, 5 April the Luftwaffe Enigma supplied proof that Rommel had circumvented the instructions given him when he advanced past Agedabia, and that he had absolutely no command to advance toward Egypt. This impelled Churchill to send his conclusions on to the C-in-C Middle East, so that the C-in-C no longer considered a large-scale offensive against Egypt to be possible.

On the same day, the intelligence officer of the *Afrika-Korps* responsible for Rommel's information on enemy positions, *Hauptmann* i.G. Count Baudissin, was captured by the British near Tobruk. A few hours later, as night fell, the British generals Neame and O'Connor, while traversing roadless country on their way to Tmimi, met a German scouting troop and were captured.

On Sunday, 6 April the Balkan campaign

Rome, April 1941: The large-scale transmitter facilities of the Superexercito, High Command of the Italian Army.

Libya, Via Balbia coast road, April 1941: Interrogating one ≫ of the first British pilots shot down by the DAK. In the background is the Arco dei Fileni, the landmark of the Via Balbia.

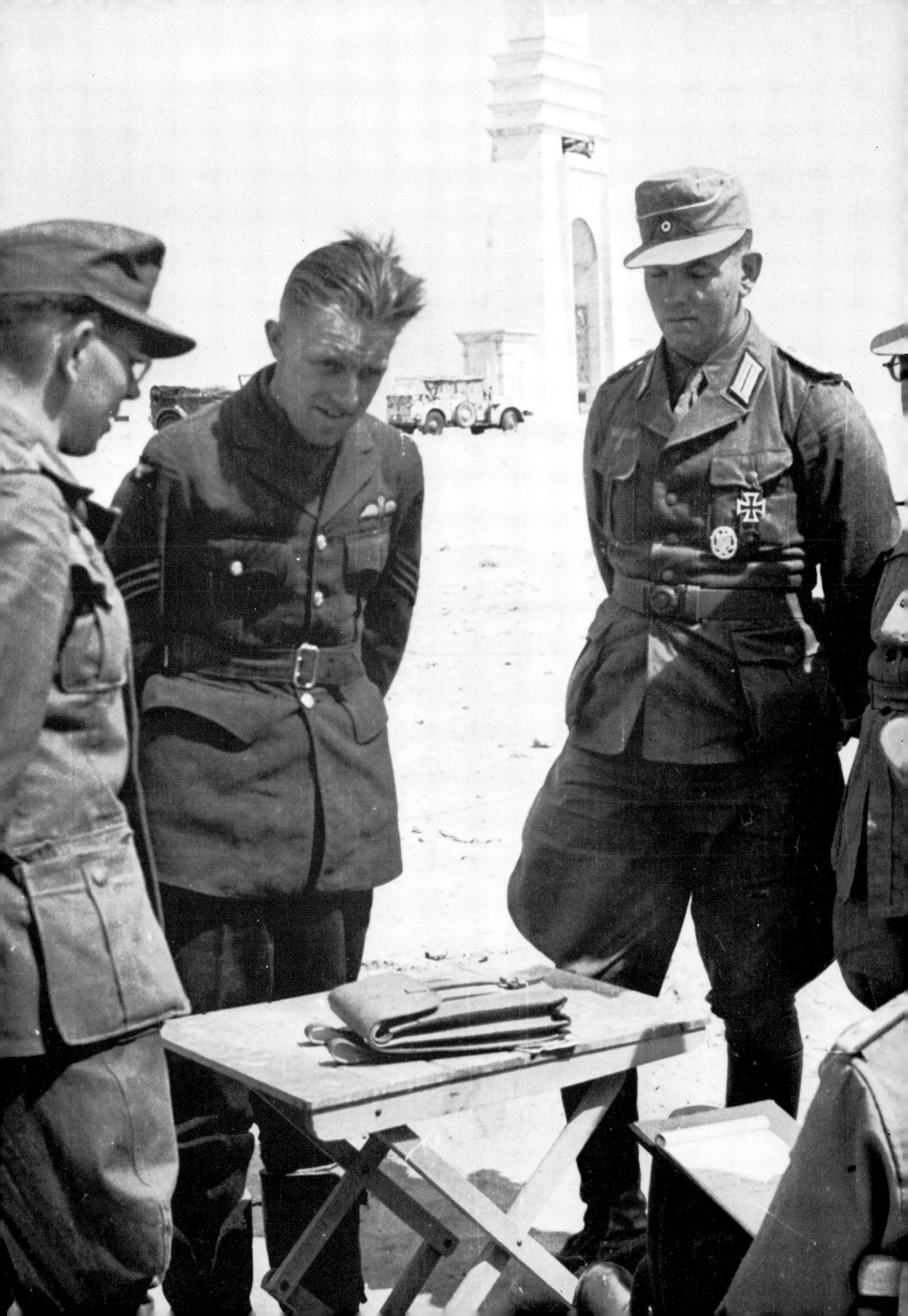

began. At the Führer's headquarters they were very busy with this new operation and barely able to pay attention to Rommel's activities.

On Monday, 7 April El Mechili was surrounded by German troops. The British forces, strengthened by an Indian motorized brigade from Tobruk, rejected German requests to surrender. After a break out attempt failed, 2000 men, with General Gambier-Parry and Brigadier Vaugham, were taken prisoner.

On the morning of the same day the British Admiralty informed the C-in-C Mediterranean that, according to an Enigma report, "advanced parts of the 15th Panzer Division had embarked from Palermo on or shortly after 9 April 1941" with the presumed destination of Tripoli. At this news, several British destroyers were ordered from Alexandria to Malta.

Likewise on 7 April, Derna and Tmimi with their gigantic British supply depots fell into German hands. The captured supplies of provisions, gasoline, ammunition and weapons made it possible for Rommel to advance further toward Egypt. On the road between Derna and El Mechili soldiers of the *DAK* found a number of important captured documents. They gave Rommel a reliable view of both the structure of the British field army and the composition of the enemy forces in the Middle East.

On Tuesday, 8 April B.P. made a bad mistake: It was reported to Cairo that the German secret service was desperately trying to find out whether Tobruk was being evacuated by the British or the fortress was being strengthened. Churchill regarded this as a bad weakening of security for Operation "Ultra Secret" and had specific instructions for the handling and dissemination of decoded Enigma reports given out.

At a desert airfield in the El Mechili area, April 1941: Air camera is installed in a Bf 110 reconnaissance plane.

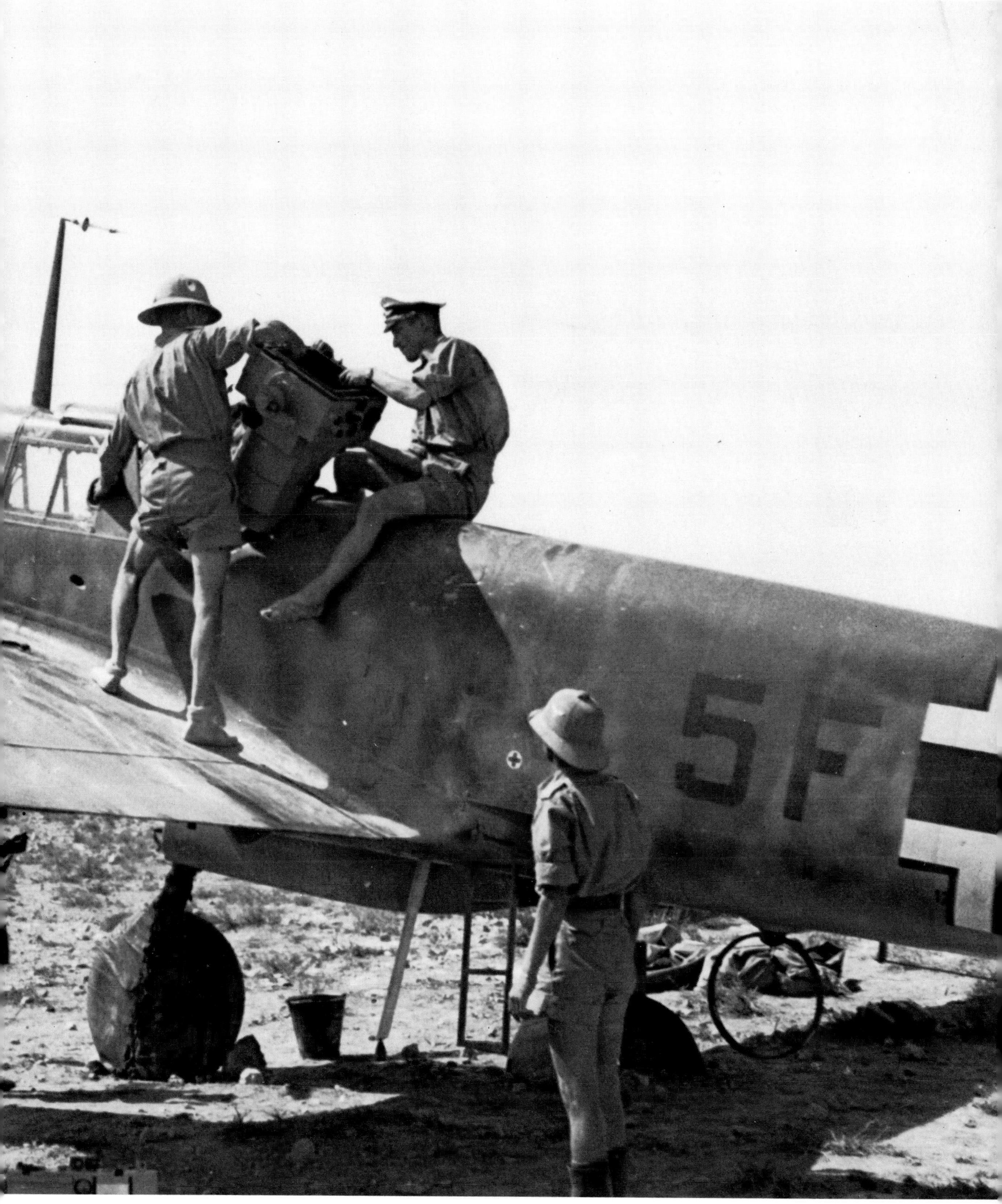
5F

Naples Harbor, April 1941: German panzers head for a loading ramp.

On Thursday, 10 April the tanks of the *Afrika-Korps* reached the fortress of Tobruk, the most important supply base for an attack on Egypt. The Australian division was able to escape via the coast road, while what remained of the British 2nd Armored Division and the Indian brigade were attacked and taken prisoner. General Wavell then transferred parts of the 7th Armored Division (Major General Creagh) to the harbor in the city of Tobruk so they could join with the Australian division and small local units.

When the advance units of the *Afrika-Korps* occupied Sollum and Bardia that day, Rommel telegraphed the OKH and asked for permission to advance further to Suez.

On Friday, 11 April Rommel's first attempt to take the fortress of Tobruk in a bold move failed.

On the same day, on account of a deciphered Italian radio message, four British destroyers were transferred to Malta. A German-Italian convoy, consisting of the freighters "Adana" (4205 BRT), "Aegina" (2447 BRT), "Arta" (2452 BRT), "Iserlohn" (3704 BRT) and "Sabaudia" (1590 BRT), escorted by the Italian destroyers "Baleno", "Lampo" (Corvette Captain Albanese) and "Tarigo" (Frigate Captain de Christofaro), was to transport units of the 15th Panzer Division to join the *Afrika-Korps.*

On Saturday, 12 April Rommel's troops fought their way into Fort Capuzzo and Sollum. The advance units of the 5th Light Division now occupied the important Halfaya Pass but were held in the highlands before the British defense lines under heavy defensive fire.

On Monday, 14 April, after the *Afrika-Korps'* advance in Cyrenaica, attacks on his supply lines were intensified, and Churchill gave this operation the highest level of priority.

increasingly more precise. They included not only more information on tactical reconnaissance, including the daily intentions of *Fliegerführer Afrika,* but also reports on the results of RAF attacks, on the supply situation and the fuel and food shortages, and on the positions and movements of the German and Italian troops. But General Wavell was scarcely in a position to evaluate this extremely valuable information operationally. In addition, these reports from B.P. were known only to an extremely limited number of persons at the SIS headquarters in Cairo. And the transmission of this information from Cairo to the various command posts entailed delays, on account of the need for particularly strict security measures, since the GC & CS realized that the Germans could read British Army codes and encoded texts. A further problem was that the B.P. cryptologists — responsible for passing the Enigma material on to Cairo — scarcely had the experience at that time to know what was important or unimportant for an army in the field. The result was that information of great importance was often simply held back.

On the evening of 16 April the destroyers "Janus", "Jervis", "Mohawk" and "Nubian" of the 14th Destroyer Flotilla (Captain Mack), belonging to the British Force K, sighted the announced convoy near the island of Kerkenna in the Small Syrte, consisting of four steamships of the German 20th Transport Echelon and the Italian freighter "Sabaudia" (1590 BRT) with supplies for the *Afrika-Korps,* and destroyed them all.

On this day Luftwaffe Enigma reported that the major part of the German troops had taken positions in the Sollum-Sidi Omar sector, and that *Fliegerführer Afrika,* under *Generalleutnant* Fröhlich, had again requested additional fighter planes. From that day on, Enigma reports confirmed that Rommel's advance through Cyrenaica was causing a severe shortage of fuel and transport vehicles.

Only as of mid-April 1941 did the reports on German intentions, which the British obtained thanks to Luftwaffe Enigma and passed on from B.P. to Cairo via their new direct service, become

Cairo, April 1941: One of the radio and teletype facilities of the C-in-C Middle East.

Off the Libyan coast, April 1941: An Italian transport attacked and set afire by the British Force F.

The Panzer's Tail   —by Illingworth.

How a London cartoonist saw the Royal Navy's disruption of the supply lines to Rommel's troops.

The Italian destroyer "Tarigo" (Frigate Captain de Christofaro) did manage to score a direct torpedo hit on the "Mohawk", but in the further course of the action the "Tarigo" and two other Italian destroyers were sunk or badly damaged. It was the first destroyer battle in the Mediterranean. Of the 3000 soldiers aboard, only 1248 could be rescued. This debacle resulted in subsequent supply problems for the *Afrika-Korps*.

On Thursday, 24 April the last units of the 3rd Company of Intelligence Unit 56 landed in Tripoli with their company leader, *Oberleutnant* Seebohm. The company was immediately transferred to its operational area on the Syrte. It was the German *Afrika-Korps'* only surveillance company.

This well-equipped radio reconnaissance unit had been established at Le Havre in 1940-41 for radio surveillance of Britain. *Oberleutnant* Seebohm, one of the best specialists in the area of radio reconnaissance, had already served with his 3rd Company of Intelligence Unit 56 in Rommel's 7th Panzer Division during the French campaign.

The *DAK*'s radio reconnaissance proved to be Rommel's most reliable source of intelligence. Their advantage: Enemy transmissions were heard at once. The well-organized transmission of the information they received provided a decisive gain in time over any other means of reconnaissance. Further sources of intelligence from which Rommel obtained his knowledge of the enemy were the statements of prisoners, captured documents, ground and air reconnaissance. For example, captured maps, orders, service instructions, personal correspondence or daybooks provided the indications needed to judge the enemy's position as well as strength, organization, command principles and intentions. Radio code charts and other codes were especially valuable prizes.

The capable questioning of prisoners of war also proved in time to be a rewarding source of intelligence information. Many of them, while still under the shock of being captured, precisely revealed their organizational positions, their commanders' names or details of organization, action and intentions. The special status of the *DAK*, though, did not include its own prison camp. All British troops taken prisoner had to be turned over, via German collecting camps, to the Italians for internment after being questioned. German position reports also were sent to the "Supercomando Libia" in Tripoli first, where they were encoded by the Italians and sent on to Rome.

On Sunday, 27 April *Generalleutnant* Paulus arrived in North Africa. He was sent by the OKH to ascertain Rommel's intentions and make clear to him that only limited means were at his disposal for his operations. Paulus' first move after learning of Rommel's intentions was to counter the clearance for the attack on Tobruk that Rommel had planned for 30 April 1941.

One of many examples: An Enigma message from the Supermarina to a subordinate naval command was decoded at B.P. and sent to Admiral Cunningham at 8:10 PM on 26 March 1941. (Document No. PRO-ADM 223 76x/PO 9755).

The popular Italian General Bergonzoli, "Redbeard", interrogated by a British intelligence officer.

Sollum area, 17 April 1941: The first German officer taken prisoner by the British being questioned by an intelligence officer.

On Monday, 28 April Luftwaffe Enigma revealed from reports made by *Fliegerführer Afrika's Generalleutnant* Fröhlich that the Luftwaffe was "seriously hampered by losses that were not replaced" in addition to being short of fuel in the advanced Tobruk-Bardia area.

At the end of April 1941, the C-in-C Middle East, General Wavell, learned from Enigma that parts of the 15th Panzer Division were still expected in Tripoli. In fact, though, the British destroyers' attack on the convoy on 16 April had ruined the plans for shipping the 15th Panzer Division out, and the arrival of the last parts of it in Tripoli could not be expected before the middle of May.

On Thursday, 1 May, at 9:00 AM, the *Afrika-Korps*, after successfully capturing several fortifications at Tobruk, had to go on the defensive, and was exposed to heavy artillery fire until evening.

Likewise on Friday, 2 May, after the first parts of the German 15th Panzer Division had already reached the front, the British were able to fight off all the German attempts to capture the fortress of Tobruk.

On Saturday, 3 May *Generalleutnant* Paulus' inspection report was transmitted to the OKW by Luftwaffe code and also routinely intercepted by the British Y Service and decoded at B.P. This report gave Churchill good reason to urge General

Wavell to go on the offensive despite his not very favorable view of the situation. On the same day the SIS learned via Luftwaffe Enigma of Rommel's requests in the last week of April: Troop reinforcements with transport vehicles plus strengthening of the Luftwaffe and U-boat action in the coastal waters between Sollum and Tobruk. All of that was necessary if he was to hold Sollum and Bardia and not miss the chance to put Tobruk out of action. In addition, at this point neither the OKH nor the SIS knew that Rommel's actual goal was Egypt.

Likewise on 3 May the JIC stated that the C-in-C Middle East had overestimated the Axis transport and supply problems and had probably overlooked "certain signs" that Rommel would attempt in May to break through the British defense positions with weaker motorized forces.

This viewpoint led the British chief of staff to accept the risk of sending a convoy with armored reinforcements through the Mediterranean to Alexandria.

On Sunday, 4 May Rommel gave up his attempts to capture Tobruk. Thus his first offensive, which had cost him heavy losses without bringing decisive success, ended.

On Monday, 5 May Churchill wired to General Wavell: "Have you read my telegram of the fourth of this month? I presume you are aware of the strictly secret and vital character of this information?" The actual text is more pointed and shows that the enemy was, "fully exhausted . . . thus strictly forbidden to make an advance past Sollum without permission in advance, except for reconnaissance."

Previously unknown photo: A bunch of bananas is a souvenir for General Paulus as he takes leave of the Fliegerführer Afrika, General Fröhlich, at his command post near Derna.

It has been reported by a reliable
source that in the morning on May 8 General
PAULUS went by plane from TRIPOLI to CATANIA.
Continuation of flight impossible due to weather
conditions. Subsequent conference with Commanding
General of X. Flying Corps.

- - - - - - -

This message must be treated as OFFICER
ONLY and should not be transmitted by telephone.

M.I.14.
1120 hrs.
9.5.41.   Distribution :

C.in C. M.E.   Personal
C.S.S.   Personal
D.D.I.   Personal
D.D.M.I.   Personal
M.E.I.C.   Personal

An Enigma message tells of General Paulus' departure from North Africa; it was given to General Wavell in Cairo just 24 hours later. (Document No. PRO WO 169/1240).

of Rommel's radio reconnaissance increased the suspicion that a British offensive could be about to begin.

On Monday, 12 May a convoy (Operation "Tiger") with 238 tanks and 43 fighter planes, escorted by a battleship, aircraft carriers, cruisers and destroyers, arrived at Alexandria. Only one freighter was lost in transit. With these reinforcements, General Wavell planned to lead a relief offensive (Operation "Brevity") toward Tobruk on 15 May.

On Wednesday, 14 May the *DAK*'s radio reconnaissance company (*Oberleutnant* Seebohm) sent the intercepted radio message to all British units and reported that the next day was "Peter."

On Thursday, 15 May General Wavell's units moved forward to break through the German front line near Sollum. At the very beginning of this battle in the early morning hours, the temperature was between 50 and 60 degrees Celsius, the air shimmered, and visibility on both sides was bad. The Halfaya Pass, Sollum and Fort

Decoded at B.P.: The first page of a highly secret report from General Paulus on his inspection of Rommel's troops.

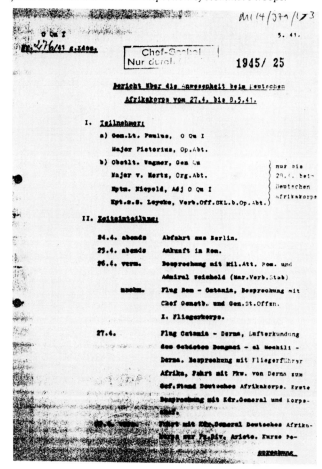

In the first week of May 1941 the Enigma information that reached Cairo was completed by captured documents and statements from prisoners of war. It was now clear that Rommel had improvised his advance in great haste. What neither the radio reconnaissance nor the Luftwaffe Enigma messages made clear was the almost catastrophic state of the British armored units in comparison to the German, plus their vulnerability to German antitank guns and, in particular, the 88mm Flak guns.

As of Thursday, 8 May B.P. sent to the C-in-C Middle East, General Wavell, the last portions of the complete text of *General* Paulus' report. Since Cairo had received the complete text of Paulus' instructions and knew that the 15th Pazner Division had not yet reached Tripoli at full strength, the C-in-C three all available tanks into the attack, though the "Tiger" supply convoy with its tanks had not yet reached Alexandria.

On Friday, 9 May the Reuters press agency sent out a brief message: "All German troops have been forced to retreat out of Egypt by the British Army of the Nile." This statement and the results

Agedabia area: Newly captured German and Italian prisoners.

Capuzzo were occupied for a short time by the British 22nd Guard Brigade, but quickly won back by a counter-thrust of the Herff battle group. The British lost about 270 tanks. The great tank battle of Sollum, which was supposed to break the ring around Tobruk in particular, now reached its zenith.

Although the Luftwaffe Enigma radio messages provided very good tactical information, they were often made obsolete by the time it took to decode them at B.P. Their transmission via Cairo to the British forces in the field was still the biggest problem. The British commanders were often not clear as to the positions and movements of either their own or the German forces at any given time.

Unlike the German reconnaissance, which correctly evaluated the obtained information and warned Rommel of enemy attacks without delay, the British commanders did not know at the right time that Rommel had moved a large portion of his tank reserves forward earlier than expected. They were still of the opinion that they had a two-to-one advantage in tanks in the combat area. Thus they were completely surprised to encounter a greater number of tanks than they themselves possessed, in spite of Rommel's serious fuel problem.

Although convoys headed for Tripoli put out to sea from Naples every three or four days between March and mid-May 1941, Luftwaffe Enigma reported only now and then on convoy instructions for the X. Air Corps. This news was reported at once to Cairo, or via the Admiralty to the C-in-C Mediterranean (Admiral Cunningham), but only in isolated cases were the Royal Navy and RAF command posts notified without delay.

On Friday, 16 May Cairo learned from B.P. that the German situation at Sollum and Fort Capuzzo had become very critical on account of Operation "Brevity."

On Saturday, 17 May the British knew from Luftwaffe Enigma radio messages that Rommel had asked for support from *Fliegerführer Afrika* (*Generalleutnant* Fröhlich) and *Luftflotte* 4 (*Generaloberst* Löhr).

On Friday, 30 May the JIC announced that the German operations in North Africa had been limited by their own recognizance of what could be undertaken by the troops already on hand. This news was of the greatest importance to the

Sollum area, May 1941: A four-wheeled armored scout car (Sd.Kfz.260) of the DAK, with frame antenna, as the regimental radio car.

Tripoli Harbor, May 1941: An Italian steamship with barrels of fuel for the DAK exploded after being bombed by the RAF.

C-in-C Middle East for planning future operations. The JIC had sent out this message after it had learned of the latest stage of German preparations for Operation "Barbarossa", the attack on the Soviet Union.

Although a total of 21 Axis freighters had been sunk on their way to Libya in April and May of 1941, including eight ships sunk by U-boats and nine by other ships operating out of Malta, this was not enough to disturb supplying the Axis troops seriously.

As of June 1941 the Italian forces introduced a new machine code system to replace Enigma D: The new device was the Hagelin C 38 machine, which was thought to be absolutely safe. This was a surprise for B.P., but since they had an almost identical French C-36 model, the GC & CS broke the Italian C-38m code in a short time and was able to reconstruct the code settings in time.

On Friday, 6 June the *DAK*'s radio reconnaissance company (*Oberleutnant* Seebohm) became aware of the completely new organization of British forces on the Sollum front, the unmistakable sign of an impending new enemy operation.

On the evening of 14 June the *DAK*'s radio reconnaissance company reported picking up the radio warning "Peter" to all British units for the next day. Rommel immediately ordered preparatory measures to begin as of 9:00 PM.

On Sunday, 15 June Operation "Battleaxe" began with a large-scale attack by the British XIII. Corps (Lieutenant General Godwin-Austin) on

*Sollum area, June 1941: **A DAK** non-commissioned officer being questioned by British intelligence officers.*

the German-Italian border positions. During the battle itself, Rommel regularly received information from his radio reconnaissance service and from captured documents. But the British enemy-position reconnaissance failed again this time: Although the strengthening of the German defensive positions had been known of before the attack, British aerial reconnaissance was unable to find any signs that Rommel had received any significant reinforcements during the past month.

From the Luftwaffe Enigma reports it was learned not only that the luftwaffe had received no reinforcements in Libya, but also that the greater part of the Luftwaffe units in Sicily had been transferred to the eastern front. All of this

made a German advance seem all but impossible. On the other hand, information about the strengths and intentions of the German armored units were insufficient; even the air-reconnaissance photographs were few in number and revealed nothing. The result: Where the British forces had expected about a hundred German tanks, they suddenly faced twice that number. Rommel had brought all his reserves from the Tobruk area at the right time without the other side noticing.

About 10:00 AM the *DAK* captured a list of British code names with detailed positions of the attacking troops, names of the commanders, code names for tanks, guns and materials. This

Sollum area, 15 June 1941: Detailed British radio information found after combat in the desert.

valuable material was passed on to the reconnaissance company of the *DAK*. Now their surveillance of enemy radio traffic resulted in quicker evaluation and immediate regrouping of the German units.

On Monday, 16 June Rommel made a wide encircling maneuver through the desert past Sidi Omar and met the British west flank. Now the British XIII. Corps was in danger of being surrounded. It was able to escape from this danger, but in the process 100 of its 180 tanks that saw action were lost. Rommel's total loss was twelve tanks; fifty more were damaged but could be retrieved later.

On Tuesday, 17 June, as night fell, the British

XIII. Corps withdrew to Egypt. Thus Rommel had won the tank battle of Sollum.

On Monday, 21 June the British tried to mount a counteroffensive with a series of tank advances in the Sollum area. But they were thrown back by the *Afrika-Korps* and the situation became quiet again.

The defeat at Sollum on 21 June had a postscript: The C-in-C Middle East, General Wavell, was relieved of command and transferred to India, and his place was taken by General Sir Claude Auchinleck.

On Monday, 23 June B.P. sent the first information from a new source to Cairo. They had just broken the Italian naval code used by the C-38m

At a desert airfield, June 1941: A German Henschel Hs 126 is prepared to take off on a short-range reconnaissance mission.

machine for May and June. And from these just-decoded radio messages the C-in-C Middle East learned of the departure of a convoy consisting of four large ships, each 20,000 BRT, with Italian troops aboard, on their way to Tripoli. When the Italians learned that all the aircraft available at Malta were concentrating on the convoy, it was halted at once.

The defeat of Operation "Battleaxe" is an example of the many factors that determined the actions of British leadership after Enigma reports had been received. Some of the most important: The experiences do practices of the commanders as well as a definitely, already available conception of political and military goals. It was exactly these well-defined strategic concepts that typified the usually wrong decisions that were made on the basis of Enigma messages. The British military leaders did not at first recognize the significance of these messages and only learned

in time to evaluate them correctly and know when the Enigma reports could be taken literally.

On the other hand, Rommel attributed great significance to radio reconnaissance. During the first part of the Libyan campaign he was aware of all the British radio traffic. Rommel did not avoid any precautionary measures to guard the security of his own communications either. Almost half of his radiomen had to monitor their own traffic in order to avoid any possible indiscretion. Rommel even gave orders to keep track of on his own motor vehicles so that radio traffic or surveillance would not be disturbed by their motors.

From the beginning, obtaining provisions and supplies was the Achilles' heel of the *Afrika-Korps*. The problem actually began on the continent of Europe, where the Italian railway lines were quite insufficient; from Rome to Naples they could handle 24 trains a day, from there to the Reggio area 12 a day, and the Reggio-Messina

In the Libyan Desert, June 1941: A radioman of a British unit sending a message.

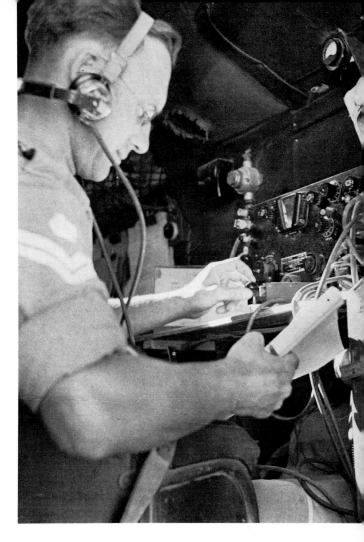

Radio situation report of the 3rd Listening Company (Oberleutnant Seebohm), dated 24 June 1941, summing up the results of radio reconnaissance.

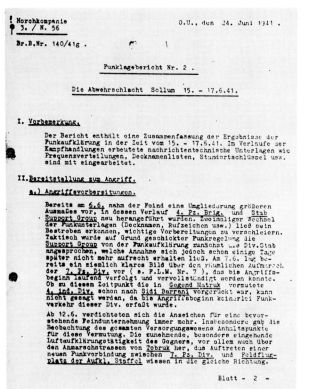

railroad ferry could transport only 400 cars per day, about 100 of which were available for German transportation.

Axis shipping, strongly endangered by the British naval fortress of Malta in any case, had to reach Tripoli, and later Benghazi and Tripoli. From here, further transport had to move on a single narrow desert road, the Via Balbia, which was also seriously threatened from the air. At times the distance to the front was more than 1000 kilometers. The supply-truck columns thus had to cover 2000 kilometers, a distance that in itself used up most of the supplied fuel, wore out trucks and required considerable manpower. The further the troops moved to the east, the more critical the supply program became.

At this time the first Special Liaison Unit (SLU), a special communications unit responsible for the security of the secret radio messages transmitted from B.P. to the Middle East, was transferred to Cairo. Its chief was "Pinky" McFarlan, who had already served at Vignolles, France as the British liaison officer to P.C. Bruno. His unit was now called "Detachment Special Signals Unit" and was later disguised from friend and foe as "No.5 Special Communications Unit."

Radio masts of the SLU unit in Cairo.

On Friday, 27 June the four large ships put out to sea again and finally reached Tripoli safely.

At the end of June 1941 McFarlan and his SLU finally reached Egypt after a long sea voyage around the Cape of Good Hope. He set up his main office at the Middle East Headquarters in Cairo and his radio station at Abassia, the communications unit to the army being ordered directly into the desert.

McFarlan was personally responsible for passing B.P. messages on to the commander (C-in-C Middle East) or authorized members of his staff. All the messages were immediately recovered by him and destroyed as soon as they had been read. No recipient of B.P. information had permission to send such a radio message further.

Every measure that was based on information received from B.P. was to be modified in a combat order, command or instruction to a form that could in no way refer to the original text or allow the enemy to suspect that his radio messages were being read. No recipient of B.P. messages was allowed to get willingly into a situation in which he might be captured by the enemy. In addition, no Enigma material could move further forward than the army headquarters.

At the Cairo headquarters, the SLU consisted of two groups, each with a radio truck to receive messages from Whaddon Hall around the clock and a secret code truck where the messages were decoded and then passed on by McFarlan. The radio messages from Bletchley Park were sent by the Whaddon Hall transmitter directly to Cairo and then from Cairo to the SLU at Royal Navy headquarters in Alexandria and to the SLU at the army headquarters in the field. Radio reception in the western desert, though, was anything but good.

Whenever General Auchinleck went to the front, he took his personal SLU along, so as to keep in touch with the "secret enemy intelligence service."

The whole Ultra system with its varying degrees of perfection depended on the quick turnover of clear radio messages. And the transmission of the messages from Cairo to the front was always a complicated undertaking. It soon became clear that it was better to send a radio message from Abbassia to Whaddon Hall by reflecting it off the ionosphere in the upper atmosphere and then sending it directly back from Britain to the army SLU in the desert than to send it from Abbassia across a few hundred miles of desert to the front.

The following SLU's were located in the eastern Mediterranean: with the desert army, with the combat forces in the desert, at Middle East forces headquarters in Cairo, partially with the navy in Alexandria, and one additional SLU each in Malta and Beirut. They were not parts of the headquarters at which they served and were not subordinated to them. Yet they had to pay attention to operational plans through which the secret of B.P. could have become known to the enemy. They also had to be sure that their superior officers did not handle these very secret messages carelessly.

HQ of the C-in-C Middle East in Cairo: Intelligence officers at work in their office. Details of the wall maps were made unrecognizable by the censors.

HQ of the C-in-C Middle East, Cairo: The mobile unit of the SLU under Captain "Pinky" McFarlan.

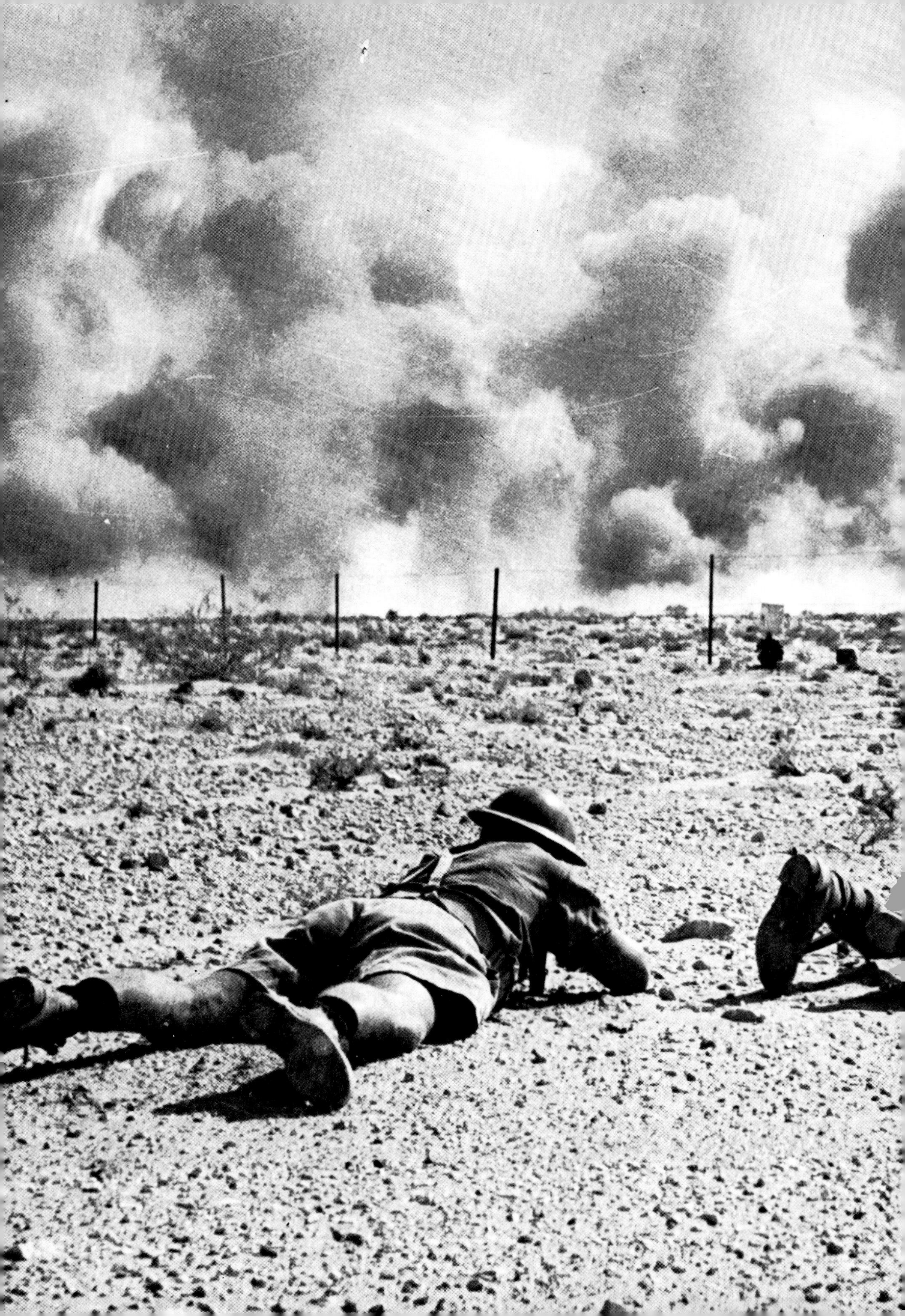

1941

July-December

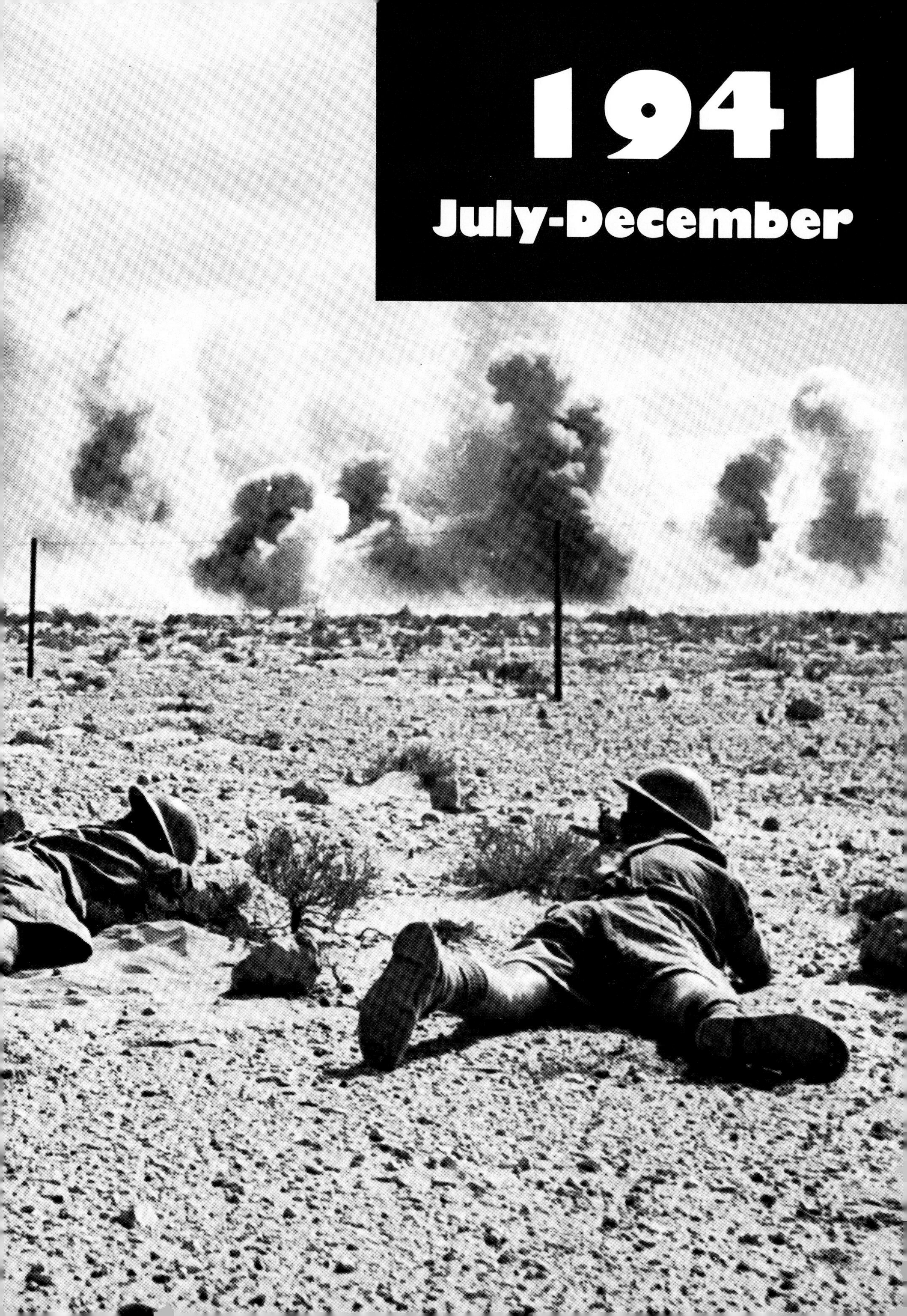

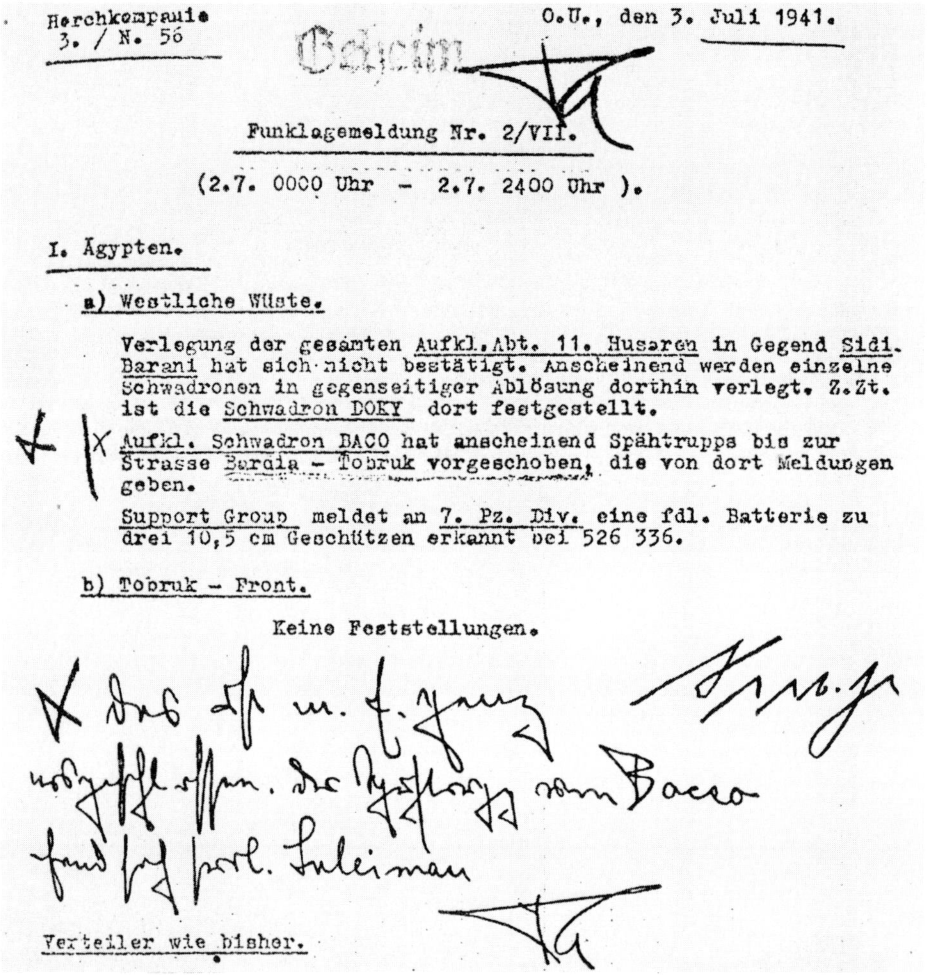

Horchkompanie
3. / N. 56

O.U., den 3. Juli 1941.

Geheim

Funklagemeldung Nr. 2/VII.

(2.7. 0000 Uhr – 2.7. 2400 Uhr).

I. Ägypten.

a) Westliche Wüste.

Verlegung der gesamten Aufkl.Abt. 11. Husaren in Gegend Sidi. Barani hat sich nicht bestätigt. Anscheinend werden einzelne Schwadronen in gegenseitiger Ablösung dorthin verlegt. Z.Zt. ist die Schwadron DOKY dort festgestellt.

X Aufkl. Schwadron BACO hat anscheinend Spähtrupps bis zur Strasse Bardia – Tobruk vorgeschoben, die von dort Meldungen geben.

Support Group meldet an 7. Pz. Div. eine fdl. Batterie zu drei 10,5 cm Geschützen erkannt bei 526 336.

b) Tobruk – Front.

Keine Feststellungen.

Verteiler wie bisher.

With a comment from Rommel: Radio situation report of the 3rd Listening Company (Oberleutnant Seebohm), 3 July 1941.

»
At a desert airfield, an RAF reconnaissance plane prepares for take-off.

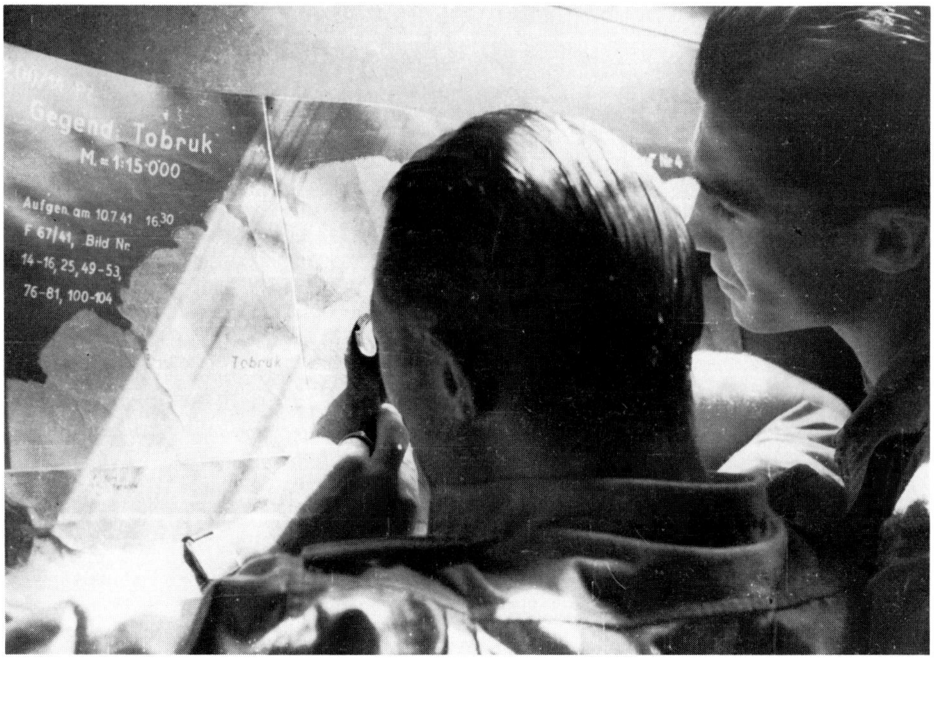

Gegend: Tobruk
M.=1:15 000
Aufgen. am 10.7.41 16.30
F 67/41, Bild Nr
14-16, 25, 49-53,
76-81, 100-104
Tobruk

The command post of the Fliegerführer Afrika, 25 July 1941: Evaluating photographs.

Early in July 1941 a pause in the fighting began that was to last almost four months: Until October only artillery activity, scouting and reconnaissance activity prevailed. Meanwhile the Germans and British refreshed their units and strengthened them.

The risks of sending supplies by convoys caused problems for both sides. Yet Rommel's supply lines were severely endangered by the British actions from Malta. The siege of Tobruk continued all the while; its occupying forces were supplied by sea and relieved regularly.

On Monday, 14 July it was reported in an Enigma message that the Germans in Tunisia were still trying to buy ex-French siege artillery. MI6 regarded this as proof that Rommel's preparations for an attack on Tobruk were presumably not yet completed.

On Friday, 25 July *"Panzergruppe Afrika"* (*Generalleutnant* Rommel) was formed of the *Afrika-Korps* and the Italian units.

On Monday, 28 July the opinion held by MI6 in London was that only supply difficulties could delay a large-scale Axis offensive in North Africa. It was also concluded on the basis of Luftwaffe Enigma reports that even an attack on Tobruk

was probably out of the question because of a lack of sufficient supplies.

Although B.P., thanks to the Enigma reports, could always report the movements of the German-Italian convoys between Italy and North Africa to the C-in-C Mediterranean without delay, there were several operative and tactical difficulties that made it almost impossible to utilize the information.

As a rule, the Enigma radio messages were deciphered at a point in time that often made the immediate action of suitable combat forces necessary, but those forces were not available on the convoy's route. The other major hindrance: So as not to reveal that the Enigma radio messages were the source of information, the convoys had to be "discovered" inconspicuously by other means of reconnaissance, such as aircraft or submarines. Only then could action be taken.

In July 1941 aerial reconnaissance of Axis shipping lanes in the Mediterranean was improved markedly. This was attributable not only to the new reconnaissance equipment that the British had brought to Malta. Along with the Hurricanes and Marylands of the 69th RAF Squadron, which were able to observe the

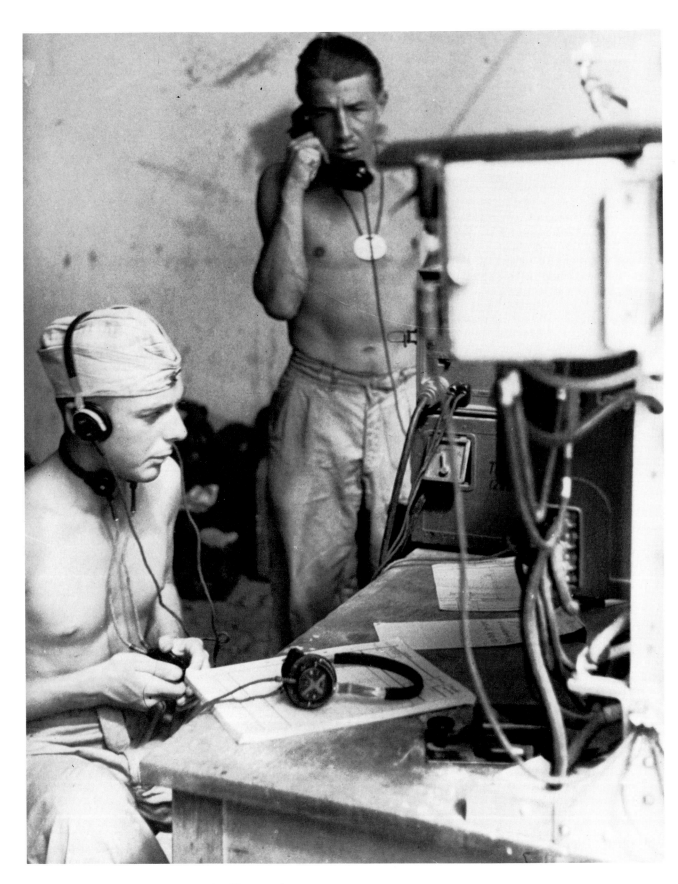

In the radio room of a Luftwaffe intelligence unit.

southern Italian seaports as well as Sicily and Tripoli, regular photographic reconnaissance missions were flown regularly as of mid-1941.

In this month the CBME was finally able, by listening to radio traffic in the mid-level code used by the Germans during their airborne operations on Crete, to break the Army Enigma codes (British code name: Chaffinch) used by the German troops in North Africa. These included, among others, simpler tactical codes such as that of the radio reconnaissance company of the *Afrika-Corps* (*Oberleutnant* Seebohm) and a code that was used to give units their direction of advance before an attack.

The support organization in Cairo was also able to reconstruct frequencies, call letters and code names used by the *Afrika-Korps* regularly. Thus in time it was possible to identify the German groups and units. But since the British navigational equipment was still rather primitive, they were rarely able to localize the radio traffic from enemy transmitters. And the advanced Y units of the British radio reconnaissance, that could decipher even simple Italian coded texts only with difficulty, lacked the necessary experience to evaluate the German messages.

In July 1941 the British captured a German Panzer IV tank in very good condition. After a routine inspection, it was sent to Britain for a detailed examination. Although information on German weapons grew regularly and even a 50mm Pak 38 had been captured, the British had practically no detailed information on the feared 88mm Flak gun.

The SIS was least successful in terms of Rommel's operational intentions from mid-1941 on. One of the reasons: The operational value of the Army Enigma reports, the newest and most important source of information on Rommel's plans, was limited by disturbances and delays in reception. Thus only a part of the radio messages could be received. The information on Rommel's supplying, organization and disposition of the *Afrika-Korps* was sufficient, to be sure, but even the reports in the highest-ranking radio traffic rarely included usable information on any newly planned operations.

In summer 1941 the Enigma reports were devoted almost completely to everyday events concerning the administration of individual units and their staffs. The GC & CS was extremely restrained when it came to passing on Enigma reports; for example, the intercepted and deciphered radio messages that were sent on by wire from the Comando Supremo in Rome to the Führer's headquarters and concerned troops, equipment, supplies and requests for reinforcements were very seldom sent to Cairo.

At this time the state of British technical

In the Libyan Desert, July 1941: Rommel's armored command car "Moritz", a captured British AEC Matador (95 HP Diesel) with all-wheel drive.

intelligence was improving steadily. Its sources were not only British combat experiences, information from prisoners of war and captured documents but also, which was most important, the chance to test captured weapons and equipment.

The Luftwaffe Enigma delivered a whole series of important operative and tactical information in the summer of 1941, including among other things the fact that six Focke-Wulf Fw 200 aircraft of *Kampfgruppe* 40 (KG 40) and six Heinkel He 111's were ready for action against the Suez Canal and the Red Sea as air support bases in the eastern Mediterranean area as of August 1941.

After combat with a reconnaissance unit of Panzergruppe Afrika, British intelligence officers examine captured documents.

The planned attacks of the X. *Fliegerkorps* on British supply convoys on their way to Tobruk, as well as mining flights in waters near the Suez Canal, Tobruk and Alexandria were all known days in advance, including detailed information on the numbers and types of planes used and the exact locations of the minefields.

On Friday, 1 August a deciphered Italian naval Enigma report stated that the fuel situation of *Panzergruppe Afrika* would become very critical if the RAF and Royal Navy continued their attacks. In fact, the Luftwaffe's fuel supply in the foremost front sectors at that time was enough for only two days' action.

On Monday, 4 August it was reported by MI6 the Axis troops' supply situation in the back-line front area had not improved, although several troop transports, freighters and tankers had been able — despite successful RAF and Royal Navy attacks — to get through to Africa.

On Sunday, 10 August the C-in-C Middle East first learned the name *"Panzergruppe Afrika"* from the Luftwaffe Enigma. MI6 believed that this new name indicated that the involvement of another corps, perhaps an infantry corps, in North Africa was being planned.

On Friday, 22 August the C-in-C Middle East was still hoping that Rommel's supply problems would certainly make it impossible to launch an offensive. At the War Office, though, the opinion was held that reinforcements that had already arrived would allow Rommel to begin his operation before the British could begin theirs.

As of Monday, 25 August MI6 ruled out any

"immediately imminent operations" against Tobruk. It had been learned from the Luftwaffe Enigma that the *Fliegerführer Afrika* would not be in this theater of war beyond mid-September. But the Luftwaffe Enigma reports on and after 25 August offered clear indications of preparation for operations against Tobruk.

In August 1941 the Germans could already decipher the operative code of the War Office, which was used for the greater part of the British 8th Army's radio messages down to the division level. Since B.P.'s success in deciphering the German Army Enigma code (British code name: Chaffinch) was increasing, it is clear that Rommel received at least as much information on the strength and battle order of the 8th Army as the 8th Army did of *Panzergruppe Afrika*. But only at the end of August was the GC & CS able to break gradually into the operative Italian naval code (C 38m). Thus it was possible, though only very rarely at first, to gain insight into the movements of the Italian naval ships.

As of September 1941 MI6 in Cairo received an important reinforcement, the RAF Y Field Unit. This unit, stationed in Alexandria, listened to the Luftwaffe's tactical radio traffic as well as that of the Regia Aeronautica and thus could complement the Luftwaffe Enigma reports.

Radio situation report of the 3rd Listening Company (Oberleutnant Seebohm) of 1 August 1941, with the results of radio reconnaissance.

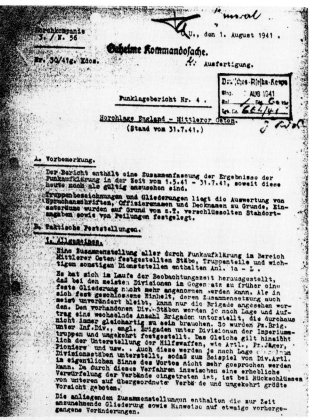

The crew of a radio truck extends the telescopic antenna.

On Friday, 5 September a new phase began for the British leadership in Cairo. On this day Bletchley Park (B.P.) was able for the first time to break the Army Enigma code so thoroughly that deciphered Army Enigma reports from *Panzergruppe Afrika* could be sent to Cairo. On the same day MI6 also learned that Regiment 361 belonged to the Division z.b.V. *Afrika,* and the 21st Panzer Division was a strengthened version of the 5th Light Division.

On Friday, 12 September the news reached B.P. that Rommel would have to give up his attack on Tobruk unless his supplying could be assured by concrete means.

On the same day the Luftwaffe Enigma report said that *Panzergruppe Afrika* had urgently requested maps and blueprints of the Tobruk defenses and the X. Air Corps had begun preparations for special missions against Tobruk.

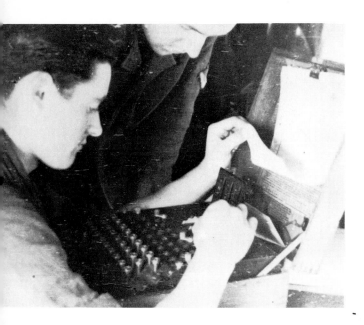

A radio station of the Fliegerführer Afrika: The Enigma daily code is set.

Cairo, 8 September 1941: Two British commanders in North Africa discuss the situation: General Sir Claude Auchinleck (left) and General Sir Archibald Wavell.

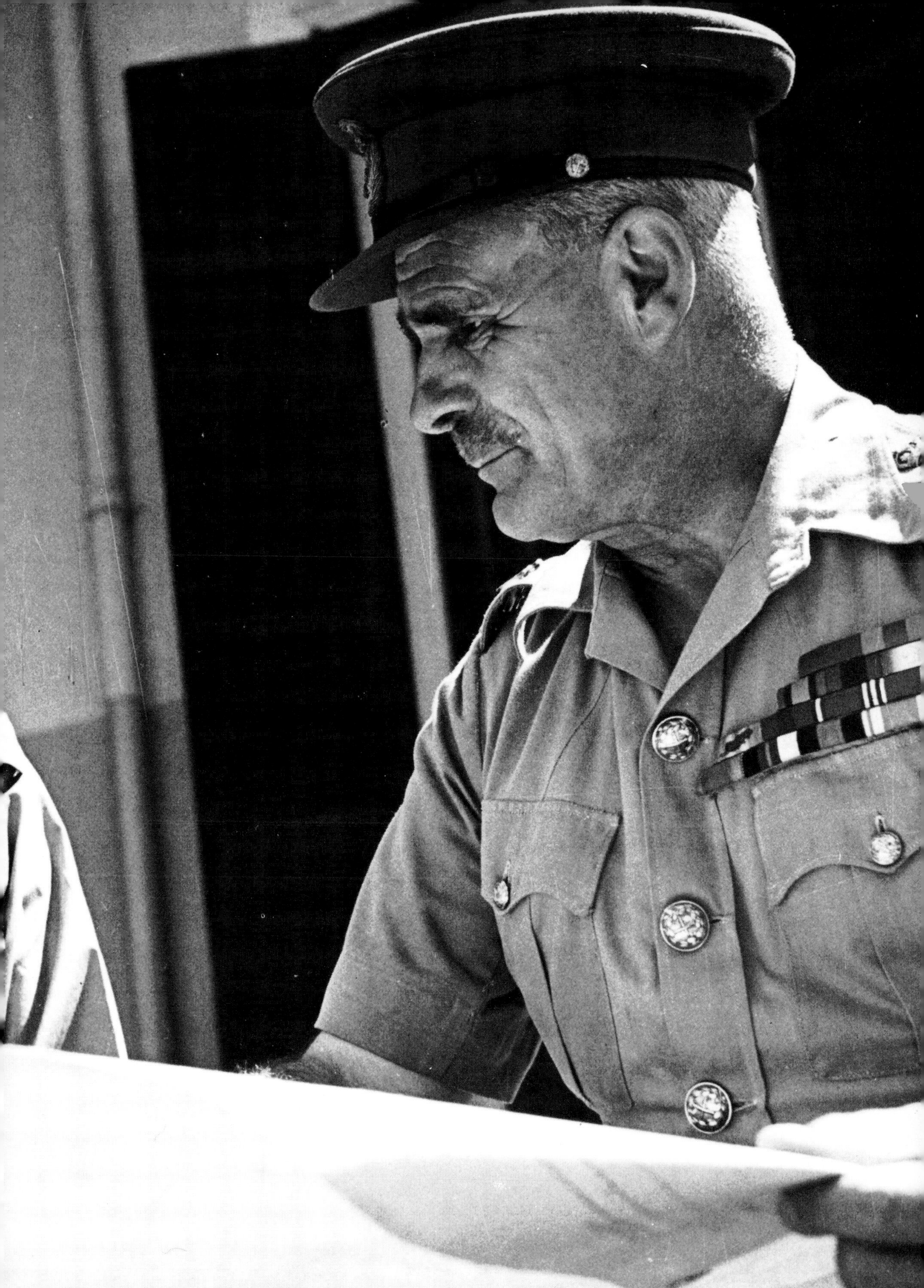

On Tuesday, 16 September the first German U-boat group ("Goeben"), with six boats, was transferred to the eastern Mediterranean. It was now under the operational command of the *Marinegruppenkommandos Süd* (Naval Group Command South) in Sofia. Despite objections from Admiral Doenitz, Hitler had ordered the group there to secure supply routes for convoys to North Africa. The U-boats scored great tactical success, but in the process they suffered heavy losses, and they could not stop the British advance in North Africa.

On Wednesday, 17 September B.P. was first to a great extent able to break the Army Enigma code (Chaffinch Code). Since that date it was read regularly, though with a great deal of trouble, until 19 October 1941. It often took a week or more until individual messages were completely translated. The Chaffinch consisted of three combined codes: Two were used within the most important supply bases in North Africa, Rome and Saloniki. The third code was for special communications between North Africa, Rome and Berlin, including the daily evaluation of the situation.

On this day, Churchill radioed the C-in-C Middle East in Cairo, because of a Chaffinch message: "The situation has worsened already . . . Various names of well-known places are gradually beginning to appear in special enemy information. Your transport movements and the formation of supply depots in the open are known to the enemy . . ."

On Thursday, 18 September, at 4:15 AM, the British submarine "Upholder" (Lieutenant Commander Wanklyn) torpedoed two large troop transporters, the "Oceania" and "Neptunia", each some 19,500 BRT, at the Heights of Homs, some 60 nautical mines from Tripoli, to which they were underway in an Italian convoy. The destroyers guarding them rescued 6500 soldiers, while 384 lost their lives. This was the result of a report that the Admiralty had received concerning the routes of the two ocean liners after B.P. had been able to decipher the Italian naval code C 38m at the right time.

On Monday, 22 September, an Enigma report said that the *Afrika-Korps* had been advised to reduce consumption of water, food and fuel. On the same day, a Luftwaffe Enigma message stating that a freighter loaded with bombs would arrive in Benghazi on the next day was decoded.

On Thursday, 25 September the British learned from the Luftwaffe Enigma that a freighter

Derna area, September 1941: the commanders of the Axis troops in North Africa, Generals Gariboldi (far left) and Rommel, discuss the situation.

carrying the whole supply of a certain type of bomb for the Axis forces in North Africa was blown up during an RAF attack on Benghazi.

By Friday, 26 September the SIS had acquired, within a week and from Army and Luftwaffe Enigma messages, much information that indicated Rommel's plans for an operation. A conference was said to have taken place at Gambut, Rommel's headquarters some 45 kilometers east of Tobruk. The headquarters of the Division z.b.V. *Afrika* had been transferred to the front lines. Several of its units were on the way from Tripoli to the front. In addition, all sections of *Panzergruppe Afrika* headquarters had been moved to Gazala, 35 kilometers west of Tobruk. Rommel was also said to have had a series of discussions with the commander of the X. *Fliegerkorps* and the German service officers in Rome.

Since 26 September, Rommel had also known his enemy's intentions very well. The irony of fate willed that the U.S. military attache in Cairo, Colonel Feller, made this possible without knowing it. Among the duties of the American colonel was that of sending a daily situation

Libyan Desert, September 1941: German troops with captured equipment on their way into position.

U.S. Colonel Bonner F. Feller.

report and the intentions of the British 8th Army to the State Department in Washington. His reports, encoded in the obligatory "Black Code" which was used by all U.S. military attaches and regarded as safe, were sent by the Egyptian Telegraph Office in Cairo to the central station in Washington.

The well-informed Feller kept his chiefs in the USA up to date, whether about international political intentions or the fighting strength, equipment, reinforcements, campaign plans or morale of their British allies in North Africa and the entire Middle East. He was able to report not only on the tactics and capabilities of every individual British commander, but also on the readiness for action of the RAF or the armored units, plus about the locations of Royal Navy units or convoy routes. It can no longer be said

One of the largest long-range antennas at the command post of the Fliegerführer Afrika.

A British radio truck in the Libyan Desert.

with assurance under what conditions the Germans were able to break the Black Code. There are many versions of the story, and it is hard to tell which one is true.

In fact, Rommel knew at the end of September 1941, 24 hours after its arrival in Washington, what Feller's report contained, thanks to a radio message from the OKW to the radio reconnaissance service that was subordinate to it. "My good source," Rommel called it. The "Desert Fox" also gained his all-inclusive view of the enemy's situation and intentions to that unit. And as his success between October 1941 and July 1942 proves (that is how long his secret was unknown to the British Secret Intelligence Service), he knew how to make use of it.

Meanwhile B.P. was able to decipher Italian radio messages in the C 38m code more and more often and to organize attacks on the Axis supply convoys which had been learned of in this way.

On Saturday, 27 September the JIC believed, on account of intercepted Luftwaffe and Army Enigma reports, that the *DAK*'s supply situation

would allow only a limited two-week campaign.

On Monday, 29 September the opinion was becoming more prevalent at MI6 that an attack on Tobruk in the immediate future was more than likely.

At the end of September 1941 the British learned from the Luftwaffe Enigma that the X. *Fliegerkorps* had been instructed to stop its missions over Egypt. Its units were now to concentrate on securing supply convoys. A long-range bomber group and a *Zerstörer* (Destroyer) unit of Messerschmitt Bf 110's were transferred to Sicily.

To be on the safe side, the Supermarina occasionally changed the schedule, composition and route of the convoys, all of which was announced via the Italian naval Enigma and decoded at B.P. If it was seen in Rome that the convoys were in danger, they were called back. Often their departure was delayed or the convoys were disbanded before departure.

Meanwhile, hours-long discussions about the operative intentions of the Axis powers took place at headquarters in Cairo. At the end of September

THIS DOCUMENT IS THE PROPERTY OF HIS BRITANNIC MAJESTY'S GOVERNMENT

SECRET.   Copy ·No. 31

C.O.S. (41) 601
(*Also W.P.* (41) 231
October 2, 1941

TO BE KEPT UNDER LOCK AND KEY.

It is requested that special care may be taken to
ensure the secrecy of this document.

WAR CABINET

CHIEFS OF STAFF COMMITTEE

WEEKLY RÉSUMÉ

(No. 109)

of the

NAVAL, MILITARY AND AIR SITUATION

from 0700 September 25th, to

0700 October 2nd,

1941

[Circulated with the approval of
the Chiefs of Staff.]

The cover of the secret weekly report of the British General Staff on sea, land and air action.

1941 Intelligence delivered fragmentary hints that Rommel was actually ready to move against Tobruk.

On Friday, 3 October a decoded Chaffinch report let General Auchinleck know for sure that he had gained some more time: The disruption of sea traffic between Italy and Africa was so decisive for troops returning from furlough that the lost time could not be made up in two or three weeks.

The report of the defense minister who sent this news directly to Cairo included the added comment: "The War Office stresses that this information is to be placed before General Auchinleck." This was one of a total of three cases in which Churchill made sure that "Ultra Secret" information from B.P. to the Middle East commander was concealed within the framework of Operation "Crusader." Churchill, who had perhaps a clearer view of all Enigma reports than anyone else, found General Auchinleck's hesitant reaction incomprehensible.

Mediterranean, October 1941: An Axis supply convoy spotted by an RAF reconnaissance plane acting on information from Enigma.

G.S.(Intelligence)
H.Q. EIGHTH ARMY

WEEKLY INTELLIGENCE REVIEW No. 1.

Based on information received up to 1800 hrs

5 Oct 1941

(a) Information sidelined in the margin is NOT to be
reproduced.

(b) Information contained herein will on no account be
reproduced for circulation below Brigade or equivalent
Headquarters.

PART I.

In the Frontier Area enemy activity during the week
appears to have been mainly directed towards the improvement of his defences. New minefields have been observed
between HALFAYA and SIDI OMAR: the suspected presence of
a new minefield some 9 miles N.W. of SIDI OMAR may indicate
that the right flank of the defensive zone is being extended in that direction. On 30 Sep one of our armoured cars
was damaged by a mine at a gap in the wire at B.P. 69.(some
12 miles NORTH of MADDALENA). Minefields so far South are
new. It is to be noted that this gap is opposite the
beginning of the track which leads North Westward towards
BIR EL GUBI and TOBRUK. If the enemy has sufficient mines
available he might be expected to distribute them along most
of the tracks leading across the frontier into CYRENAICA.

Movement of tracked vehicles in the HALFAYA Area
during Night 29/30 Sep is believed to have been connected
with exercises.

On 27 Sep a ship of 2000 tons entered BARDIA harbour
carrying a cargo believed to have been M.T. petrol.

*Page 1 of the first part of the weekly intelligence report of
the British 8th Army . . .*

PART II

G.S. (Intelligence) H.Q. Eighth Army. Weekly Intelligence Summary.
No. 1.

1. ENEMY METHODS.

(a) Enemy Armd Car patrols took bearings on our own patrols
at frequent intervals during their withdrawal on 29 Sep towards
SHEFERZEN. Formerly, the enemy has more often relied on air for
the location of our patrols.

(b) R.A.F. at TOBRUK again report the use of tin cans on wire
as a warning signal. Our patrols on the coastal area (frontier) report
the same device in the 'ADI SHAEA night 29/30 Sep.

2. ENEMY EQUIPMENT. (a) ITALIAN.

Armament of C.V.3s. A captured photograph from a letter
posted in Italy on 15 Sep 41 shows a C.V.3s Light Tank with a
SOLOTHURN A/Tk Rifle on an outside mounting for A/Tk Defence.
There were instances of C.V.3s being found equipped with
SOLOTHURN Rifles, during the campaign last February.
Small numbers of this rifle were issued to the Italian forces
in CYRENAICA in autumn 1940, and it now appears that it is part of
the regular equipment of the infantry regiment on the scale of One
per platoon, and One per Company in reserve.
One of the advantages of this weapon, which is of SWISS origin,
is that it can use the 20mm BREDA H.M.G. ammunition.

(b) German.
(1) With reference to Eighth Army Intelligence Summary No 3 Captured
Documents reveal that the Tank Regt in the German Army has a high
proportion of recovery vehicles.
8 Tank Regt for an establishment of 148 Tanks has 12 Tractors
which are presumably provided with Transporters. These are probably
issued on a scale of two to each squadron.
5 Tank Regt for an establishment of 158 Tanks had 16 such
machines, also issued at two per squadron.

. . . the first page of Part II of the report.

The report of the defense minister who sent this
news directly to Cairo included the added
comment: "The War Office stresses that this
information is to be placed before General
Auchinleck." This was one of a total of three cases
in which Churchill made sure that "Ultra Secret"
information from B.P. to the Middle East
commander was concealed within the framework
of Operation "Crusader." Churchill, who had
perhaps a clearer view of all Enigma reports than
anyone else, found General Auchinleck's hesitant
reaction incomprehensible.

On Wednesday, 8 October the Operative Intelligence Center (OIC) sent the radio message from
Supermarina, newly decoded at B.P., to the
Admiralty at Malta: Casaregis convoy with ships
"Casaregis", "Zeno", "Giulia", "Bainsizza" and
"Proserpina" departs Naples today at 2130 hours,
runs westward past Malta and then in the direction
of Tripoli at a speed of nine knots. Time of
arrival: 10/11/1941 at 1800 hours. Accompanied
by four destroyers. The "Nirvo" and a T-boat
"Cascino" join the convoy off Trapani." It is
noteworthy that the convoy had not yet left
Naples when this news had already arrived at
Malta.

On Thursday, 9 October the OIC radioed to
Malta: "Casaregis", "Zeno", "Giulia", "Bainsizza", "Proserpina" and "Nirvo", accompanied
by five destroyers, left Naples at 2130 hours on

*Mediterranean, October 1941: RAF bombers attack one of
the Italian supply ships.*

Rommel at his command post, discussing the situation.

compelled Rommel to put off his attack on Tobruk, first from September to October and later until the end of November.

The Luftwaffe Enigma messages at this time contained almost daily reports of the *DAK*'s strength and readiness for action, the condition of its airfields, troop reinforcements and the supply situation, plus details about daily goals, the intended scope of action and reports of operational success.

On Friday, 17 October SIS was still receiving new reports from radio reconnaissance that referred to Rommel's preparations for an attack on Tobruk, so that Churchill was convinced that it was soon to come.

On Tuesday, 21 October Force K (Captain Agnew), consisting of the cruisers "HMS Aurora" (Captain Agnew) and "Penelope" (Captain Nicholl) and the destroyers "Lance" and "Lively", reached Malta. Their activities in the next two months are an example of the operational action of intelligence.

Today it can't be determined how many sinkings of German-Italian supply ships since the breaking of the Italian Supermarina code are directly attributable to this fact.

Tobruk area: Radiomen of a DAK unit set up an antenna.

October 8, 1941. Speed nine knots. Arrival at Tripoli at 1800 hours on 11 October."

On Friday, 10 October, at 10:45 PM, flares suddenly illuminated the "Casaregis" convoy. In two waves, British planes attacked the surprised convoy, and the steamships "Casaregis" and "Zeno" were hit by torpedoes. At 4:30 PM on the next day, only the tanker "Proserpina" and the freighter "Giulia" reached the harbor of Tripoli.

In mid-October 1941 a Supermarina radio message revealed that the Italians were halting all convoy traffic to Tripoli because of the steadily mounting losses on this shipping route since 18 October.

MI6 learned from the same source that the German leadership pressured their Italian allies to take measures to maintain the transport of important supplies at any price. Troop reinforcements, if necessary, were to be transported by air or in destroyers. The U-boats had been sent to Derna and Bardia with fuel and equipment.

At that time there was, of course, no reliable information as to Rommel's plans and their delay in time, but it was obvious that the supply difficulties had operational consequences: They

On Saturday, 25 October the British Force K (Captain Agnew), with the cruisers "Aurora" and "Penelope" and the destroyers "Lance" and "Lively", carried out its first mission from Malta, though without success. A group of Italian destroyers with reinforcements for North Africa aboard was able to escape from Force K unseen, although B.P. had gained sufficient information about this destroyer group from Supermarina radio messages. The problem was the complicated and time-consuming route of sending the decoded radio messages from B.P. to the posts that could have used this information if they had received it at the right time.

For example, the C 38m messages intercepted at Malta were encoded again in a complex manner and then sent to B.P. by radio or telex. After the code messages were deciphered, B.P. sent them by telex to the SCU/SLU in Cairo, which passed them on to the Vica-Admiral at Malta. After the original texts had been departed from further for security reasons, the Vice-Admiral in Malta gave them out in the form of action commands. The Senior Officer of Force K, Captain Agnew, received these commands, but because of his low rank, he received no direct information from B.P.

Derna area, October 1941: An air photo processing site of the Regia Aeronautica.

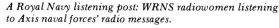

A Royal Navy listening post: WRNS radiowomen listening to Axis naval forces' radio messages.

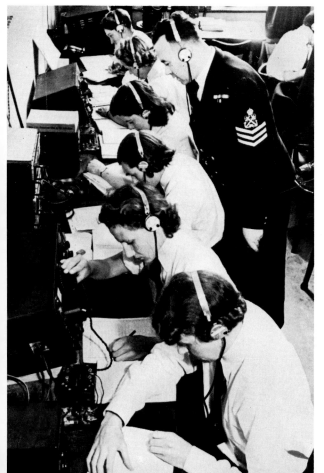

To simplify this complicated method of communication, GC & CS suggested to Churchill that the decoding of C 38m Supermarina radio messages be done not at B.P. but on the spot in Malta, which would enhance the operative value of the decoded messages considerably. Although this should have been of benefit to the Admiralty, they declined to support the suggestion.

This was also the first suggestion for simplifying the communication process that B.P. submitted to Churchill and that the Prime Minister took up.

Since 25 October the intercepted Supermarina code messages were decoded at Malta by a team of specialists sent there from B.P. for that purpose.

On Sunday, 26 October B.P., at Cairo's request, composed an analysis of the enemy's intentions. The Cairo headquarters wanted most of all to know whether Rommel might have discovered the top-secret British preparations for Operation "Crusader." B.P. came to the conclusion "that the enemy was expecting a British offensive and was straining every nerve to be ready for it, and that he was nowhere near ready to undertake an attack of his own."

. . . the developed pictures are dried

In an Italian photo evaluating office . . .

This was proved by, among other things, the shipping of new Messerschmitt Bf 109F fighter aircraft, which were superior to any RAF fighters in that theater of war, as well as increased German-Italian air reconnaissance activity and the hasty shipping of German reinforcements on Italian destroyers.

The constant need for more fuel and the ceaseless search by the German radio intelligence service for signs of a British offensive also attest to this view. The situation analysis closed with a decoded radio message from the high command of the Regia Aeronautica that said that a British offensive was expected and the Germans had also spoken of it.

In July 1941 some 40% of the fuel that had been loaded had been lost. In September and October 1941, an average of 13,000 of 16,000 tons of fuel arrived, while in the first three months of 1941 28,000 of an average of 31,000 tons had reached North Africa.

Thanks to the eventual breaking of the Italian C 38m naval code, B.P. was able as of July 1941 to report every convoy and every single shipment of significance precisely, with the ships' names, type and weight of their cargo, number of troops carried, the ships escorting them and security measures, as well as their planned routes, to headquarters in Cairo.

For the cryptologists, though, this was no easy task. The carefully coded messages from Italy as to the ships' routes, ports, lighthouses, beacons and such were mentioned only in code names. The code system of the C 38m machine was extremely complicated and made even more difficult by additional encodings of the planned departure and arrival times.

Between June and the end of October 1941 some 16% of the supplies for North Africa did not reached their intended destinations.

While the German radio reconnaissance service functioned almost perfectly, the British Army's Y organization was still in its infancy. The British code radiomen were quite casual about their tactical code and the whole radio traffic. The use of uncoded language and the lack of surveillance on radio traffic in the front lines, from brigade to battalion level, made it possible for Rommel to get at least some idea of the enemy's tactical plans.

Sunday, 2 November was a great day for B.P.: For the third time since 5 September, they were able to break the army Enigma code (Chaffinch code). The deciphered texts included requests for precise serial photographs, as large as possible, of the city of Tobruk and maps of the harbor, city and fortress. Rommel requested further shipments of assault equipment and at the same time expressed his concern as to whether it would arrive at the right time.

In his next radio messages, Rommel requested a hundred more antitank guns, and the X. *Flieger-korps* absolutely wanted a better supply of aircraft fuel no later than 20 November 1941.

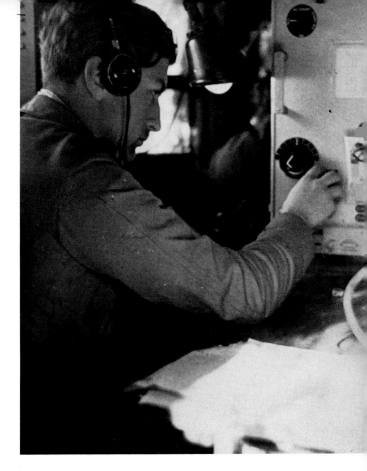

In the Libyan Desert, November 1941: An Italian radioman searches for frequencies.

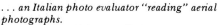

... an Italian photo evaluator "reading" aerial photographs.

In the Army Enigma radio messages intercepted and decoded on Friday, 7 November the "coming attack" was mentioned for the first time. Breaking into the "Chaffinch code" took place sporadically at that time but was done regularly from the middle of the following year on.

Early on the afternoon of 8 November the officer on duty with the 69th RAF Squadron at Malta received a call. A crew was to take off in a reconnaissance plane of the Maryland type immediately to observe an Italian convoy. Force K was likewise placed on standby.

Except for a few men in the know, nobody knew that the takeoff of the Maryland reconnaissance plane was just meant to deceive the enemy: A few hours ago, B.P. had just deciphered a C 38m radio message that contained precise details of the route, composition and type of cargo of a large convoy that was to use the Tripoli route, which had been closed on 18 October 1941 because of heavy losses. This news reached the Vice-Admiral at Malta, via the C 38m decoders sent to Malta by Churchill, soon enough.

Shortly after midnight on the night of 8-9 November, Force K attacked the big Italian convoy, which had been reported by the Maryland reconnaissance plane late in the afternoon, on its way to Tripoli. With the help of radar, Force K was able to maneuver into a favorable attack position unnoticed and open fire on the convoy without giving the radar-equipped Italian cover group, consisting of the heavy cruisers "Trieste" (Sea Captain Rouselle) and "Trento" (Sea Captain Parmigiano) or the 13th Destroyer Flotille (Sea Captain Capponi), with the ships "Granatiere", "Fuciliere", "Bersagliere" and "Alpino", a chance to attack them effectively.

Force K was able to sink all seven transports: "Duisburg" (7389 BRT), "San Marco" (3113 BRT), "Maria" (6336 BRT), "Sagitta" (5153 BRT), "Rina Corrado" (5180 BRT), the tankers "Conte di Misurata" (5014 BRT) and "Minatilan (7599 BRT). One of the six escort destroyers, the "Fulmine", and the two securing destroyers "Grecale" and "Euro", were damaged.

On Sunday, 9 November a radio message from Supermarina confirmed the tragedy that had

Mediterranean, November 1941: An large Italian convoy on course for Tripoli ...

taken place off the North African coast the previous night. With the entire convoy, a great number of tanks, the assault equipment urgently needed by Rommel and the fuel required by the X. *Fliegerkorps* had been lost. This debacle was one more indication to the German leadership that there was a traitor among the Italian Supermarina commanders who was reporting the movements of the Italian fleet to the British. The highest-ranking officers of the Italian Navy held this opinion for years after the end of World War II.

On Monday, 10 November the B.P. decoders read that furloughs had been halted for *Panzergruppe Afrika,* and that the Italian "Trento" motorized division was to see action in the attack on Tobruk. There was also talk of a plan of Rommel's to land troops from the sea near Tobruk by means of rubber rafts and other craft.

During the second week of November 1941 the preparations for a British counteroffensive, Operation "Crusader", were completed. General Auchinleck intended to smash Rommel's tank units, relieve Tobruk and take Libya and Tripo-

... one of the Italian freighters sinks after being attacked by Force K.

litania away from the Italians. Churchill was hoping for a victory comparable to Waterloo. To handicap his opponent from the start, an attempt on Rommel's life was planned, with which Operation "Crusader" was to begin.

Likewise on 10 November, a 59-man commando troop (Colonel Laycock) went aboard the submarines "Talisman" and "Torbay." Their mission was to attack Rommel's headquarters near Apollonia.

On Wednesday, 12 November a very casual radio message mentioned the coming offensive of the Rommel troops: The Army Enigma reported that the 15th Panzer Division (*Generalmajor* Neumann-Silkow) requested the delivery of 800 assault medals to recognize the bravery of their soldiers.

On Sunday, 16 November B.P. decoded an Enigma report in which it was said that the Italian Navy's "San Marino" Battalion had just arrived in North Africa — a further confirmation that Rommel was planning an attack from the sea as well as the operation of his motorized units

Silence! Whoever talks, is a traitor — as placards of the Italian forces warn.

87

SEA·POWER BOXING BOOTH

LIBYA CONVOY KNOCK·OUT

ALL COMERS TAKEN ON

HUGE PRIZES!
KNOCK THEM OUT AND THE WORLD IS YOURS

You next?

It's all right, it's only musso!

PAY HERE

—by Illingworth.

A London cartoonist's view of the British strikes against Italian supply convoys for the troops in North Africa.

against Tobruk.

On Monday, 17 November the commanders of the British XIII. Corps (Lieutenant General Godwin-Austen) and the XXX. Corps (Lieutenant General Norrie) were informed confidentially by General Headquarters that Rommel was planning an attack on Tobruk and was determined to beat back decisively any British attempt to take action.

To be sure, the two generals were amazed, for just a few days before they had been convinced that Rommel's plans were "completely defensive" and the German commander intended to withdraw.

General Headquarters cited the questioning reports of prisoners of war as the source of their news. The truth, though, was that this conclusion was based on decoded Luftwaffe and Army Enigma reports. It is possible that the statements of prisoners had confirmed this information.

On the same day, B.P. learned via Army Enigma that Rommel had flown to Rome on 1 November and was expected back at his headquarters in North Africa on the evening of 18 November. This information was rushed immediately to the C-in-C Middle East.

In the night of 17-18 November the commando under Colonel Keyes, set ashore near Appolonia by two British submarines, attacked the prefecture building in Beda Littoria, in which, according to information from the British Secret Service, was

Tobruk area, November 1941: The crew of an eight-wheeled armored scout car (Büssing-NAG) during a scouting mission.

"Secret Command Materials", a radio message of 17 November 1941 for General Rommel: "An attack on Tobruk is wanted soon."

General Cunningham), began. The army rolled out of the area of the desert fort at Maddalena in the direction of Tobruk to help the besieged fortress and occupy Cyrenaica.

The British units included 724 tanks, the Germans and Italians had 558. In spite of that, the situation was not unfavorable for *Panzergruppe Afrika:* As the attack began, both German armored divisions were east of Tobruk and could intervene in the battle at once.

At first the British were able to outflank the German southern group through the desert and meet the Axis forces at Sollum. Although they were able to close the encircling ring in the Sidi Rezegh area, the British tank units broke up in individual combat, so that no coordinated action resulted.

Heavy rainstorms turned the German air support points into swampy fields and made it impossible for reconnaisaance planes to take off. After Rommel's return on the evening of 18 November he said that on the basis of the available situation report the British attacks were certainly not the expected counteroffensive. Rommel's opinion was that it was merely a strengthened, powerful reconnaissance.

Libyan Desert, 1941: The Chief of the RAF in North Africa, Air Vice-Marshal Coningham (left), with General Ritchie and Brigadier Galloway.

located the headquarters of Rommel, whom they wanted to liquidate along with his entire staff.

In pouring rain some thirty men of the commando troop fought their way into the building half an hour after midnight. After a brief but heavy exchange of fire, the commandos had to withdraw. A stormy sea prevented the two submarines waiting offshore from taking the men back on board.

At daybreak they were encircled by the Germans and the survivors were taken prisoner. Only two of them were able to escape. After a day-long march through the desert, they reached their own lines again. In addition, Rommel's headquarters had never been in the prefecture building that had been attacked, and besides that, the general was in Athens that night.

When Rommel heard about the attack, he ordered the commandos treated as normal prisoners of war, although they wore overalls instead of uniforms and their status as combatants was questionable.

On Tuesday, 18 November, during a rare desert cloudburst, Operation "Crusader", the counteroffensive of the British 8th Army (Lieutenant

Libyan Desert, Tobruk area, November 1941: The Commanding General of the British XXX. Corps, Lieutenant General Norrie, beside his command car.

Picture evaluators of the British 8th Army examine the newest aerial photos.

One of the causes of this decisive failure was that both the RAF and the British Army knew how to make the enemy air and ground reconnaissance much more difficult and hold them back from the important preparation areas. Only from that evening's radio silence from the otherwise so chatty British radiomen did Rommel draw the wrong conclusions.

The commander of the British 8th Army (Lieutenant General Cunningham) relied considerably on his enemy situation reporters in planning the operation. According to them, for example, the XIII. Corps (Lieutenant General Godwin-Austin) should advance along the coast, mainly with infantry divisions, but only in case Axis units became invloved in the fighting. The preparations for the XXX. Corps (Lieutenant General Norrie) were also chosen according to the known locations of the enemy armored divisions.

Army Enigma reports provided valuable details about the German battle order that helped plan the British offensive. They added to the meager information about the Axis ground forces that MI6 had gained via Luftwaffe Enigma at the time. From these two sources the British leadership acquired their information, filled out from British air and ground reconnaissance, for the planning of Operation "Crusader."

Thanks to the Army Enigma radio messages, MI6 was able in numerous cases to identify the German units and groups and gain a clear picture of the composition of the armored brigades. The information gained from the Army Enigma reports was of incalculable value on the subject of enemy movements that were supposed to start immediately before Operation "Crusader", such as the transfer of the Italian "Ariete" Division to Bir Gubi. As verified by the statements of prisoners of war and reports from British reconnaissance, the presence of the Italian "Trieste" Division in the southern area, near Bir Hacheim, became known.

About noon on Wednesday, 19 November B.P. reported, on the basis of an Army enigma message, that at Rommel's headquarters they were still of the opinion that the British were only carrying out large-scale armed reconnaissance.

In the evening the British headquarters learned from the first reoprt of the highest-ranking radio traffic of the German leadership's reaction to the British operation. The Luftwaffe had called Stukas and other air assault forces from Crete to North Africa "because of a strong British advance in the direction of Tobruk." The Italian Supermarina, though, believed that the movements of the British Mediterrenean fleet that they had spotted were linked with the beginning of an offensive in Cyrenaica.

After a battle in the Tobruk area, November 1941: A British intelligence officer gathers captured papers.

"Keep it under your hat!"

CARELESS TALK COSTS LIVES

Placards warn the British soldiers to keep quiet.

Meanwhile Rommel orders his Panzer divisions into the foremost line. After examining the latest situation reports he recognized that the British would try to disrupt his attack on Tobruk.

After the troops in Tobruk had tried and failed to break out, two German armored divisions attacked the flanks and rear of the two British divisions moving toward Tobruk from the southeast, causing heavy losses.

Likewise on 23 November the British XXX. Corps was thrown back out of Sidi Rezegh, which it had taken shortly before. *Panzergruppe Afrika*'s armored units and the whole Italian XXI. Corps caused heavy losses: 200 tanks were lost and the South African units were hit hard again. The "Battle of Dead Sunday" was a complete success for Rommel. (Note: All Souls' Day is Sunday of the Dead in German).

On the same day, the C-in-C Middle East received a summary of *Panzergruppe Afrika*'s

General Rommel in his "Greif" command vehicle, an armored radio car, Sd.Kfz.250/3.

report on the operations of 21 November. It made clear to him that Rommel's fuel shortage was still an unsolved problem. The other information available from radio messages told that the enemy was occupied until late the previous evening in evacuating Gambut. In addition, numerous reports confirmed that Rommel was concerned about his back-line area during an advance toward Benghazi.

On Monday morning, 24 November B.P. delivered, for the first time during the war, an uo-to-date report about the enemy's operational intentions: Now the headquarters of the British 8th Army knew from a Luftwaffe Enigma message of *Fliegerführer Afrika* on the previous day that, "the *Panzergruppe* was reliable and planned on wiping out the British fighting forces at Rezegh, in order then to be able to carry out operations on the Sollum front."

It was learned from this information that Rommel intended to cut the lines of the 8th Army and relieve the Halfaya Pass. The tragic side of it was that despite this timely warning, the British 8th Army could not prevent Rommel from over-running the headquarters of the XXX. Corps and throwing the British back-line area into chaos.

On the same day *Panzergruppe Afrika* broke off its combat against the decimated British armored brigades in the area south of Tobruk and moved eastward in the direction of Egypt. But Rommel made one decisive error: He went too fast and covered too much space. Thus the German armored units lost some of their cohesiveness and suffered considerable losses from British artillery fire, without essentially weakening the enemy troops.

At about 12:00 noon, Force K, with the two cruisers "Aurora" and "Penelope" and the destroyers "Lance" and "Lively", intercepted the tankers "Procida" and "Maritza." The two ships were sunk shortly thereafter.

On Tuseday, 25 November, Churchill — concerned about the "Ultra" material — radioed to General Auchinleck: "Please burn all the special material and telegrams at the front."

On the same day, B.P. learned from a Luftwaffe Enigma report that the sinking of the two steamships "Maritza" and "Procida" had caused "a real

Tobruk area: British soldiers bring in a German eight-wheeled armored scout car, the so-called "weapon wagon" (20mm KwK), a valuable catch for the British technical intelligence unit.

Radio operator of a DAK intelligence unit at his equipment in a small radio truck.

danger" for German operations in North Africa. Now the transportation of fuel had to be handled by using all available aircraft, Italian submarines and destroyers.

The German counterattack to the east confused the British leadership to the extent that General Cunningham already wanted to order the withdrawal of the entire 8th Army when General Auchinleck appeared at his command post and had him replaced by General Ritchie.

On Wednesday, 26 November the British 8th Army (now under General Ritchie) again attacked Tobruk, which was still besieged by the Axis troops. After breaking out at El Duda, the troops from Tobruk were able to make contact with the advancing British tanks. Rommel's attempt to concentrate his forces and make a counterstroke gained no success, primarily because of the British aerial superiority.

A British prisoner being questioned.

On Thursday morning, 27 November the British Y Service listening posts of the 8th Army picked up radio messages in which Rommel ordered his units back to the approaches to Tobruk. He described the situation as "extremely critical."

At the same time, Luftwaffe Enigma reports confirmed the constantly worsening fuel situation of the X. *Fliegerkorps* as well as its chronic shortage of fighter planes and the oppressive British air superiority.

On Friday, 28 November some important documents fell into British hands: During a battle with the German 15th Panzer Division, they captured many secret files and maps, including Enigma codes for the month of November 1941.

Now B.P. was able to read the radio messages it had not yet been able to decipher. The same secret documents enabled the GC & CS to decode a week's worth of *Panzergruppe Afrika* radio traffic at the operational level between the headquarters of the army, the corps and individual divisions. Likewise on November 18, 1941 the British learned, via the Supermarina's C 38m code, of Italian destroyers that were carrying barrels and canisters of fuel to Derna as deck cargo. The containers were tipped overboard onto the quay at once to keep the time in harbor to a minimum, because of the danger of an RAF attack.

On Sunday, 29 November 1941 troops of the New Zealand 2nd Division (Lieutenant General Freyberg) made an amazing capture: *Generalmajor* von Ravenstein, commander of the German 21st Panzer Division, who was on his way in his *Kübelwagen* to a morning issuing of orders for the 15th Panzer Division, lost his way in the desert. In his briefcase were maps of minefields

plus operational materials for the newly opened German attack.

Meanwhile B.P. was able to decipher Rommel's operational commands for the enclosing attack on the same day, intercepted from the Army Enigma, so quickly that they reached Cairo before the attack began.

On that afternoon the British radio reconnaissance service reported the positions of the enemy tanks that were just preparing to attack.

On this day the Luftwaffe Enigma announced the appointment of *Generalfeldmarschall* Kesselring, the chief of *Luftflotte* 2, as Commander South (OB Süd). Rommel was, to be sure, subordinate to *Generalfeldmarschall* Kesselring but not directly under him, though Kesselring, as OB Süd and *Luftflotte* Chief, reserved the right to discussion and veto power. The OKW felt responsible, of course, but Rommel was also subordinated to the Comando Supremo via General Bastico.

Meanwhile the significance of Bletchley Park had been confirmed again: From a deciphered C 38m message the Admiralty learned details of the next supply convoy, its route and destination, as well as its cover group. This was the first convoy that the Italians protected with battleships. This information arrived just short of 24 hours before the obligatory monthly change of the C 38m code.

In November 1941 it was decided to set up an

Tobruk area, November 1941: A British armored command car (AEC Matador), known as the Mammoth, is stuck in the desert.

ME CIU evaluation office for enemy information, with branches in the Western Desert, the Levant, Iraq and Malta. How important recognition of the enemy situation was for warfare in the desert is shown in that valuable information that was not passed on meant an advantage for the enemy. For example, during November 1941 the British technical inttlligence had learned that a number of German Panzer III and IV tanks were equipped with special armor plates and had new, more effective guns.

Yet technical intelligence had neglected to pass the news of these two tank versions, which were far superior to most British tanks, on to the troops. This fact came to light only in the latter half of January 1942, when Rommel and his new tanks were able to wipe out the British XXX. Corps at Agedabia.

Early on the morning of Monday, 1 December an army Enigma message reached the commander of the British 8th Army: On the previous evening, Rommel had given orders to the army. The contents stated that on the morning of 1 December the attack was to be commenced again.

On Tuesday, 2 December only a single ship of the six transports that were carrying tank fuel, ammunition and rations for *Panzergruppe Afrika* and were heavily guarded at sea arrived at the harbor of Benghazi. Three transports with a total load of 15,992 BRT were sunk, and two badly damaged transports were able to save themselves only by quickly turning back.

Tobruk area, 28 November 1941: Numerous secret files are found on the battlefield after a fight with the German 15th Panzer Division.

Lost in the desert: Generalmajor von Ravenstein during a first "cautious" interrogation.

A morning report in the desert: GFM Kesselring (right) greets Rommel.

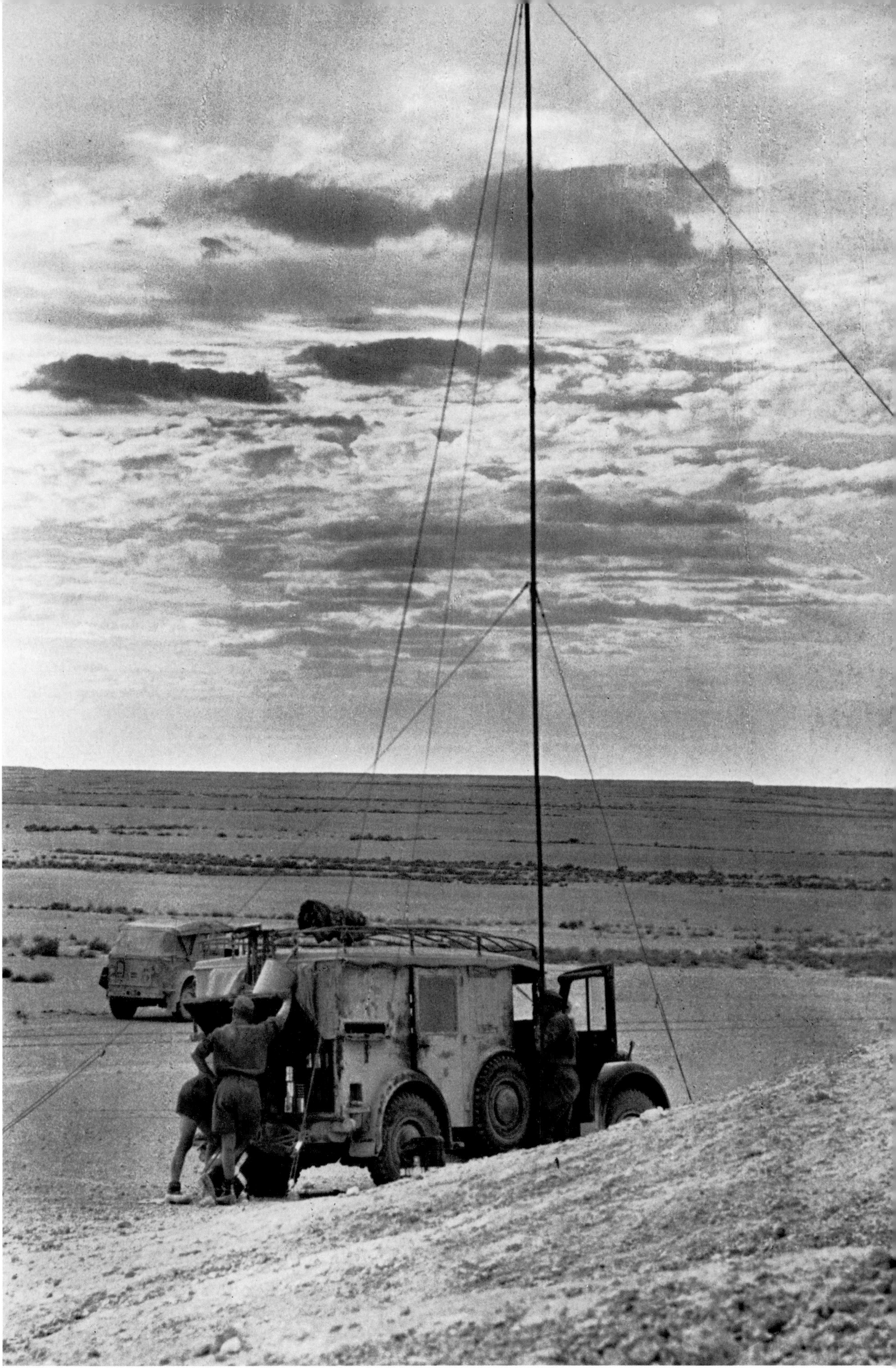

« Libyan Desert, November 1941: A radio truck of the 3rd Listening Company (Oberleutnant Seebohm).

Starve him with Silence

WAR Secrets

THIS POSTER IS PUBLISHED BY THE HOUSE OF SEAGRAM AS PART OF ITS CONTRIBUTION TO THE NATIONAL VICTORY EFFORT

With these and similar placards, the British leadership tried to warn its troops of the German secret service activities.

Success or failure for Rommel's forces was now more than ever a supply problem. Rommel now had to realize that he had overestimated his powers. Continuing to fight on the spot would have been senseless for the weakened *Panzergruppe Afrika,* and so Rommel considered a withdrawal.

Early on Friday morning, 5 December both the Y Service and the air and ground reconnaissance picked up the first signs of *Panzergruppe Afrika*'s withdrawal. All Axis units — with the exception of the border garrisons — were withdrawn; even the armored divisions left the Rezegh area.

Despite the pursuit begun immediately by the British 8th Army (General Ritchie), *Panzergruppe Afrika* set out to the west in proper order and even took more than 9000 prisoners along.

On the same day, B.P. learned from a C 38m message that the Supermarina had decided to use the cruisers "Alberico di Barbiano" and "Alberto di Giussano" to transport fuel to North Africa. The two warships were to use the Palermo-Tripoli route.

On Saturday, 13 December the cruisers "Alberico di Barbiano" (Sea Captain Rodocannacchi) and "Alberto di Giussano" (Sea Captain Marabotto) put out of Palermo, bound for Tripoli. The critical fuel situation of the Axis troops in North Africa now compelled the use of the two warships as freighters. While the two cruisers were still at their piers, the OIC was already able to inform Alexandria and Malta of their departure time, speed and destination. The British destroyers "Sikh" (Commander Stokes), "Legion" and

A reconnaissance unit of the DAK on a scouting mission in a captured British truck.

"Maori" and the Netherlands destroyer "Isaac Sweers" met the two cruisers off Cape Bon and sank them with torpedos.

On the same day, five steamships, escorted by eight destroyers, were to set out in three convoys. The cover group was formed of the battleships "Littorio" and "Vittorio Veneto" plus four destroyers. Thereupon the C-in-C Mediterranean immediately sent three cruisers out from Alexandria. Force K, Force B and the "Sikh" destroyer group were to join them from Malta. Because of a lack of destroyer escorts, the stronger units "Queen Elizabeth" and "Valiant" remained in harbor, but the Italians were fooled by a radio message that these two battleships had also left Alexandria.

When the German observation service (B-Dienst) spotted the British Mediterranean fleet on the sea, the convoy and the Italian fleet turned back to their point of departure. On the way, the British submarine "Urge" (Lieutenant Commander Tomkinson) torpedoed the battleship "Vittorio Veneto" and damaged it badly.

Likewise on 13 December the Luftwaffe Enigma report confirmed that Gazala "was held." It was also said that Rommel was considering returning to the Derna position within 48 hours. The Luftwaffe, on the other hand, was opposed to leaving their Derna support base. Another message said that Kesselring had made Rommel responsible for holding the position before Derna unconditionally, for supporting the Luftwaffe without it would be impossible.

On Monday, 15 December, under the leadership of *Generalfeldmarschall* Kesselring, the decisive German-Italian discussions about a continuation of the operations in North Africa took place. Rommel radioed the results of the talks to the OKW, namely that "the army therefore still

A dangerous ocean voyage: German and Italian troops on their way to North Africa.

intended to hold the area around Gazala on 16 December. The retreat via El Mechili and Derna, in the night of 16-17 December, would be unavoidable, though, to avoid being surprised by the superior enemy forces and thus wiped out."

On Wednesday, 17 December B.P. gave Admiral Cunningham a decoded radio message in the C 38m code which showed an extraordinary interest on the part of the Supermarina in the Royal Navy support points in Egypt. In the report it was said, among other things, that the two battleships (Author's note: "Queen Elizabeth" and "Valiant") were at their usual anchorages and the sea was calm. In B.P.'s opinion, this could only concern plans for an air attack.

Discovered by British bombers thanks to Enigma information: An Italian supply convoy headed for Tripoli.

At the photo evaluation office of an RAF reconnaissance unit, a evaluator combines the serial aerial photographs.

Not quite 24 hours later, on the morning of 18 December, Admiral Cunningham was informed by B.P. of another C 38m radio message, which said "that renewed reconnaissance of Alexandria was urgently needed." Admiral Cunningham, uneasy about these secret messages, suspected some desperation act by the Italians, who wanted at any price to prevent any interference with the shipping of supplies to North Africa, while Rommel was already in retreat.

At 10:25 AM a general alarm was given at the naval support base: "Attacks on Alexandria are to be expected from the air, from ships or manned torpedos, if the hitherto calm weather lasts. Sentry posts and patrols should be informed."

On the same day, the C-in-C Middle East informed his subordinate group commanders of the enemy situation on the basis of the most recent decoded radio message: "The enemy fuel, ammunition and general supply situation is probably so critical that if convoys with supplies do not reach Benghazi or Tripoli in the next few days, Rommel will be confronted with the choice of losing his troops in Cyrenaica or withdrawing out of Cyrenaica."

What the C-in-C Middle East did not suspect was that both his staff and the staff of the 8th Army possessed indications from air reconnaissance reports that one of the ships then underway to North Africa had a load of new-type 22 Panzer III tanks on board.

Meanwhile, both air reconnaissance and the Y Service simultaneously reported clear signs of a retreat of the German troops to below Derna. And the C-in-C Middle East learned from a decoded radio message that the Supermarina had ordered all available empty ships to to to Benghazi immediately. It was left to the Italian commanders

Fortunately landed in Tripoli despite all the dangers: Fuel for Rommel's tank forces.

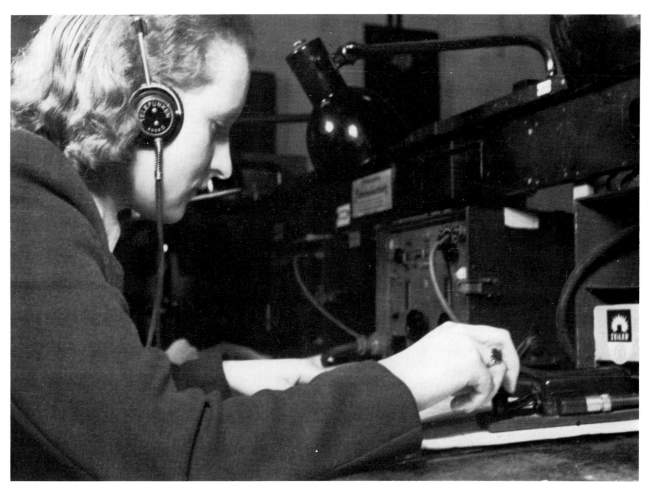

At GFM Kesselring's headquarters, an intelligence assistant transmits a radio message — and the British listen in.

to make preparations for an evacuation of the troops across the Mediterranean Sea.

Shortly after midnight on the night of 18-19 December, the Mediterranean fleet had to accept another serious setback: While in pursuit of the Italian convoy, Force K, the terror of the Italian-German supply convoys, got into an Italian minefield. The destroyer "Kandahar" and the light cruiser "Neptune" sank, the two cruisers "Penelope" and "Aurora" were badly damaged. Now Admiral Cunningham had only submarines, a few destroyers and a couple of cruisers to fight the convoys.

On Friday, 19 December the Italian convoy reached Tripoli and Benghazi with reinforcements for Rommel's tank units. The Italians could attribute the success of this brave action to the fact that at that time B.P. was only able to decipher the highest-level Supermarina code. This is why B.P. had not been able to learn of the actions of Italian torpedo riders against Gibraltar from radio reports previously.

Likewise on 19 December the German motor ship "Ankara" (4768 BRT) entered the harbor of Benghazi. The "Ankara Case" is an example of the fateful role brought on by listening to Enigma reports. The freighter, built for the German Levant Line of Hamburg, had 22 brand-new tanks on board, ready for Rommel to use.

Just a few days before, the C-in-C Middle East learned from B.P. that the "Ankara" was to arrive at Benghazi. The Royal Navy specialists, though, considered that harbor to be fully unsuitable for unloading tanks. The destruction of the port facilities at Benghazi by British commandos and RAF bomb attacks was so great that the British thought the action was impossible. Thanks to a strong tide, though, the "Ankara" was able to get through the blocked harbor canal, reach the pier and accomplish the unloading.

Well hidden: A supply truck at a British command post in the desert.

The 22 tanks were taken over at once by the 15th Panzer Division. This raised the strength of *Panzergruppe Afrika* to 68 tanks ready for action. This was a big help to Rommel, for he was planning a counterattack for 23 December.

Brigadier Shearer, General Auchinleck's enemy situation officer, thought the strength of the enemy armored units to be less that it really was.

On Saturday, 20 December B.P. received a Luftwaffe Enigma report in which Rommel complained about the lack of fighter-plane pro-

tection, which hindered his movements. At the same time, he urgently requested the use of all available transport planes to bring in supplies of fuel.

On 20-21 December, while reconnaissance was reporting the retreat of the Italian XXI. Corps through Benghazi, Enigma messages were saying that *Panzergruppe Afrika* was preparing to hold the line east of Benghazi as long as possible, so that supplies could still be sent out.

It was also thought that, in view of the slow

The safest means of transport so far: The Ju 52/3 transport planes bring in supplies for Rommel's troops.

Attacking Malta in waves: A Junkers Ju 88 bomber is prepared for take-off from an airfield in Sicily.

British pursuit, Benghazi could be held until 22 December. Further Enigma reports included complete information about airfields that were being used by the Luftwaffe for operations as well as to transport fuel.

On Sunday, 21 December the units of *Luftflotte 2* that had been transferred from the eastern front to Sicily began their waves of attacks on Malta. The main thrust was aimed at the island's airfields and the Kalafrana flying-boat support base. While the British Hurricane fighters tried to drive the bomber units off, the Blenheims flew counter-attacks on the Sicilian air support bases.

On Monday, 22 December, at 6:45 AM, the commander of the British 8th Army sent his staff officer to the XIII. Corps with a message to General Godwin-Austin, which read: "I am of the opinion that I made clear to you yesterday that there were important indications that the enemy will do anything imaginable to cover the with-drawal of his forces in the south while he holds a line east of Benghazi. I have learned from the best

secret sources that this is true." In this message, General Godwin-Austin was urged to attack Magrun, which is southward of Benghazi and was "absolutely vital" to the enemy operation.

On this day Rommel, knowing of his local superiority in tanks, decided to begin a counter-attack at once. He kept his decision very secret and did not inform either Rome or Berlin. Thus no Enigma message could warn B.P.

Through the arrival of Axis supply ships at Benghazi and Tripoli, and particularly through tank reinforcements, the tactical situation in North Africa had changed. This development, one important factor in the success of Rommel's counteroffensive in January 1942, was attributable to, among others, the elimination of Force K, as well as the arrival of the II. *Fliegerkorps (General der Flieger* Loerzer) in Sicily, an event that considerably decreased Malta's importance as a sea and air support base.

On Tuesday, 23 December the 15th Panzer Division began its attack. This operation

Rommel on a reconnaissance mission.

surprised the British leadership all the more because their intelligence had not noticed any sign of preparation for it.

On Saturday, 27 December Rommel unexpectedly attacked the British 22nd Tank Brigade (Brigadier Scott-Cockburn) with sixty tanks. This surprise attack cost the British 37 tanks, but Rommel lost only seven.

On the same day, the 22nd Tank Brigade reported to Cairo that in the Agedabia area it had encountered a new type of Panzer III tanks, for they were freshly painted but bore no *DAK* emblem. The British were able to capture one of the Panzer III tanks, whose odometer showed only 400 kilometers. MI6 noted in its report that the 8th Army was completely surprised by the strength of these German tanks.

As early as Monday, 29 December B.P. gained information from the C 38m radio traffic about the next supply convoy, which was to go to Tripoli with battleship protection. In addition to the information that it consisted of nine ships, each of 10,000 BRT, the type of load and the ships' route were given in detail.

On Tuesday, 30 December Rommel repeated his successful attack and lost seven tanks in the process. The British, on the other hand, had to leave 23 tanks on the battlefield. Thus in two attacks the Germans had destroyed sixty tanks of the British 22nd Tank Brigade (Brigadier Scott-Cockburn), or two thirds of their total strength. Now Rommel had smashed the tank spearheads of Operation "Crusader" and driven the British back to the Gazala position.

To obtain at least a fraction of the supplies that he considered necessary, Rommel always painted a gloomy picture of his tank strength and fuel supply, so that the OKW in Berlin — as well as B.P. — would believe his pessimistic situation reports. But there was one unexpected result: When Churchill read the decoded supply reports that were turned over to him, he was always so impressed that he urged the British commanders in North Africa to take the offensive against their will, and as before, all their efforts failed.

The Enigma reports played an important role in Churchill's decisions. His imagination and intuition, linked with information from this source, show this. "Where are my eggs?" Churchill always asked when he inquired about the availability of new Enigma reports. Those closest to him called them "Boniface", while in the Middle East they were known as "Uncle Henry"; the Admiralty simply called them "Z Information."

At the end of December 1941 *Panzergruppe Afrika* moved back into the tactically favorable Marsa-Brega position on the Big Syrte, west of El Agheila, where Rommel had begun his first offensive so successfully in spring 1941. It was a hard loss, but the gain and loss of territory in desert warfare are scarcely of importance. The only decisive factors were that the units suffered no heavy losses and the situation stabilized. Thus for the time being, Cyrenaica and the port of Benghazi were in British hands again.

Toward the end of 1941, B.P. had only sporadic success in breaking the Army Enigma codes used by *Panzergruppe Afrika*. But the Luftwaffe Enigma made up for it: The basic Enigma code (Red) and a modified code were used by *Flieger-führer Afrika* (*Generalleutnant* Fröhlich) and the X. *Fliegerkorps* (*General der Flieger* Geisler) until 1 January 1942 (Light Blue). In the radio traffice of these two offices, which concerned Luftwaffe activity, there was also a quantity of valuable information that concerned *Panzer-gruppe Afrika*.

At the end of December 1941 the British sea and air forces' ability to disturb Axis supply lines was severely limited by the loss of Force K and by German Luftwaffe action in the Mediterranean area.

Agedabia area, December 1941: Radiomen of an Italian unit sending a radio message . . .

. . . "The enemy is listening in" in Italian.

1942
January-June

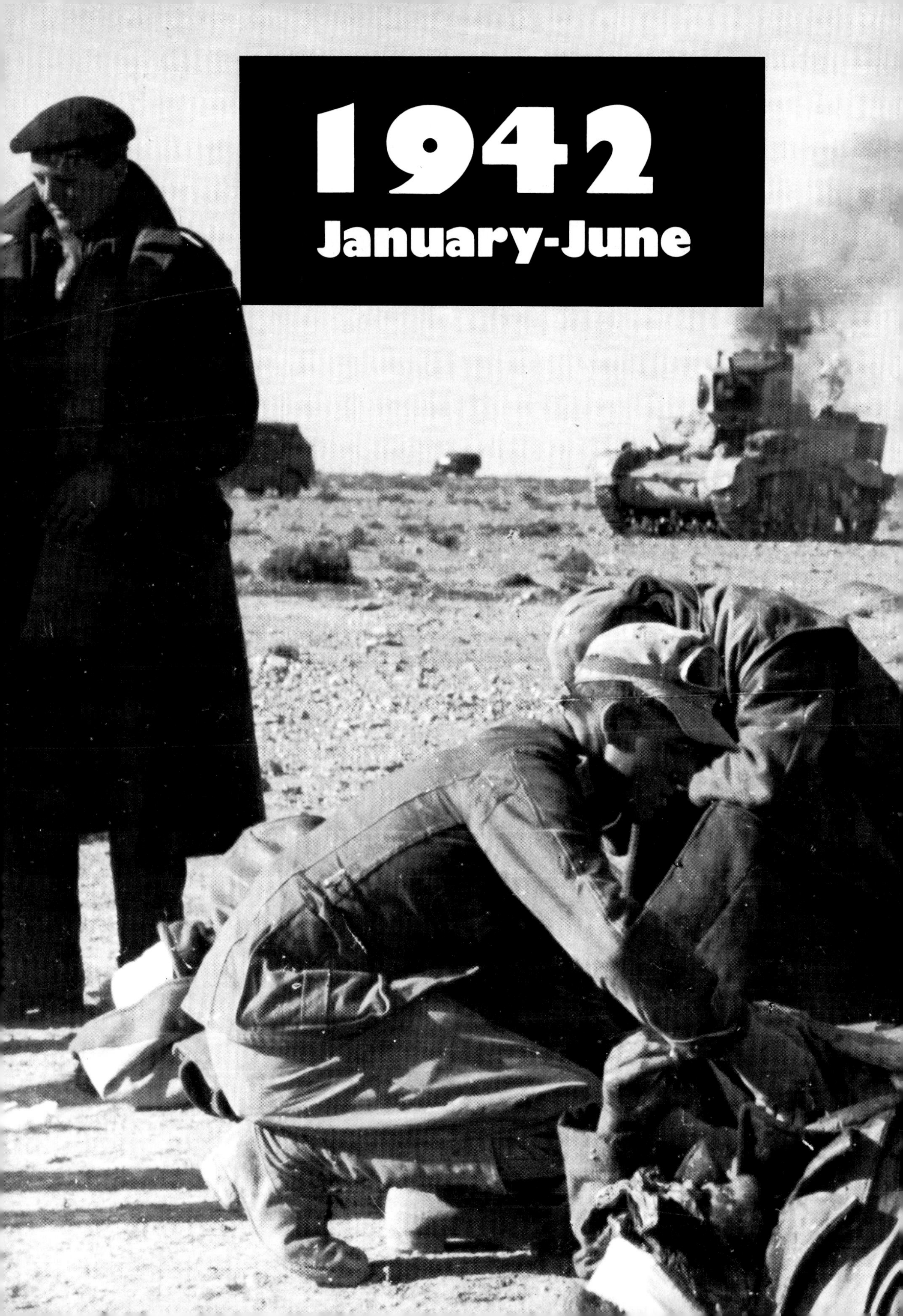

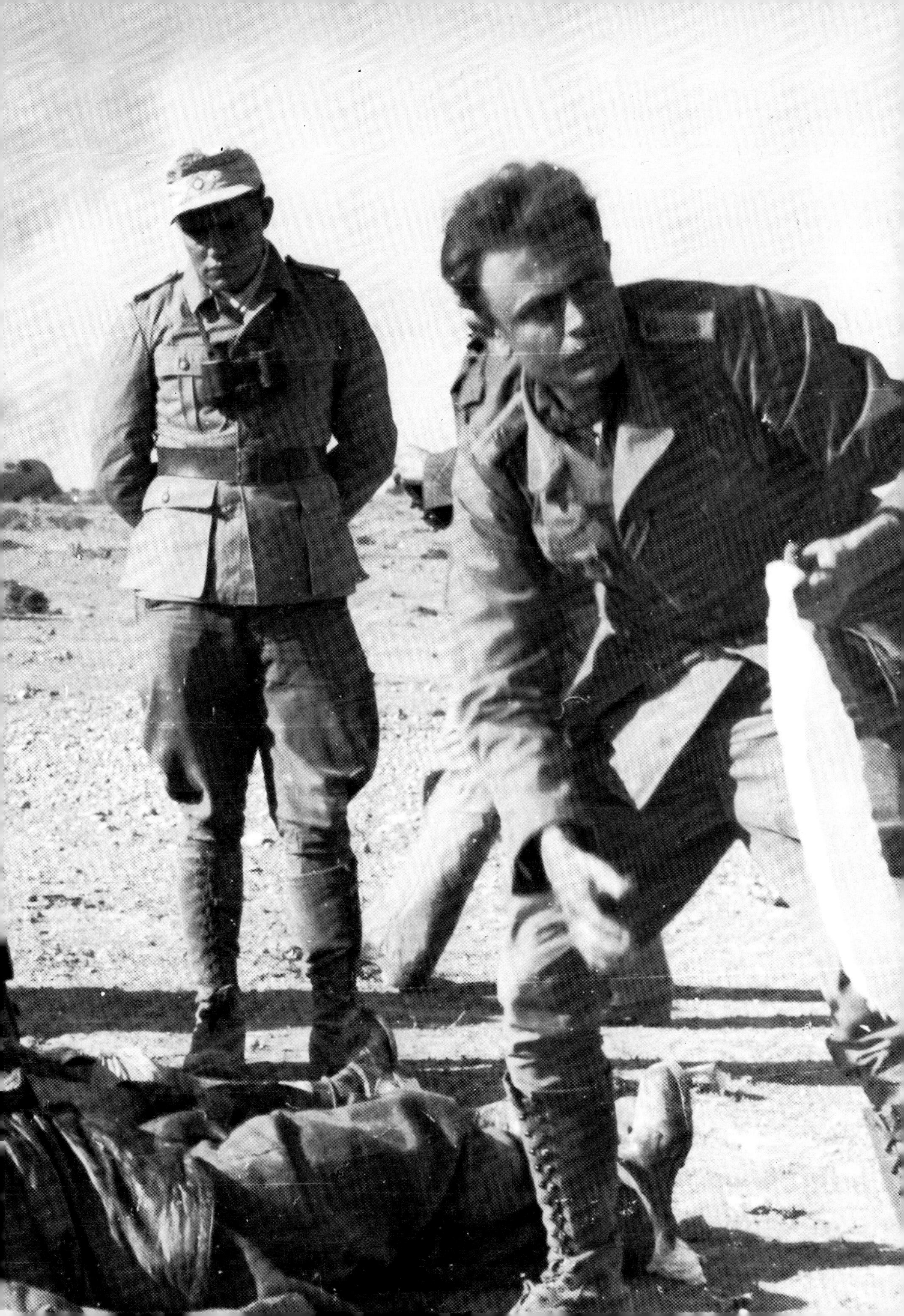

Rommel talking with the Fliegerführer Afrika, General Fröhlich.

Since the beginning of 1942 the chiefs of staff in London did not rule out the possibility that the Axis forces would try to put Malta, the most important British support point in attacking the German-Italian supply lines to North Africa, out of commission through an airborne operation —as had been done in Crete.

On Friday, 2 January 1942 *Generalmajor* A. Schmitt and his troops, who were surrounded in Bardia, laid down their arms. He was the first German general to surrender in World War II.

On Monday, 5 January the Italian Navy reported the safe arrival of a convoy at Tripoli. The lack of British reconnaissance planes on Malta and the constant attacks on the island prevented the RAF from spotting the convoy in time. The supply ships were seen only a short distance from their goal. What B.P. had not learned was that the load of supplies included 54 tanks.

On Thursday, 8 January a Supermarina radio message said that this convoy had brought not only great quantities of fuel for the air forces and ground troops, but also equipment "of the greatest importance to *Panzergruppe Afrika.*"

In January 1942 a member of the Operational Intelligence Center (Admiralty), OIC, was ordered from London to Alexandria to set up a tracking room there for C-in-C Mediterranean (Admiral Cunningham). The reason for such belated activity: The Enigma radio messages to date had provided scarcely any information about the movements or positions of the German U-boats operating in the Mediterranean.

The "Ankara Case" gave the C-in-C Middle East the impetus to improve the organization of intelligence coordination and evaluation. In January 1942 an office of the forces was set up in Cairo to select targets for fighting against enemy supplying. Among its tasks were comparing

Enigma and C 38m reports with all other sources of intelligence and issuing a daily synopsis of all enemy ship movements for all command posts in the Mediterranean, an analysis of the enemy supply situation and the preparation of a priority list of targets. This department maintained constant contact, via the SCU/SLU network, with all command posts for the purpose of planning all operations against Axis supply lines.

On Monday, 12 January 1942 the C-in-C Middle East reported in his evaluation of the situation that the Axis forces "were very disorganized and lacking in both experienced officers and material. They do not seem to be as strong in reality as their total strength makes one suspect."

General Auchinleck said: "I am convinced that the enemy is under more pressure than we realize." As proof of his evaluation of the situation, the C-in-C cited "very thorough and interesting pictures gained from the daily conversations between the captured Generals von Ravenstein and A. Schmitt."

These two generals, von Ravenstein and Schmitt, were housed in special quarters for higher officers at the Combined Services Detailed Interrogation Centre (CSDIC) near Cairo. They visited each other in their rooms, had long conversations and exchanged experiences: "They made no secret of their opinion of Rommel's leadership. But there was one thing that neither of them suspected: MI6 had carefully built a complete listening apparatus into their rooms, and their move into special quarters did not happen by chance. By this tried-and-true method MI6 was able to gain firsthand, emotionally unfalsified information that was of incalculable use in the evaluation of other sources. *General-major* von Ravenstein revealed many details of which the British had formerly known nothing: *Panzergruppe Afrika*'s heavy tank losses, its faulty leadership, and above all the widespread "dissatisfaction with Rommel's leadership."

On Tuesday, 13 January the Joint Intelligence Committee (JIC) issued its latest information on the estimated strength of Rommel's units. The JIC assumed that, as opposed to previous estimates, the following was correct: "a higher beginning number of 108,000 men, but a lower estimate of 11,000 losses, total losses 49,000. According to this calculation, Rommel should still command more than 59,000 men. Just 24 hours later, the C-in-C described the JIC's estimation of Rommel's losses as "much too low."

Bardia area, January 1942: A rest during a reconnaissance advance; at left is a Fieseler Fi 156 Stork staff plane.

Cairo area: A complete listening post at the special prisoner-of-war camp of the CSDIC.

On Wednesday, 14 January B.P. decoded a C 38m radio message in which it was asked whether the unloading of 25-ton tanks in Tripoli harbor was possible.

On the same day, Rommel informed the staff of *Panzergruppe Afrika* of his intention of undertakimg a strong counterthrust with limited targets. "I must attack before the British" — Rommel, plagued by misapprehensions, disclosed his plans to neither the OKW nor the Comando Supremo.

Rommel even went one step further: He did not send out the command for the units subordinate to him to attack by radio as usual, but posted it on bulletin boards in all rest houses along the Via Balbia as far as the front, with zero hour set at 8:30 AM on 21 January. And this decided the success of his operation, for there was no Enigma report on it.

On Thursday, 15 January the C-in-C Middle East asserted in his evaluation of the enemy's situation that it was hardly likely that Rommel would receive any new German troops as reinforcements in the time being. But it was not ruled out that within a month a fresh Italian division with some 140 tanks could be available. General Auchinleck's advisers, though, thought it impossible that the Axis troops who had taken part in the heavy fighting in the El Agheila area would be refreshed and strengthened by now and sufficiently equipped for a counterattack.

They also doubted that the convoy that got through on 5 January had tank reinforcements on board. Their judgment was based on the Enigma information made available to them, which certainly did not mention any tanks among the convoy's load. In reality, though, this convoy had unloaded a goodly number of tanks: 54 of them, according to a later message. Another report even mentioned 80 tanks (40 German and 40 Italian).

On the same day, the C-in-C Middle East reported to the JIC: Rommel's supply problem was "obviously acute." It was reckoned that Rommel would stay where he was at that time until either a British offensive of supply difficulties compelled him to retreat.

On Friday, 16 January 1942 the British 8th Army's Intelligence Summary of the enemy's situation gave out the newest information: Rommel's troops were still at the defense lines and were digging themselves in now.

On Saturday, 17 January a Luftwaffe Enigma report included a complaint from *Fliegerführer Afrika* to *Generalfeldmarschall* Kesselring: He pointed out the shortage of 50-kilogram bombs and urged Kesselring to take any means to deliver at least fifty bombs to the advanced airfields "in view of the operations in the next few days."

On the same day, the German-Italian troops (*Generalleutnant* de Georgis) surrounded by British units in the Sollum-Halfaya Pass surrendered.

On Sunday, 18 January prisoners of war interrogated by MI6 gave the information that at the complete Panzer Regiment 9 of the 15th Panzer Division had taken up a position in Wadi Faregh. In fact, the 15th Panzer Division began to attack from there on 21 January.

On 19-20 January the Intelligence Summary of the British 8th Army mentioned no noteworthy enemy activities. And on the afternoon of 20 January the local Senussi appeared unexpectedly at the British front lines. He stated that the Germans were just about to get ready to move their troops further back to the west.

On the same day, an RAF reconnaissance plane that took off in spite of sandstorm and rain reported that the enemy was moving its supplied, which had been brought by ship, into its positions near El Agheila. Equally unusual was a strong concentration of vehicles just in front of the enemy lines. On the other hand, the British army observation posts did not notice anything special.

A radio truck of the 3rd Horchkompanie (Listening Company) —Oberleutnant Seebohm — with a star antenna.

Radio reconnaissance, which was limited at that time to the information that B.P. gained from Luftwaffe Enigma and C 38m reports, could not recognize Rommel's true intentions at the right time either.

On Wednesday, 21 January the C-in-C Middle East was in Palestine and the commander of the British 8th Army was in Cairo, preparing for an advance in the direction of Tripoli.

On this day the British 8th Army's latest Intelligence Summary stated without commentary that an RAF reconnaissance plane had observed a

A load of fuel for Rommel's troops aboard a Junkers Ju 52/3m transport.

observation and his connections with the highest-ranking British officers.

Rommel's success, especially in the first three days of his counterattack, led the C-in-C Middle East to realize that the 8th Army had been taken completely by surprise. One of the reasons was that the British intelligence service had not warned of either a possible enemy operation or its time and extent.

Neither did the RAF combat forces, limited by bad weather and the loss of several advanced bases, gain any valuable information. The British Army Y service, to be sure, was able to identify a few enemy units but was incapable of finding out any details of their movements or intentions.

Even on Saturday, 24 January the C-in-C Middle East still believed Rommel's operation would turn out in the end to be just another

An observation post of the DAK on ground reconnaissance duty.

First questioning of prisoners: Important information for the enemy situation specialist.

large number of enemy vehicles on the coastal road the day before.

At that time, no reconnaissance planes could take off because of severe sandstorms. The British soldiers had no way of knowing that Rommel was beginning a counteroffensive until the moment when German tanks rolled over their foremost positions. Rommel owed his surprising success not only to the fact that he had succeeded in keeping his preparations secret, but also to the U.S. military attache in Cairo, Colonel Feller, who radioed really accurate reports of the situation and intentions of the 8th Army to Washington thanks to his remarkable powers of

typical disruptive attack, and so he was optimistic. And the commander of the 8th Army, Major General Ritchie, was convinced that Rommel had already reached the limits of his capability.

Only the commanding general of the XIII. Corps, whose units were now in combat, saw the situation in a less rosy light. He insisted on pulling his forces back to El Mekili and called attention to the fact that the fighting power of Rommel's troops had been seriously underestimated.

On this day another convoy, escorted by battleships, reached Tripoli almost undamaged. B.P. had learned details of its composition and route in advance from a C 38m radio message, as well as of the great number of motor vehicles on board, but the most important detail was not included in the Supermarina radio message: There were also 71 tanks in the convoy's freighters.

On Sunday, 25 January the commander of the XIII. Corps arranged to withdraw. Naturally he had permission — if necessary — to take appropriate measures for the retreat. But all the same, the headquarters of the 8th Army disapproved his decision and assured him at the same time that the advance of Rommel's troops "did not amount to a counteroffensive."

In the process, the 8th Army headquarters cited information from its intelligence service, according to which Rommel had already overextended his forces. The commander of the XIII. Corps was instructed "to take offensive measures" and take on "the greatest risks" to stop Rommel's advance.

On Monday, 26 January Rommel learned from his Ic officer, the enemy situation advisor, that the British were already considering the evacuation of Benghazi, and that there were serious differences of opinion among the British commanders. They also expected that Rommel would advance northeastward from Msus to El Mechili.

The new German offensive was a success from the start. Within a few days, the former advance of the British 8th Army turned into a panic-stricken retreat, made even worse by their shortage of fuel

A German short-range reconnaissance plane brings back intelligence material.

Mediterranean, January 1942: An RAF bomber attacks an Italian supply convoy.

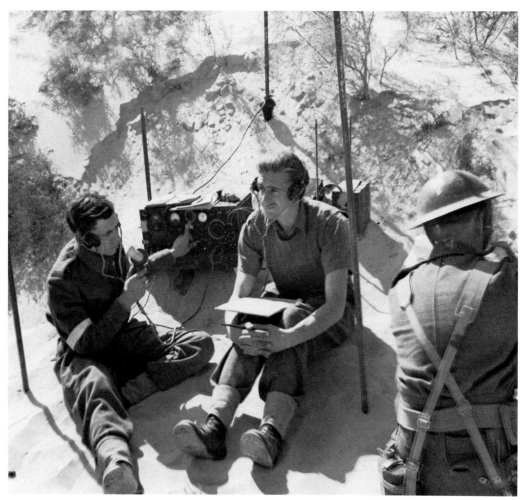

Benghazi area,
February 1942:
During a rest in the
desert, Rommel
talks with his staff
officers.

and a leadership that leads one to believe that they lacked unified planning. Now Rommel decided to anticipate a British advance.

On Tuesday, 27 January Rommel commanded his troops, who were pushing forward in three spearheads, to unite for a surprise attack on Benghazi and march northwestward. Meanwhile *Panzergruppe Afrika* was also to carry out a pretended attack on El Mechili, so as to show the British their superiority.

MI6 helped them inadvertently. It all began with the decoding by GC & CS of a C 38m radio message sent from Regia Aeronautica Command to Rome. Since the Italian allies knew nothing of Rommel's planned deceptive moves, it was stated in the message that the German-Italian forces were continuing their offensive advance in the direction of El Mechili and would try to reach Benghazi at the same time.

When the contents of this message were presented to the commander of the British 8th Army,

he acted at once and transferred his powerful 1st Armored Division (Churchill: The 1st Armored Division was one of our best) from Benghazi in the direction of El Mechili on the same day, "in order to turn back the dangerous German advance", while the Indian 4th Division received the command to move forward against the Axis troops marching in the direction of Benghazi. The two British units were just barely able to avoid complete encirclement and annihilation, and suffered heavy losses.

Since the C-in-C Middle East had received no information about Axis losses from Enigma reports, Cairo underestimated the enemy's remaining total strength by more than 100%.

On Wednesday, 28 January *Panzergruppe Afrika* rolled into Benghazi and pushed further along the coast road in the direction of Derna. Rommel was able to push the British troops back to the El Gazala line westward of Tobruk. Churchill said: "This retreat of almost 500 kilo-

meters destroyed our hopes and brought about the loss of Benghazi and all the depots that Auchinleck had built up for the hoped-for mid-February offensive.''

On Friday, 30 January Rommel, after taking Benghazi — and despite disobeying Hitler's strict instructions — was promoted by him to *Generaloberst*. With that the "Desert Fox" reached a new high point in his career.

After the taking of Benghazi, the combat activity came to a stop again for several months, till the end of May 1942. The enemy troops lay along the so-called Gazala position, a line of well-built field positions and desert forts, in close communication with each other, running from the Mediterranean coast far to the south near Bir Hacheim and able — so the British command hoped — to bring the Germans to a stop. But the quiet situation was deceptive: Both sides were preparing for a new attack.

At the beginning of February 1942 the time

needed to decode an Army Enigma (Chaffinch) message was 24 hours as a rule, which meant that a day usually passed between the reception of an Army Enigma message and the decoding of its text. But if one day's "captures" by the radio reconnaissance unit were especially numerous, so that the GC & CS could not proceed with decoding quickly enough, there was a further delay, since the decoded messages had to be looked over again, placed in a file, sorted and gone over to extract every clue as to their origin.

The messages were then passed on to the C-in-C Middle East in the form of a condensation. And the commanders of the 8th Army could consider themselves lucky if they received information about the movements and intentions of Rommel's troops in time to be able to evaluate them operatively or tactically.

In order to speed up the process, B.P. now gave the Rommel troops' Enigma messages the highest priority, and the daily summaries about *Panzer-*

The men of a DAK intelligence unit erect their antenna.

was replaced. At the end of 1941 he had estimated Rommel's tank strength wrongly in the "Ankara Case", and this became his fate. The C-in-C Middle East now appointed Colonel de Guingand, an officer of his planning staff, to be Deputy Director Military Intelligence (DDMI). At de Guingand's urgent protests that he had no experience in the area of intelligence, General Auchinleck replied: "Splendid, that's exactly why I appointed you." Colonel de Guingand later became the chief of General Montgomery's general staff.

On Tuesday, 10 March B.P. sent a Luftwaffe Enigma report to Cairo that excited the C-in-C Middle East and his staff greatly. The *Fliegerführer Afrika* again asked the Luftwaffe high command (OKL) for photographs of the fortifications in and around Tobruk — as he had already done in November 1941 — when Rommel was planning an offensive. And now Rommel's headquarters also needed all sorts of information about all the forts, fortifications, fixed flak

Msus area, February 1942: A Luftwaffe unit's radio truck with a star antenna.

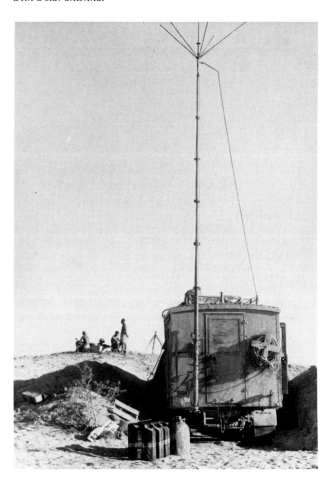

armee Afrika were finished late the same evening.

Until the end of the first week in February, General Auchinleck was still completely unclear about Rommel's next intentions. Only in the night of 8-9 February did intercepted Enigma radio messages reveal Rommel's plans to the British SIS. The *Afrika-Korps* was to be moved forward from Msus, as was the Italian XX. Corps, which at that time was being refreshed south of Benghazi.

On Saturday, 21 February, *Panzergruppe Afrika* commanded by *Generaloberst* Rommel was renamed *"Panzerarmee Afrika."* At that time Rommel had at his disposal two German panzer divisions, one German light division, one Italian armored division, one Italian motorized infantry division, and four Italian infantry divisions.

On Monday, 23 February a large German convoy, the fourth since mid-December 1941, reached Tripoli. The convoy, escorted by the Italian fleet, arrived in port unharmed.

In February 1942 the Desert Air Force received twelve Spitfire D reconnaissance planes. These brand-new aircraft replaced the obsolete Hurricanes with which the Photographic Reconnaissance Unit (PRU) had to muddle through until then. Now aerial reconnaissance could be upgraded considerably and was less dependent on weather conditions.

At the end of February 1942 Brigadier Shearer, General Auchinleck's enemy situation specialist,

Cairo, 29 March 1942: A conference of the three Middle East service chiefs: from center to right, C-in-C Sir Moncton, Admiral Cunningham and Air Marshal Tedder. At left is General Auchinleck.

batteries, electric stations and water supply facilities between the Egyptian border and the Suez Canal.

In these days the British SIS was rather confused and unsure of how to judge Rommel's intentions. They were of the opinion that the Axis activities were being carried out intentionally in the southern front sector in order to prepare the troops for a later advance in an easterly direction. MI6 stressed, though, that they were "chiefly of a defensive nature."

On Friday, 13 March B.P. picked up a Luftwaffe Enigma radio message with information on the strength of Rommel's armored forces, the first that B.P. was able to provide for the C-in-C Middle East since November 1941. The list included all tanks ready for action, listed by type, including 87 Italian and 159 German tanks. Surprisingly, the numbers agreed fairly closely with the MI6 estimations of 27 February: 100

Italian and 160 German tanks under Rommel's command, as the British SIS had estimated.

On Sunday, 15 March the JIC gave out its latest strategic situation evaluation. According to its view, the Axis fighting forces in Libya were not strong enough to expand their position before mid-June 1942.

In February and March 1942 the Axis powers lost only 9% of the supplies they shipped to North Africa.

On Wednesday, 1 April MI6 suffered a severe blow in Cairo: The Luftwaffe, presumably for radio-technological reasons, changed their code for air-to-ground radio traffic (Auka). Until then the results of the reconnaissance service for tactical radio traffic were collected in Cheadle (Britain) and sent from there to the RAF Y-Base Unit's radio reconnaissance department in Cairo, where the radio messages were decoded. By breaking the Auka code, the RAF T service had been able up to

Tmimi area, 21 April 1942: Two German prisoners talking with a British intelligence officer. At left Feldwebel Kurt Gerhardt, Ph.D., beside him Rifleman Erich Frystazki, General Schmitt's chauffeur.

then to provide regular reports on the general air situation and, above all, to give timely warnings of attacks on British convoys, as well as on Alexandria and the Suez Canal.

How changeable the situation in the North African intelligence service area was can be seen in the fact that just ten days after the Auka code had been changed, on 10 April, the GC & CS was able to break the Army Enigma (Chaffinch) code again. The deciphering of this complex code was extremely difficult, and at first it was only possible to decode about half of the intercepted radio messages bit by bit, often with a delay of six or more days.

On Friday, 17 April the 3rd Company of Intelligence Unit 56 was renamed Long-Range Reconnaissance Company 621 for reasons of secrecy and concealment.

On Sunday, 19 April, a few days after Rommel had decided to begin his offensive at the end of May, Luftwaffe and Army Enigma reports contained numerous references to *Panzerarmee Afrika*'s preparations for an operative action. The only questions still open were: Where? and When? Now even the upper-level Intelligence personnel in Whitehall were sure that Rommel would take the initiative without waiting for a British offensive. And they were convinced that this could still occur before mid-June.

On Friday, 24 April B.P. was able to decode a Luftwaffe Enigma radio message with an enemy situation evaluation by *Generalfeldmarschall* Kesselring. MI6 had to recognize with amazement that the german field marshal stressed in his message that he could depend on information that came from an absolutely reliable source and knew that "a British attempt to advance to Benghazi was not possible before the beginning of June." Kesselring added, "Because it is not possible before June, it will come too late."

Now a great guessing game began at SIS. They did not yet suspect at that time that the "absolutely reliable source" named by Kesselring was the U.S. military attache in Cairo, Colonel Feller, whose radio messages were decoded regularly by the German intelligence service. The idea that the British attempt to advance would come "too late" gave MI6 headaches. Did it mean an attack on Malta or Rommel's new advance in the direction of the Egyptian border? Since the Luftwaffe units, according to the latest Enigma reports, were to return to Sicily almost without exception, it was MI6's view that Rommel's new counteroffensive was in the works.

On the next day, 25 April, B.P. learned from a Luftwaffe Enigma report that a German paratroop brigade was to be transferred to Africa in the latter half of May to support "an operation against the British 8th Army and for an attack on Tobruk." (Author's note: This was the *Ramcke Fallschirmbrigade* (Paratroop), which did not actually arrive until the end of July 1942).

In his situation analysis of 25 April 1942 the C-in-C Middle East admitted that Rommel could try to attack Tobruk early in May, but he believed that it was scarcely likely, since May was a remarkably bad month for such an operation.

On Thursday, 30 April B.P. decoded an Army Enigma (Chaffinch) radio message that confirmed to MI6 that most of the Axis armored units were in the northern front sector. Only weak units of the *DAK* were in the southern part of the front, "in order to secure the south flank."

On this day too, the results of questioning a major from Rommel's staff were evaluated. This officer had been captured during a reconnaissance mission. MI6 had used a special trick in this case: An Austrian-born officer of the British 8th Army staff had been dressed in a *DAK* captain's uniform and housed in the same tent as a fellow prisoner of the major.

After initial greetings and a cigarette, the two discussed the situation of their troops. The major voiced a little criticism of Rommel's decision but declared once more that his reconnaissance mission was completely of a defensive nature, as he was supposed to determine the possibility of a British advance to surround the Axis positions in the southern front sector. In addition, the information found on the major agreed with this.

Now Churchill made it perfectly clear that, because of the constant mobile war and the danger of being captured, as well as the presence of German radio reconnaissance, none of the front commanders was to be informed of the

A ground reconnaissance troop of the DAK.

Enigma reports. The dissemination of these reports was limited to a minimum by his order. Thus at the Middle East headquarters only the commander, General Auchinleck, the chief of his planning staff and the chief of the military intelligence service, as well as the enemy situation evaluator, Colonel de Guingand, received these reports. Even the commander of the 8th Army, General Ritchie, did not get to see them. In the

Tobruk area, April 1942: A German specialist interrogates a British prisoner.

event that the Enigma reports were of importance to General Ritchie for operational plans, General Auchinleck had to produce a written version without naming the source. After being seen by General Ritchie, this document was burned immediately. In most cases, though, the enemy situation evaluator flew to the headquarters of the 8th Army and informed General Ritchie personally, without mentioning the source.

From the end of April to early May 1942 *Luftflotte* 2 (GFM Kesselring) was able to disturb the activities of the RAF and Royal Navy units stationed at Malta by frequent bomb attacks.

As a result, supplying *Panzerarmee Afrika* became easier at this time, and sufficient supplies were guaranteed. But after *Luftflotte* 2 was needed to support the combat in the Gazala-Tobruk area to a greater degree, the RAF and Royal Navy were once again able, from Malta, to disturb the supply lines to Rommel's troops.

Even the C-in-C Middle East was not quite sure of Rommel's intentions. On 2 May 1942 General Auchinleck admitted in his situation report that one might possibly regard the activities of Rommel's troops as preparations for an advance in the direction of the Egyptian border, but in his opinion they were just for a defensive operation.

On the same day, B.P. gave the War Office and Churchill a new Army Enigma (Chaffinch)

Flying low over the Mediterranean toward North Africa: A group of Junkers 52/53m transport planes.

April 1942: General Auchinleck on a reconnaissance mission along the coast road in the Tobruk-El Gazala sector.

message, from which it could be seen that *Panzer-armee Afrika*, thanks to their favorable supply situation, would very soon have sufficient supplies of fuel for a thirty-day operation. Since then, the British leadership firmly believed that Rommel was planning an offensive for the end of May.

On Sunday, 3 May the C-in-C Middle East wrote a message to the War Office. General Auchinleck indicated in his evaluation that he did not intend to began any operations during summer 1942. He assured them again that even his supply shortages would not prevent Rommel from starting some significant operation in the course of the next three months. His suggestion: It would be more reasonable to stay on the defensive in the Middle East, give up all thoughts of a North African offensive during summer 1942, and transfer all available land forces to India because of the danger of a Japanese invasion.

It would turn out to be fateful for MI6 that at this time nothing of Hitler's strategic intentions in the Mediterranean area had leaked out or been mentioned in Enigma reports. Except for a few minor allusions in deciphered fragments of Axis diplomatic radio traffic and a few rumors, no information on the subject was available.

On Tuesday, 5 May Rommel briefed his commanding generals at El Kerima on Operation "Theseus", the new counteroffensive. His goals were the encircling and elimination of the British 8th Army and the conquest of Tobruk. Rommel's intentions: After holding and distracting the British forces by an apparent frontal attack on the Gazala position, he wanted to circumvent the enemy in the south, near Bir Hacheim, with three German and two Italian motorized divisions and strike the 8th Army in the back. After that Tobruk was to be taken in a bold move, to make supplying his *Panzerarmee* easier via its harbor. In addition, he hoped to gain rich booty from the supply depots there.

On the same day, B.P. learned from a Luftwaffe Enigma report of the repeated request for photos and maps of Tobruk and its vicinity.

On Wednesday, 6 May B.P. stated in a situation evaluation that, on the basis of the latest Enigma reports: "A German offensive in Cyrenaica for the purpose of capturing Tobruk will probably begin about 20 May. If this offensive is successful, Rommel could make an attempt to prepare for a large-scale attack on Egypt in the coming winter months."

On Friday, 8 May Churchill, in a personal

message to the C-in-C Middle East, emphatically stated that it was correct to begin an offensive in May, especially in view of "the fact that the enemy is planning an attack for the beginning of June."

On Saturday, 9 May the JIC's new situation analysis said: "The enemy attack on Tobruk is possible any time after the third week in May. Despite several indications that Rommel is interested in beginning a further operation — perhaps an advance to the Nile delta — in June, this would scarcely be possible on account of his fuel shortage in the second half of June."

On Sunday, 10 May the War Cabinet received the report of the Middle East Defence Committee of 9 May 1942, in which the opinion was stressed that there were "scarcely any signs" of an enemy attack at the beginning of June.

Meanwhile, though MI6 did not yet know it, Rommel had already almost completed his extensive troop movements in preparation for Operation "Theseus."

On Friday, 15 May the C-in-C Middle East informed the Chief of the Imperial General Staff (CIGS) that, on the basis of available information, an attack by Rommel around 20 May could be suspected after all, "possibly even earlier, but probably some time between this date and the end of May." The C-in-C Middle East was sure, though, that "our plans are made in view of such an attack, and all enemy preparations are under observation."

On Saturday, 16 May the 8th Army received a report from its reconnaissance unit that new troop concentrations, trenches and AA gun positions had been observed in the Asida area. B.P. learned from a Luftwaffe Enigma report that as of 17 May *Generalfeldmarschall* Kesselring had a command post in Derna.

As of Monday, 18 May the first reports from the British advance posts reached MI6, telling that the enemy had intensified his reconnaissance activities. Meanwhile the Luftwaffe began to make systematic attacks on British field air bases and supply lines. Again and again, aerial battles took place between German fighters and British reconnaissance craft, and German patrols did everything to disturb British scouting troops during their missions.

On Wednesday, 20 May the JIC ME's report on the C-in-C Middle East's situation evaluation stated that, since it "is quite likely that the enemy did not know that we know of his planned actions, he hopes to achieve a high degree of surprise effect." For these reasons the 8th Army —

« *Tobruk area, May 1942: A smashed British reconnaissance unit.*

Air photo from a British reconnaissance plane: Italian bombers at the edge of an airfield near Agedabia.

according to JIC ME — was not to undertake anything that might indicate that Rommel's attack was expected.

On Thursday, 21 May British reconnaissance aircraft spotted unusually large gatherings of vehicles and tents in the Asida area. The 8th Army immediately reported to the War Office that this information was further proof of the regrouping of the Axis troops and simultaneously indicated Rommel's interest in the southern desert sector. The 8th Army, though, lacked corresponding reconnaissance material as to what was going on in the northern sector of Rommel's front lines.

Still on Friday, 22 May, the information provided by MI6 convinced the C-in-C Middle East leadership that Rommel would carry out a feint operation against Bir Hacheim as well as his frontal attack. But the C-in-C reckoned on the Italian XX. Corps, known to be in the south, being able to deal with the feint. The two German armored divisions and units of the 90th Light Division still seemed to be located in the northern sector.

On the same day, B.P. learned from a Luftwaffe Enigma report that *Generalfeldmarschall* Kesselring had called a conference in Derna on that day. Another important piece of information,

Personal papers of a British 8th Army soldier: Valuable information for the enemy situation specialist.

Tobruk area, May 1942: Intelligence officers of the 8th Army examine a German 150mm heavy 13/1 howitzer on an armored carrier (ex-French Lorraine tractor).

the German attack . . . would be made from the west in the coastal area, the radio reconnaissance reports of troop concentrations in the south merely represented the enemy's concern about his exposed flank, although radio messages had made it clear that the 21st Panzer Division was now located in the south.

Worse yet, so little faith was placed in these facts that despite short-range reconnaissance reports of tents, vehicles, positions and connections in the original concentration area of the 21st Panzer Division, MI6 explained to general headquarters in Cairo that the reconnaissance must be in error. Thus MI6 was taken in by Rommel's feint maneuver.

Since General Headquarters in Cairo was so convinced by the results of the short-range reconnaissance, no effort was made to carry out reconnaissance further south. And this was the decisive error. If short-range reconnaissance planes had been ordered into the southern sector, the 21st

this one from the Army Enigma (Chaffinch) radio traffic, said that *General* Crüwell, Commander of the *Afrika-Korps,* was expected back in North Africa from his furlough in Berlin on 24 May or, at the latest, 25 May.

On both 22-23 May British patrols reported increased German reconnaissance activity being carried out, this time in the staff car.

On Saturday, 23 May a non-commissioned officer from the staff of the 90th Light Division was captured in the southern front sector of the British XIII. Corps. During questioning he explained that his staff company and Infantry Regiment 155 of the 90th Light Division were located in the southern front sector. Two other motorized regiments of the light division had likewise been transferred southward from the coast. A great number of German tanks — he estimated them to be about 300 — belonged, he believed, to the 21st Panzer Division, and were gathered behind his company's positions.

According to information from an officer of the XIII. Corps who had been present when the German NCO was questioned, the German had given his information so "willingly" and had "tried so hard to remember as many details as possible", that "several of those present were of the opinion that this was a case of deception."

As the JIC later ascertained, what the German NCO had said was actually true, but the general headquarters in Cairo was firmly convinced that

Panzer Division would have been discovered there.

In addition, on Tuesday, 26 May the officer responsible for the Y service (radio listening) at the headquarters of the 8th Army as yet knew nothing of what the NCO of the German 90th Light Company had said. On the other hand, the XXX. and XIII. Corps and the General Headquarters in Cairo did not yet have the results of the Y Service, from whose report one could not help but realize that Rommel intended to carry out his main attack in the south.

The lesson that GS Int of the 8th Army later learned from this error: The intelligence staffs of the Y groups, which were responsible for the evaluation of Y material heard on the radio, were linked more closely with their Operations Intelligence Staffs. Since the Y officers, for reasons of security, still had no access to Enigma reports, they now received information that reached the Operational Intelligence Staff from other sources.

On this day the listening company of Seebohm, who had been promoted to captain by now, was divided into two units for Operation "Theseus." One of them was transferred south of Tmimi, the other joined the staff of *Panzerarmee Afrika* and maintained direct connections with Rommel.

Likewise on 26 May the Y Service picked up the code word "Venezia" more than 24 hours before the attack and correctly interpreted it as the disguised name for the German-Italian operation. B.P. also anticipated the impending attack from a decoded Enigma message and immediately sent a warning to the C-in-C Middle East.

About 3:00 in the afternoon, a short-range reconnaissance plane in the northern front sector discovered several tanks that were identified as German, but they were not as numerous as had been expected. A few hours later, another RAF short-range reconnaissance plane further south spotted a larger tank unit moving forward toward the central British front sector.

Derna area, May 1942: Siesta at a field air base. While awaiting their call to combat, the crew and ground crew seek shelter from the searing sun under the wing of a Ju 52/3m.

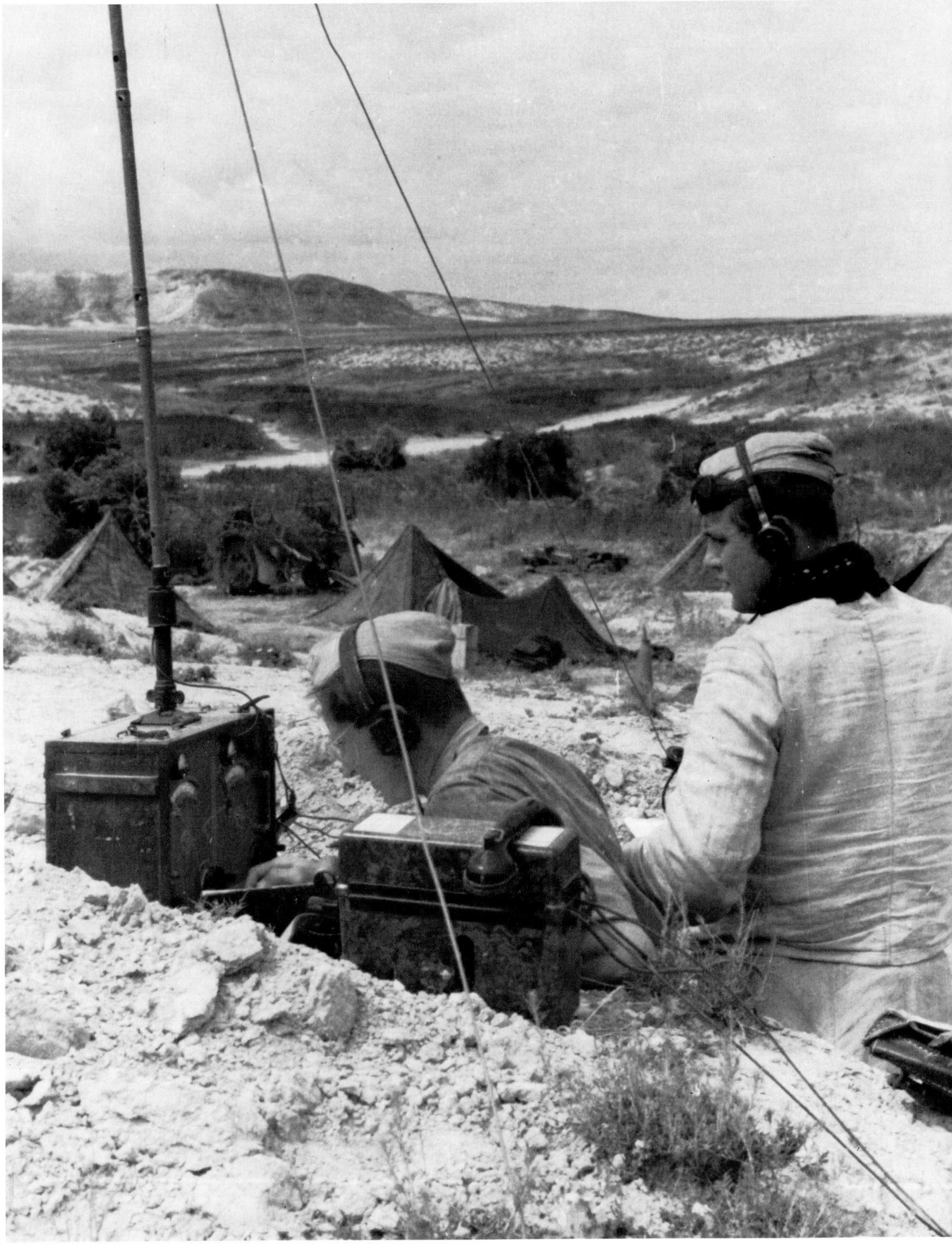

Libyan Desert, Cyrenaica, near Via Balbia, May 1942: An observer of the Long Range Desert Group (LRDG) observes the supply traffic of the Axis troops on the coast road.

Without suspecting it, the British pilots were witnesses to a very clever deceptive maneuver: Rommel had ordered his tank forces to march northeastward in daylight, so as to confuse the enemy. After night had fallen, they were to turn around at once and move to the southeast.

In the British XXX. Corps' situation report, the reported tank advance was regarded as a powerful reconnaissance undertaking. At 11:00 PM the commander of the 8th Army recorded in his situation evaluation: The enemy has begun his offensive, but it cannot yet be ascertained where his main attack will take place.

To hold the British forces on the Gazala line and enable reinforcements to be brought up, Rommel ordered Italian infantry to attack there. Meanwhile, tanks and trucks drove around and threw up clouds of dust to simulate considerable tank readiness procedures. And while the Italian infantry held the British on the main front with their frontal attack, tanks and motorized units drove around the southern flank of the Gazala line, which ended in the open desert, in a wide arc.

On Wednesday, 27 May the desert fort of Bir Hacheim had already been circumvented to the south at daybreak. After a brief gathering, the units moved behind the British front line. About 11:00 AM parts of *Panzerarmee Afrika* met the British 4th Tank Brigade and the Indian 3rd Motorized Brigade, with their new Grant tanks, on the old Trigh el Abd caravan route northeast of Bir Hacheim.

Now a tank battle began that proved costly for both sides. The Indian 3rd Motorized Brigade was overrun and the British 7th Armored Division was badly beaten. The Italian "Ariete" Armored Brigade tried in vain to advance on Bir Hacheim. Here the Foreign Legion and colonial troops under General Koenig, commander of the French 1st Brigade, fought bitterly.

West of El Gazala, May 1942: Radiomen with their equipment in the battery position of a German light field
« *howitzer; the British Y service was listening.*

West of El Gazala, near Chechiban, May 1942: A disguised radio truck of the DAK's Intelligence Unit 200.

They also opposed the "Trieste" Division and the 90th Light Division successfully and cost them heavy losses. When night fell, Rommel's troops were exposed to vigorous counterattacks from the British XXX. Corps. The Axis motorized units were cut off and lost contact with each other in the minefields.

On Thursday, 28 May, and on the next day, the situation of the German-Italian attacking troops became very critical. The British had recognized the threatening danger and now pulled all their available forces together to wipe out the parts of Rommel's army that were fighting separately.

The Grant tanks caused considerable losses to the German tank units fighting in back of the Gazala line, and when the battle ended, *Panzerarmee Afrika* ran into a British antitank barrage. Rommel's troops were able to push the British back to the El Adem area, but here the British 4th Tank Brigade was able to stop long enough for the British tank forces that were hurrying to the scene to intervene in the battle.

Until Friday, 29 May B.P. had not one single hint from Enigma messages as to the positions and intentions of Rommel's offensive. Only in the evening did the Y service (radio surveillance) give the commander of the 8th Army an extensive report. It said, "Supply difficulties for all German units. Individual tank companies have already run out of fuel. The 15th Panzer Division had begun the operation with a water supply for only four days, and the soldiers are now suffering from severe thirst. The division has been urged to use ammunition very sparingly."

On Saturday, 30 May the battle on the Gazala line moved into its decisive phase: Amid the minefields of the British defense, the Germans encountered a defensive position (box) of the British 150th Brigade, hitherto unrecognized by reconnaissance, which halted the further advance of Romell's forces. The German tanks, caught behind the minefields and the defensive line (box), were almost out of fuel, ammunition and supplies. But while the British generals spent two days thinking, Rommel was regrouping his forces.

On the same day the C-in-C Middle East finally received various Army Enigma reports of 27-29 May from B.P., including the daily evening reports of the *Panzerarmee*. This informed the C-in-C Middle East, General Auchinleck, of the supply crisis for Rommel's units.

On this day, Churchill intervened personally in the transmission of the Enigma reports to the C-in-C: He instructed the "C" (traditional code for the chief of the SIS) to take the following measures immediately: first — contrary to his previous instructions — to turn over two Enigma situation reports in their full text, word for word, to the C-in-C Middle East, and second, "During the combat activities at the time . . . all messages of strategic significance which show the enemy's intentions and position are to be sent personally and in full text to General Auchinleck."

Churchill's decision meant that in addition to the usual service and dissemination, which had to be supervised strictly, the C-in-C Middle East would now receive all Enigma reports. This lifted the B.P. ban on letting decoded Enigma texts in their original wording leave their hands. Previously they had to be rephrased carefully for security reasons, so their true origin would remain a secret.

Despite the present simplification in disseminating highly confidential reports, the danger could not be ruled out that the leadership in London, on the basis of the Enigma reports, would draw different conclusions than the C-in-C Middle East in Cairo.

On Sunday, 31 May the C-in-C Middle East

learned from an Enigma report that Rommel knew of the 8th Army's attack, which was planned for the following night. He did not intend, though, to draw his troops back, but regarded the British operation as a good chance to strike an effective blow at the enemy.

At this time the RAF, along with the 8th Army, set up a joint headquarters, in order to coordinate the PR (photographic reconnaissance) operations of their aerial reconnaissance better. This measure had some advantages, to be sure, but it did not succeed in attaining a successful blend of the results of aerial reconnaissance with information from other intelligence sources for a better determination of the enemy's position.

At the end of May 1942, B.P. was finally able to break the new Army Enigma code (British code name "Thrush"). Now the GC & CS was able to supply important information about the daily air transport of supplies and troop reinforcements to North Africa. And Chaffinch was not the only Army Enigma code that could be deciphered.

As of June 1942, the 24-hour daily Enigma code was changed every eight hours, so as to make the coding machine "even more secure." The inherent changes to the code roller arrangement were introduced according to a definite system, though, which made decoding the new code system considerably easier for the British cryptologists.

On Monday, 1 June the British "Box" defense system that barred the German advance fell after heavy dive-bomber attacks. Now Rommel turned to the south to capture Bir Hacheim, simultaneously fighting off several weak British advances from the north. A supply train with food, fuel and ammunition finally reached the German units, which were suffering from a shortage of supplies. Thus at one stroke the situation on the battlefield changed: Rommel's offensive forces, which the British believed to be on the verge of collapse, were now pushing eastward in the direction of Egypt.

Early in the morning the C-in-C Middle East received an Enigma report that B.P. had sent out at 6:04 AM, and that showed him Rommel's further intentions: *Panzerarmee Afrika* intended to attack the strong enemy antitank positions and, after disposing of the British tanks and antitank guns, embark on a counterattack.

From this day on, B.P. could take credit for further success: Until the end of May 1942, the decoding of the daily Army Enigma reports had taken up to ten days and was often only fragmentary. Thus the operationally important information was scarcely of any use by the time it was decoded. Now the time from interception of a radio message to passing its decoded text on to the C-in-C Middle East averaged only 24 hours. The reason was that the transmission of news from

A field teletype station in the camp of Intelligence Unit 200: A teletype message is passed on by telephone.

Here at SIS headquarters in Cairo, the communication lines come together in a tangle of telephone and teletype cables.

Tobruk area, May 1942: Rommel personally questions the British officers captured on a reconnaissance mission.

North Africa to Italy and the OKH, and vice versa, was now done mostly by radio and not by teletype as before.

In the night of 1-2 June the 90th Light Infantry Division and the Italian "Trieste" Division pushed toward Bir Hacheim, the southernmost corner post of the British front, and enclosed the desert fort from the east. The demand to surrender was refused by the commander of the French 1st Brigade, General Koenig.

At noon on Tuesday, 2 June the Italian "Trieste" Division and the German 90th Light Infantry Division moved in from the south to attack the desert fort at Bir Hacheim. The surrounded troops defended themselves stubbornly. "Only rarely was I given such a hard fight in the African theater of war," said Rommel.

At the beginning of June 1942 the British radio reconnaissance, the Y Service, was already able to listen to the busy radio traffic of the Seebohm listening company and locate their position. The intercepted radio messages, decoded at B.P. and presented to the C-in-C Middle East along with other important Enigma reports, showed beyond a doubt that it was Rommel's most important source of information.

Since the end of the first week in June, the British surveillance of the enemy became more and more successful. Captured documents and equipment, the statements of war prisoners and regular air and ground reconnaissance completed the picture offered by the Enigma reports. But this did not necessarily protect the 8th Army from severe reverses.

After the battle had gone on for a week, Rommel was hoping he could advance further through Sollum and Bardia. He gave the left flank instructions to fake preparations for a major offensive by using smoke screens, false tanks, dust-raising vehicles with propellers and captured enemy tanks. The commanding generals were the inform their division commanders and then burn all written commands.

Mediterranean, June 1942: An Italian freighter with supplies for Panzerarmee Afrika after an RAF bomb attack. »

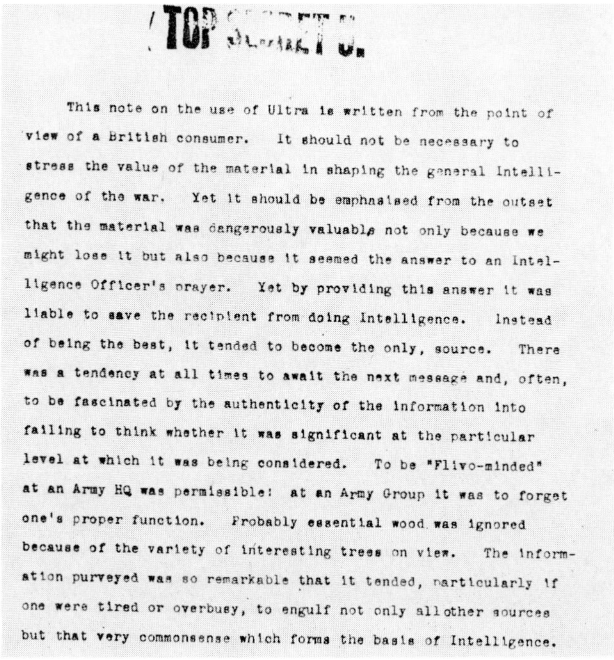

TOP SECRET U.

This note on the use of Ultra is written from the point of view of a British consumer. It should not be necessary to stress the value of the material in shaping the general Intelligence of the war. Yet it should be emphasised from the outset that the material was dangerously valuable not only because we might lose it but also because it seemed the answer to an Intelligence Officer's prayer. Yet by providing this answer it was liable to save the recipient from doing Intelligence. Instead of being the best, it tended to become the only, source. There was a tendency at all times to await the next message and, often, to be fascinated by the authenticity of the information into failing to think whether it was significant at the particular level at which it was being considered. To be "Flivo-minded" at an Army HQ was permissible: at an Army Group it was to forget one's proper function. Probably essential wood was ignored because of the variety of interesting trees on view. The information purveyed was so remarkable that it tended, particularly if one were tired or overbusy, to engulf not only all other sources but that very commonsense which forms the basis of Intelligence.

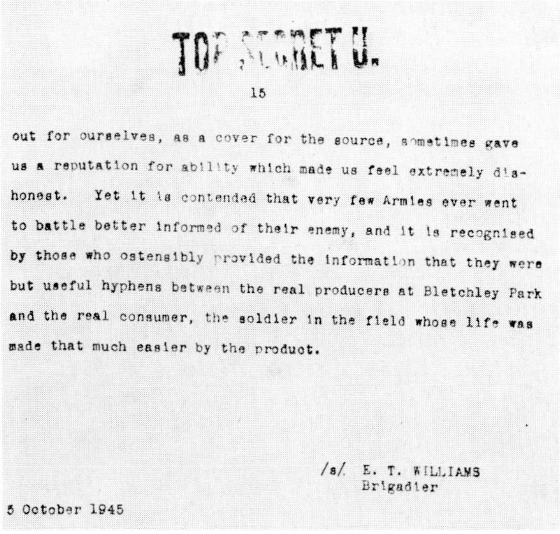

TOP SECRET U.

15

out for ourselves, as a cover for the source, sometimes gave us a reputation for ability which made us feel extremely dishonest. Yet it is contended that very few Armies ever went to battle better informed of their enemy, and it is recognised by those who ostensibly provided the information that they were but useful hyphens between the real producers at Bletchley Park and the real consumer, the soldier in the field whose life was made that much easier by the product.

/s/. E. T. WILLIAMS
Brigadier

5 October 1945

"On the use of Ultra reports", written by Brigadier Williams, General Montgomery's intelligence chief: Still treated as TOP SECRET in October 1945 and only released more than 30 years later (Document No.P20 WO 208/3575).

On Monday, 8 June the C-in-C Middle East received *Panzerarmee Afrika*'s evening situation report of 7 June. It said that Rommel had lost 40% of his tanks and men since the beginning of the offensive.

Several hours later another Enigma report arrived in Cairo: on 6 June Rommel had given priority to the attack on Bir Hacheim and personally taken over the leadership of this operation.

On Tuesday, 9 June an Enigma report with an

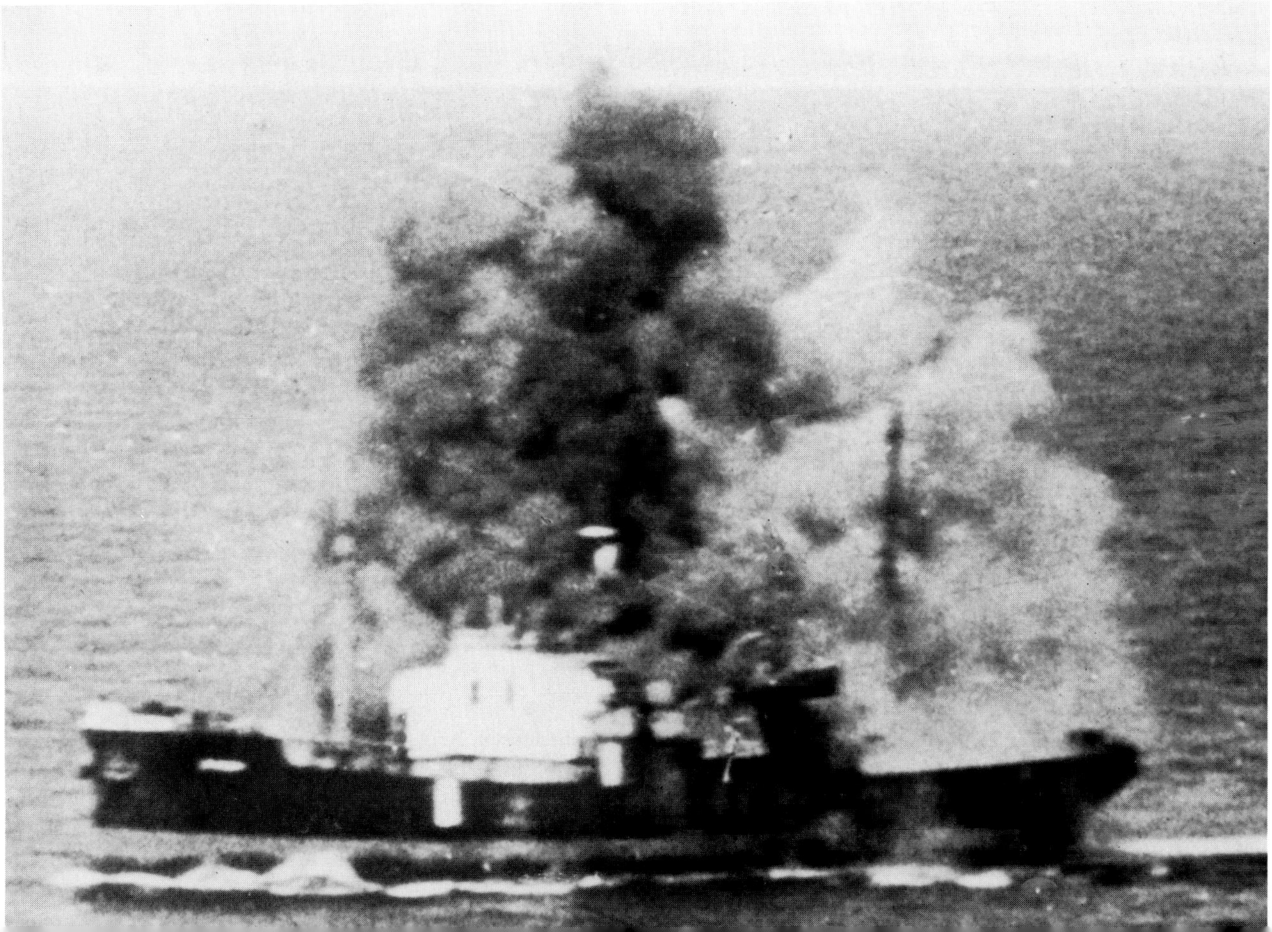

Tobruk area, June 1942: Rommel at the front after his promotion to Generalfeldmarschall.

With acknowledgments to Tommy Handley's postcard pedlar in the "ITMA" shows
—by *Illingworth*.

Rommel's offensive toward Alexandria as seen by a London cartoonist.

important bit of news reached the C-in-C Middle East: Rommel supposedly refused to use tanks against Bir Hacheim. He feared this would have a negative effect on his plans to move toward Tobruk with the least delay. Colonel de Guingand flew immediately to General Ritchie's headquarters to warn the army commander. He brought the news to Ritchie, but did not mention that the news came from an Enigma report. Ritchie, who apparently suspected that Rommel's deceptive maneuvers and faked operations had influenced General Auchinleck's viewpoint, disregarded the warning.

On Wednesday, 10 June, after several days of steady dive-bomber attacks, the Darmstadt Rifle Regiment 115 (*Oberst* Baade) succeeded in pushing far into the defenses of Bir Hacheim from the north. Despite German security measures, part of the fort's garrison, under the direction of their commandant, *General* Koenig, broke out to the west under cover of darkness and was able to fight its way to the British 7th Motorized Brigade.

The combat in the desert now moved further eastward to the El Adem area. Around the district nicknamed "Knightsbridge" there developed a tank battle that lasted for several days. The American Grant tanks and the British 57mm antitank guns cost the Germans heavy losses. The Germans in turn fired their 88mm Flak guns, destroying numerous tanks and smashing two British armored divisions. After that the British troops withdrew from the battlefield.

By the morning of 12 June the headquarters of the 8th Army had received a decoded order which Rommel had given for an advance several days earlier. This time, though, it had not come from B.P. as usual, but was a radio message that the 8th Army's Y Service had deciphered.

It contained a command of Rommel's to the 90th Light Division to advance in the direction of El Adem. Meanwhile, the 15th Panzer Division was to advance to the El Adem airfield, while the 21st Panzer Division and the "Ariete" Division were to seek out the British XXX. Corps in the area west of Knightsbridge. After the two divisions that were advancing on El Adem had taken the airfield and the RAF fuel depot, they were to swing around and encircle the Gazala position.

On Saturday, 13 June the 8th Army received another Enigma report with Rommel's instructions for the next phase of his operation. After smashing the British armored forces in the Knightsbridge area and before Bir Hacheim, Rommel planned to roll over the Gazala position. To do this, he wanted to cut across the coast road and then attack the fortress of Tobruk via Acroma and El Adem.

On Sunday, 14 June the SIS scored another success: B.P. was able for the first time, about 5:30 AM, to include in a quick report to the 8th Army the almost complete contents of *Panzerarmee Afrika*'s daily report that had been radioed to the OKH the previous evening. According to this report, Rommel wanted to continue his attack and try to encircle the whole Gazala front.

At 1:00 PM the 8th Army received an Enigma report that included all the details of Rommel's intentions for the day. And shortly before sunset, the Y Service surprised the 8th Army again with the news: "Rommel has observed the beginning of the British withdrawal from Gazala and ordered his units to blockade the coast road at once."

That evening B.P. sent the C-in-C Middle East a further report from *Panzerarmee Afrika*'s radio traffic: After the situation had been reviewed by Mussolini, Kesselring and Cavallero on 9 June, General Bastico had received new orders. He was to limit himself to the capture of Bir Hacheim and the Gazala positions and the defeat of the British tank forces. The ensuing enclosing of Tobruk was not necessarily to be the next step, although it possibly could be. The situation after the fall of Bir Hacheim and Gazala would have to be reviewed again, and the losses and supply pro-

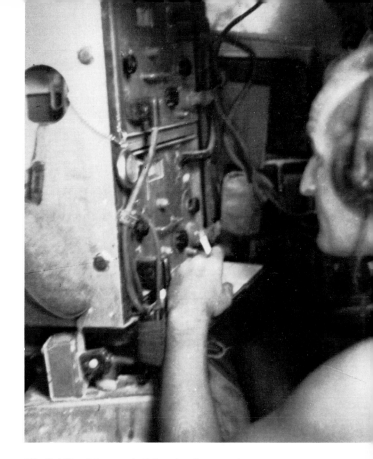

The 3rd Horchkompanie (Listening Company) — Hauptmann Seebohm) — June 1942: A radioman at the radio, as the British listen in.

Mediterranean, June 1942: An Italian freighter sinks in flames after an RAF bomb attack.

blems would have to be studied carefully. The exhausted troops were under no conditions to be thrown into a new attack. *Generalfeldmarschall* Kesselring did consider extending the operation four or five more days after 20 June, but after that there had to be a pause for rest.

Likewise on 14 June B.P. gave the C-in-C Middle East several Enigma reports at the same time. From them it could be seen clearly that the *Panzerarmee* had an acute shortage of fuel. The *DAK* scarcely had any fuel left, the Luftwaffe was using its last reserves, and supplies from Naples were requested for the *Panzerarmee.*

At 5:00 AM on Tuesday, 16 June the C-in-C Middle East was able to learn from an Enigma report that Rommel planned to extend his positions on the heights around Tobruk and capture the big British supply depot at Belhamed during the course of the day.

Although the Italian-German advance was brought to a stop, the bitter fighting in the depths of the British Gazala positions caused such heavy losses that General Ritchie ordered the 8th Army to withdraw. In this critical situation, the British leadership decided to defend the city and fortress of Tobruk.

But before the British could grasp the new situation correctly, Rommel suddenly played a trick on them. He stopped his units abruptly and had them turn toward the west. At a fast speed, the German motorized units now rolled back, directly at momentarily peaceful Tobruk. The amazed British troops, exhausted from the combat on the Gazala line, scarcely had time to take defensive measures. Within four hours, the 15th Panzer Division (now commanded by *Oberst* Crasemann) was able to break into the ring of defenses around Tobruk, now protected only by incomplete mine-fields.

On Wednesday, 17 June, at 6:00 AM, the C-in-C Middle East received the new Enigma report for the day. It was Rommel's command to the *DAK*, which was to capture the Gambut airfield, then cut across the road east of Tobruk to complete the encirclement of the fortress. About 8:00 PM on the same day, the C-in-C received a further Enigma report, in which the Panzerarmee requested that a reserve of 8000 men be sent to North Africa by plane as fast as possible. The answer stated that the lack of transport planes allowed at most 75 men per day to be sent.

On Thursday, 18 June the C-in-C Middle East learned from an Enigma report from the *Panzerarmee* that Hitler had approved, on 13 June, the commands that Mussolini had given General Bastico on 9 June.

At GFM Kesselring's headquarters, June 1942: The teletype office. One of the safest methods of communication.

In the Libyan Desert, June 1942: A native guides a reconnaissance unit.

At about 5:00 in the afternoon, B.P. sent the C-in-C Middle East an Enigma report which revealed that Rommel had just finished his last preparations for an attack on Tobruk.

On Friday, 19 June the C-in-C Middle East received an Enigma report of the same day, including daily commands from *Generalfeldmarschall* Kesselring, "The fate of North Africa will depend on Tobruk . . . Everyone must know this tomorrow and act accordingly."

On the evening of 21 June the Y Service of the 8th Army picked up a message signed by Rommel: "The garrison of the Tobruk fortress has surrendered."

The South African 2nd Division and other Commonwealth units, with a total of 32,200 men, including the commandant of Tobruk, Major General Klopper, were taken prisoner. In Cairo, British government personnel began to burn secret documents, and the Royal Navy prepared to put out into the Red Sea.

Meanwhile, Mussolini landed in Tripoli, bringing a white horse, the Sword of Islam and a marching band along, so as to be prepared for the triumphal march into the capital of Egypt. Hitler promoted Rommel to *Generalfeldmarschall* — at 50, the youngest in German history. The OKW, looking ahead, had military medals made for the capture of Egypt and the Suez Canal. The occupation currency was already being printed.

On Monday morning, 22 June B.P. gave the C-in-C Middle East the latest Enigma report, which was addressed to *Reichsmarschall* Göring. It stated that Kesselring and Rommel had agreed that the troops would be concentrated for an attack on Maddalena, Halfaya and Sollum on 26 June. Rommel planned to have his infantry forces make a feint attack on the 8th Army's border positions. Meanwhile the *DAK* was to advance to the south to encircle the 8th Army's flank.

On thursday, 23 June *Panzerarmee Afrika* crossed the Libyan-Egyptian border. Rommel's next target was Alexandria; within a week, by 30 June, it was to be taken and the Nile Delta and Cairo were to be reached. Rommel then wanted to push forward to the Suez Canal. Kesselring, though, was opposed to that and pointed out that only the capture of Malta could secure the supply situation in North Africa.

In reality, though, the British leadership in the Mediterranean area did not have enough submarines, ships and aircraft to fight the supply convoys successfully in the first half of 1942. And the operational-tactical potential of the Royal Navy had been reduced greatly. The causes were the success of the German U-boats and Italian small craft, the work of the Luftwaffe as well as the Regia Aeronautica, and the successful German-Italian mining operations.

Likewise on 23 June B.P. gave the C-in-C Middle East several Enigma reports, including a detailed plan of Rommel's for encircling the British border positions. His attack was to be supported by air forces from Crete, as there were barely any fuel supplies or bombs left at the Libyan air bases. The capture of several extensive supply and fuel depots in Tobruk was confirmed. The *Panzerarmee* was also to receive maps of Sollum, Sidi Barrani, Marsa Matruh, El Daba and Alexandria. From all these reports the SIS could learn one important fact for the further course of the campaign: Rommel did not by any means intend to pause at the Egyptian border.

At 2:30 AM on Wednesday, 24 June SIS received information from B.P. that made it stop and take notice: According to Enigma reports, the Germans had learned that the British, in the view of the U.S. Military attache in Cairo, were decisively beaten. Now the moment seemed to have come for Rommel to overrun the Nile delta. On this day the 8th Army learned before sunset, from Y Service and aerial reconnaissance reports, that the main forces of Rommel's two Panzer divisions, the 90th Light Division and the "Ariete" Division, plus reconnaissance units, were at most 75 kilometers west of Marsa Matruh and moving eastward fast.

On Thursday, 25 June General Ritchie was relieved. Because of the serious situation, the high commander in the Middle East, General Auchinleck, personally took command of the British 8th Army and decided to withdraw further into the El Alamein area, the last defensive position before Alexandria.

The British positions at El Alamein, built up into a strong line 75 kilometers long, reached the Mediterranean with their right wing and the El Qattara Depression, impassable for tanks, with their left. It was scarcely possible to go around them on account of the lack of connecting roads and the great distance. Another disadvantage for the attackers was that the British supply lines were very short, while the German supply lines grew longer constantly. The British units had suffered high losses, to be sure, but they were still ready for battle and were being strengthened constantly.

On this day, preparations began in Alexandria to evacuate the ships as well as the most important facilities at the naval support point and the headquarters of the Mediterranean fleet.

Likewise on Friday, 26 June the advance of *Panzerarmee Afrika* toward Marsa Matruh and that of ground patrols and short-range reconnaissance forces were observed. Although the 8th Army was being informed almost constantly of the enemy's immediate intentions, this scarcely influenced its critical position. Even the transmission of this information to the fighting forces was scarcely possible, on account of the total disorganization.

On Saturday, 27 June B.P. reported to the C-in-C Middle East that an Enigma radio message had just been decoded. It said that Rommel had requested that the X. *Fliegerkorps* (Air Corps) in Crete should supply aerial photographs of the El Alamein fortifications as soon as possible.

In the night of 27-28 June the New Zealand 2nd Division (Lieutenant General Freyberg) broke out of the Marsa Matruh area, which was being encircled by Rommel's forces. Even *Hauptmann* Seebohm's listening company took part in the bitter firefights that were meant to prevent the breakthrough. Several days later, Seebohm moved his company back to the west again.

The medal struck at the Duce's orders in the summer of 1942 for the triumphal entry into Cairo. "Summa audacit et virtus" is on the back. The medal bears the date "28 October 1942."

*Capuzzo area, June 1942: Bringing in a newly captured,
undamaged British "Crusader" tank.*

At 5:15 AM on Sunday, 28 June the C-in-C
Middle East received a Supermarina radio message
decoded at B.P.: Rommel now intended to encircle
Marsa Matruh from the south and east. In the
afternoon the C-in-C learned from an Enigma
report that the Luftwaffe had just finished its
reconnaissance of the El Alamein-El Qattara
Depression area.

On the same day, *Panzerarmee Afrika* reported,
according to an Enigma report sent to the C-in-C
Middle East from B.P., that they "had met stronger
opposition that expected at Marsa Matruh."

After sunset, General Auchinleck was given a
further Enigma report: Rommel planned to attack
the new British positions as soon as possible.

On Monday, 29 June the German 90th Light
Infantry Division (*Generalmajor* Veith) captured
Marsa Matruh and took 5000 prisoners.

On the same day, Rommel lost his second-best
(to *Hauptmann* Seebohm's radio reconnaissance
company) source on intelligence: The despatches
of the U.S. military attache, Colonel Feller. This
"good source", which since the autumn of 1941
had made decisive contributions to Rommel's

A German airfield near Heraklion, Crete, June 1942: Bombs for Rommel.

Sunset in the harbor of Tobruk, captured by Rommel.

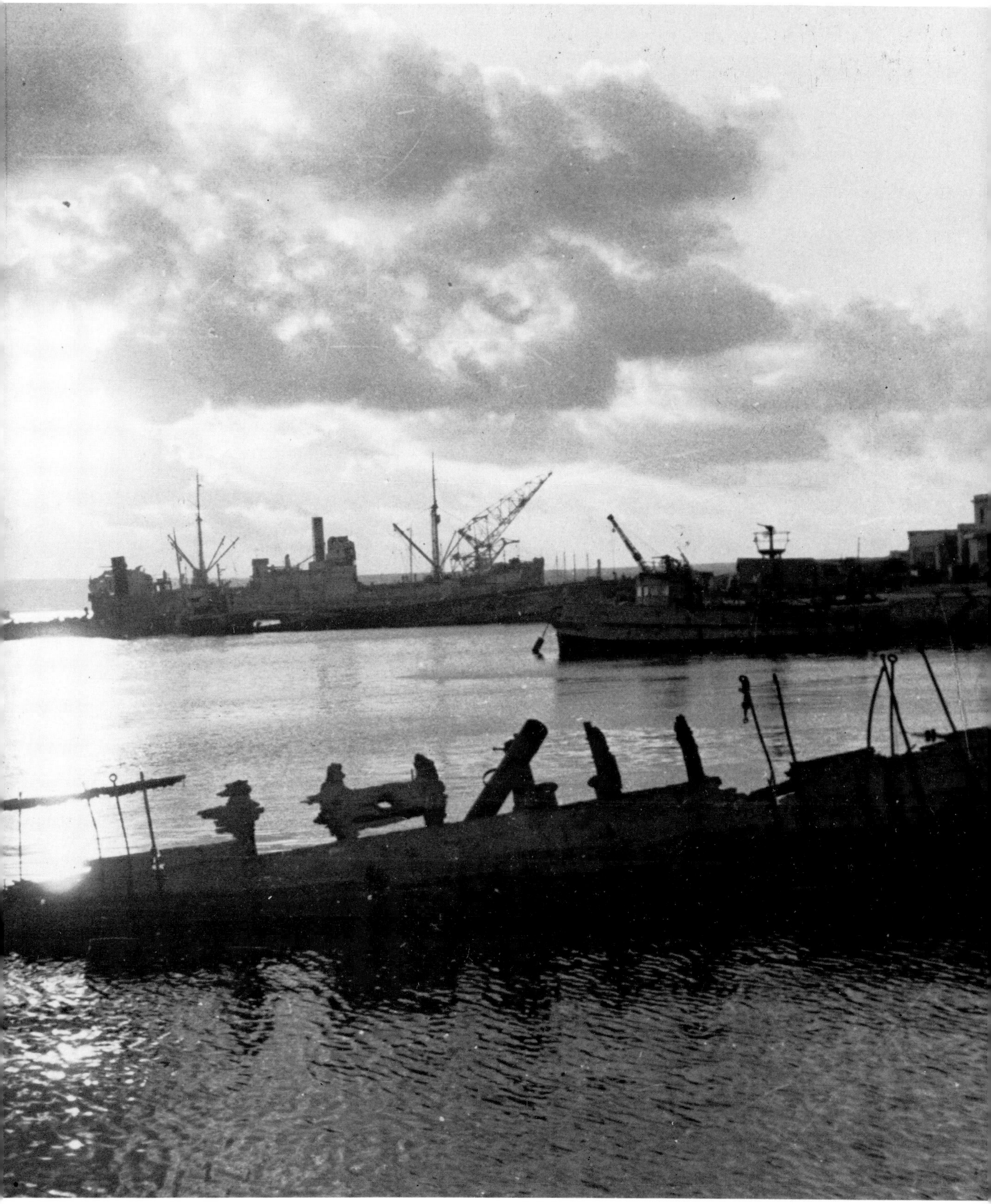

estimations of the enemy's situation through the reliability of its information and made a considerable contribution to his success, was silent now.

In the night of 29-30 June the C-in-C Middle East received a hasty message from B.P. It was learned from a just-decoded Luftwaffe Enigma report that Rommel intended to resume his attack at 3:00 PM on 30 June. That same morning he intended to make a feint attack on the El Alamein positions, and only then would he begin the main attack.

A further Enigma report delivered to the C-in-C that day said that Rommel had ordered the main body of his forces to move southeastward for an encircling movement south of Bab El Qattara.

On the morning of 30 June all units of the 8th Army received the order: "All defensive measures must be completed as soon as possible, because it can be expected that the Alamein positions can be attacked any time after noon today." At 10:50 AM B.P. sent a new quick report, based on a Luftwaffe Enigma message, to the C-in-C Middle East: Since the troops had not yet reached their points

of departure at that time, the Luftwaffe doubted that the *Panzerarmee* could open the attack as planned.

The 90th Light Division was still some 20 kilometers away from El Alamein. The 21st Panzer Division had to halt their advance on account of fuel shortages. A violent sandstorm had unexpectedly delayed the transfer of the Luftwaffe units to the advanced front-line airfields.

About 4:00 PM the C-in-C Middle East received another Enigma report from B.P., stating that Rommel had changed his plans on account of the latest developments. The attack was now to begin the next day, presumably at 1:00 PM.

In a further Enigma report that reached the C-in-C Middle East it was stated: "Precise information concerning preparation areas of individual units before the opening of the attack. The planned thrust direction of the 15th *Panzerarmee*: between El Alamein and the El Qattara Depression. The Luftwaffe had received the command to carry out attack waves, between 4:00 and 6:00 AM on the next day, 1 July, on the British key positions in the El Alamein area and troop concentrations to the east, south and west of this area.''

On this day *Panzerarmee Afrika* reached the town of El Alamein, some 95 kilometers west of Alexandria, but an immediate attempt to break through the lines failed, thanks to the stiffening British resistance.

At the end of June 1942 *Hauptmann* Seebohm moved his reconnaissance company far forward. He chose a location for his NFA Company 621 directly on the coast, near the highlands known as ''Jesus Hill'' northwest of the Tel el Eisa halting place, not quite 1000 meters behind the Italian troops that held that sector of the front. The reason for such an exposed position was its guarantee of clear, interference-free reception of the most important enemy radio traffic, as well as good connections with the listening posts in the rear section of the front area.

Even the RAF reconnaissance planes that turned up again and again and showed a particular interest in the radio trucks, antennas and tents of the company in the dunes, could not impel Hauptmann Seebohm to move his listening post further back. The company belonged, though it was fully independent and worked according to instructions from Berlin, to Panzer Intelligence Regiment 10.

It consisted of five platoons and was divided into two echelons. The 1st Echelon with the company staff and the 3rd platoon was located with the staff of *Panzerarmee Afrika*. It was responsible for decoding and evaluating all intercepted enemy radio traffic. The 2nd Echelon, with its two platoons, was now located at Tel el Eisa. *Leutnant* Wischmann of NFA Company 621, assigned by Rommel to his front-line staff as a permanent escort officer, and two radiomen maintained contact with the parts of the company at Tel el Eisa.

Every enemy radio message of importance intercepted by Seebohm's intelligence service was sent on to *Leutnant* Wischmann, decoded, and given to Rommel, after which it was noted on a radio situation chart. *Hauptmann* Seebohm was also assigned a decoding unit led by a code specialist.

The company was equipped with two powerful 100-watt receiver-transmitters and used the Army Enigma code machines on all the main communications lines. It operated on the main frequency of 1057 kilohertz.

The average age of the company members was about 25 years; they were intelligent and well-trained radiomen with fluent knowledge of English. Seebohm's company regularly provided daily reports and a monthly summary of information, known as radio situation reports.

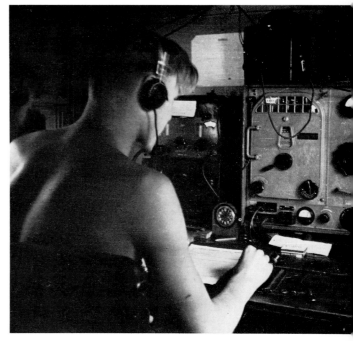

Marsa Matruh area, June 1942: A German radio man sends a message.

Mediterranean, June 1942: An Italian motor ship with a load of fuel for Panzerarmee Afrika blows up after being torpedoed by RAF bombers.

*On the rim of the El Qattara Depression, June 1942:
German observers on a ground reconnaissance mission.*

*Tel el Eisa area, June 1942: A radio truck of the 3rd
Listening Company (Hauptmann Seebohm).*

The exhaustive daily radio situation reports for the German and Italian staffs in North Africa included information on the organization and locations of the enemy troops. A summarized short form was sent to the Listening Evaluation Office (HAS) in Berlin, the commander of the Listening Troops Southeast in Athens, the Chief of the General Staff of *Panzerarmee Afrika*, and others.

The intercepted, operationally important radio traffic of the C-in-C Middle East, transmitted in a complicated code, was immediately sent to the main evaluating office in Berlin, since no high-level German cryptologists were located in North Africa.

Radiomen of the 3rd Listening Company locate a transmitter.

Radiomen of the 3rd Listening Company receiving a radio message.

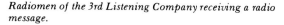

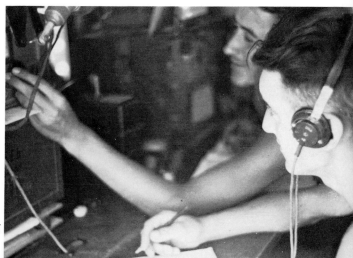

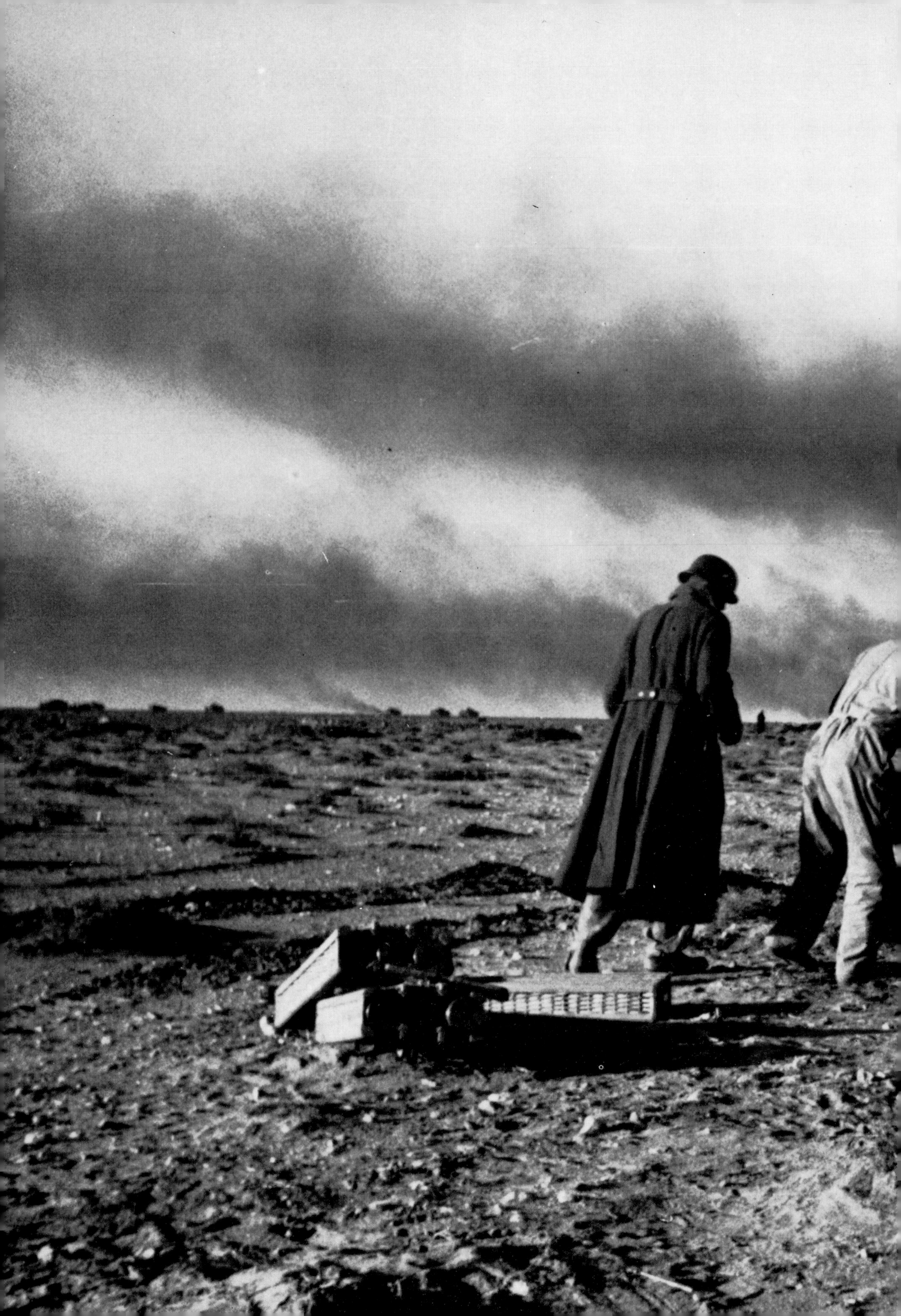

1942
July-December

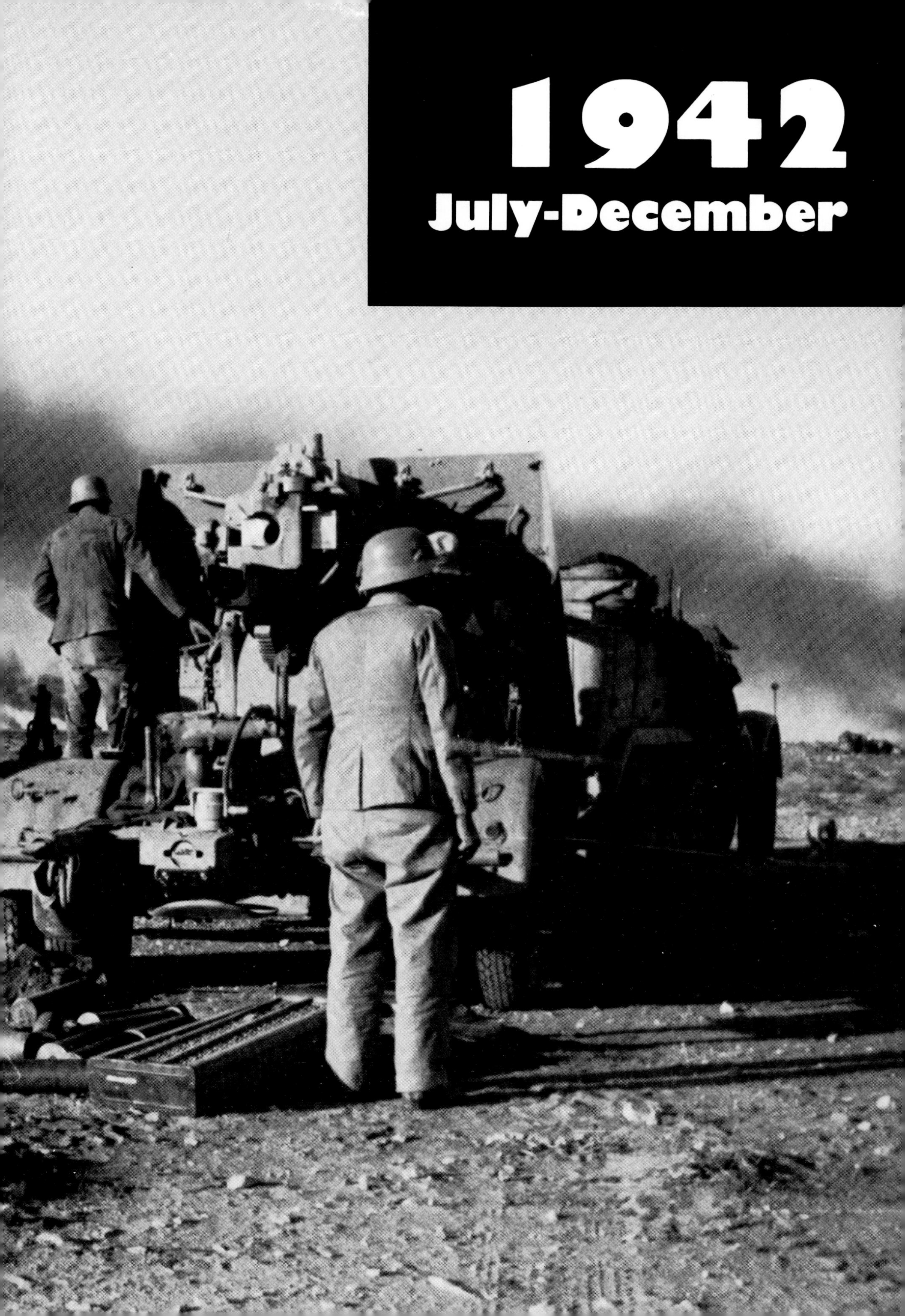

Berlin, 3 July 1942: According to Dr. Goebbels, the occupation of Egypt is about to take place.

At the Fliegerführer Afrika's headquarters, July 1942: Two enemy situation analysts, Oberleutnant Dietrich (left) and Major Janke.

On Wednesday morning, 1 July B.P. sent the C-in-C Middle East a decoded radio message: *Panzerarmee Afrika* urgently requested 10,000 maps of the largest Egyptian cities in the Nile delta from OKH.

Now Rommel's Panzer units, that had reached the narrows by El Alamein the day before with only 48 tanks and armored scout vehicles ready for action, began an advance against the positions of the British 8th Army, but it came to a stop under enemy fire.

At about 5:00 PM General Auchinleck learned from Enigma reports and information from the Y Service that the 90th Light Division's advance had been stopped. The "Littorio" Division had made a mistake. On the other hand, a report from Rommel said that the 90th Light Division "had succeeded in breaking through." When this news reached Berlin, Dr. Goebbels made known in a press release that "the occupation of Egypt is about to take place."

On Friday, 3 July B.P. sent the C-in-C Middle East another important bit of news early in the morning. A just-decoded Enigma report revealed Rommel's intentions: Despite heavy losses the day before, another attempt would be made to roll over the British defensive positions around El Alamein and cut the coastal road.

On the same day, though, the exhausted *Panzerarmee Afrika* had to break off its operation begun on 1 July the breaking of the British defense lines near El Alamein, and go on the defensive with its weakened forces.

Likewise on 3 July B.P. sent the headquarters of the Mediterranean fleet, C-in-C Mediterranean, a decoded report from the Supermarina: The Axis leadership had learned that Alexandria was on the verge of being evacuated. They had decided to allow the French squadron (Admiral Godfroy) interned there passage to its home ports.

Early in the morning of Saturday, 4 July B.P. sent the C-in-C Middle East a decoded command that had been given to *Panzerarmee Afrika* the evening before: Rommel had no intention of continuing the attack on 4 July. First he intended to deal with the serious supply problem.

On this day the number of decoded Enigma reports that B.P. sent to the C-in-C Middle East reached a record high. There were over 100 radio messages, and their operational value was incalculable. They even included tactical details,

such as precise information on the supply columns and their marching routes, the locations of individual unit headquarters and their command posts, the location, strength and activity of the positions. In addition, the strength, losses and intentions of the *Panzerarmee* and the Luftwaffe on that day were cited. General Auchinleck said: "If it had not been for "Sigint" (Author's note: the decoded enemy radio messages), Rommel surely would have gotten through to Cairo."

Now the C-in-C Middle East decided on a course of action that was to decide the fate of the North African campaign and thus that of Rommel's troops like scarcely any other: He gave the strengthened Australian II/26 the Infantry Brigade and Battalions II/24 and II/48 the order to attack Tel el Eisa and put the German listening company out of action in a shock-troop undertaking. General Auchinleck and his enemy situation specialist, de Guingand, believed that in

German General Staff map of 1942: The arrow marks the position of the 3rd Listening Company (Hauptmann Seebohm) near Tel el Eisa.

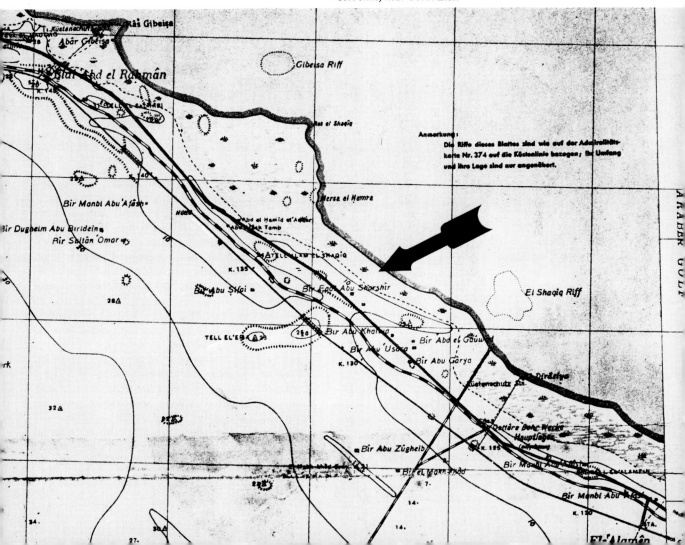

this way they could gain important information and insights into Rommel's intelligence activities. Lieutenant Colonel Hammer of Victoria was given this assignment along with the 2nd Company of the 48th Battalion of the Australian 9th Infantry Division (Major General Morshead), which had been transferred to the front a short time ago and placed under his command. The time set for this bold move was the night of 9-10 July 9-10.

On the evening of 4 July the enemy situation specialist gave the 8th Army his new situation evaluation: "Since the enemy has been busy all day with placing his supplies of ammunition and fuel behind a strong barrier of tanks, this indicates that Rommel will accept the resulting slight rearward movement of his troops in order to undertake a much greater advance later."

After Rommel's summer offensive, the front gradually settled down on a line 50 kilometers long, from the swampy El Qattara Depression, impassable for tanks, in the south to El Alamein

in the north on the Mediterranean coast, a few kilometers east of Tel el Eisa.

Early in July 1942 *Panzerarmee Afrika* was composed, after the arrival of Italian reinforcements, of four Panzer divisions, two of them German, and eight infantry divisions, two of them German as well. The British 8th Army (General Auchinleck) was meanwhile reinforced by two divisions from the Middle East, American Sherman tanks and self-propelled artillery. At that time the 8th Army included three armored divisions, seven tank brigades, and seven infantry divisions. The forces were now more or less equal, but the RAF was supreme in the air.

On Tuesday, 7 July B.P. sent the C-in-C Middle East, among others, the following Enigma report: Rommel was now receiving reinforcements from Crete, namely Infantry Regiment 382 of the 164th Infantry Division. The OKH informed Rommel, though, that it could provide only a few units in addition to the reinforcements already agreed on. Their transfer, to be sure, would still take some time.

On Wednesday, 8 July the C-in-C Middle East learned from a new Enigma report that Rommel had just moved his main fighting force, the 21st Panzer Division, the 90th Light Division and the "Littorio" Division, into the southern sector of the front.

In the morning hours of 9 July 1942 the II. Battalion of the Australian 26th Infantry Brigade received the order to make a bold attempt to capture the sector in the Tel el Eisa area, near the Mediterranean coast. The target of the attack was

« *The railroad line between El Daba and El Alamein, July 1942: the abandoned desert station of Tel el Eisa, very close to Hauptmann Seebohm's listening company.*

Tel el Eisa area, July 1942: The position of part of the 2nd Echelon of the 3rd Listening Company, seen from the shore.

The Mediterranean coast at Tel el Eisa, July 1942: A radio truck of the 1st Platoon, 2nd Echelon, 3rd Listening Company.

*Tel el Eisa area, July 1942: Camouflage nets to prevent
enemy pilots from seeing part of the 2nd Echelon of the 3rd
Listening Company.*

*El Alamein area, July 1942: Soldiers of the Australian 26th
Infantry Brigade prepare for a surprise attack against Tel el
Eisa.*

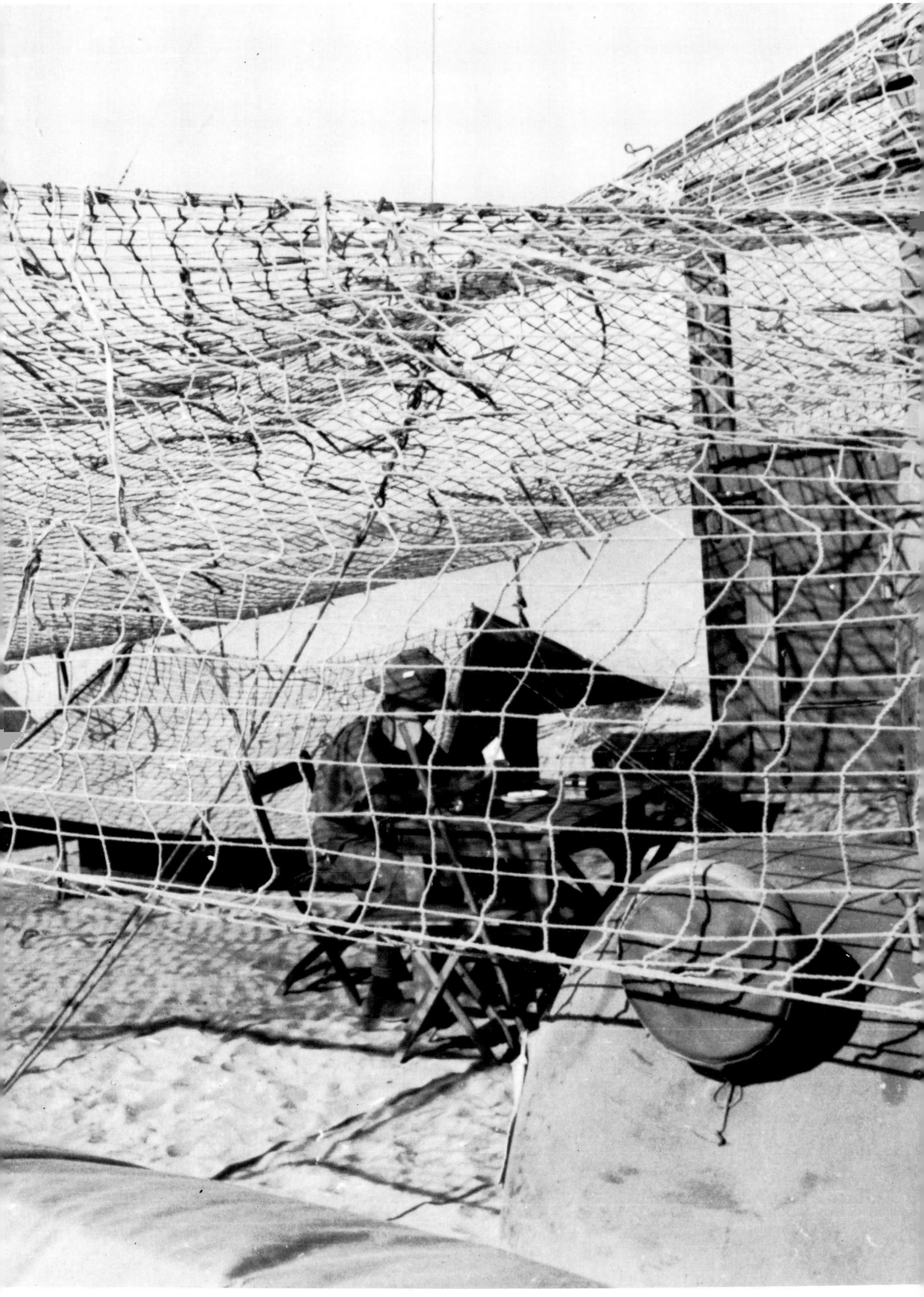

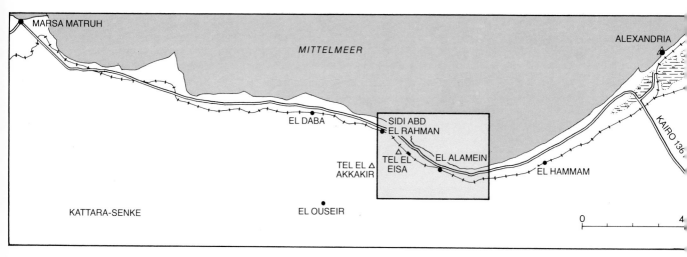

The Mediterranean coast between Cyrenaica and the Nile Delta, with the Tel el Eisa area.

the coastal highlands with Hills 33, 26 and 23, the Tel el Eisa ridge and the railroad station of the same name, which was some 600 meters east of the ridge.

The actual target, known to only a few specially informed officers of the infantry brigade, was the 3rd Company of *Hauptmann* Seebohm's Intelligence Unit 56. It was situated in an advanced position close to the sea, near the railroad station. It was secured by Italian field artillery grenade launchers and machine gun nests of the 7th

Regiment "Bersaglieri", plus the parts of the inexperienced Italian "Sabratha" Division that were north of the railroad line. To drive off the enemy, the South African 3rd Brigade of the South African 1st Division (General Pienaar), with tanks and artillery support, was simultaneously to attack the highland positions of the Axis troops in the Tel el Eisa area.

At 3:40 AM British time on Friday, 10 July Lieutenant Colonel Hammer and his Australians moved forward. The men, equipped with boots wrapped in sackcloth, made their way soundlessly through the sand dunes in the darkness. The 7th Regiment "Bersaglieri", securing the listening company, was surprised while asleep. Ten minutes later, the New Zealand artillery opened massive fire, first using explosive shells, then smoke-screen shells to conceal the advance of the tanks moving westward along the coastal road.

The 2nd Echelon of the listening company, about 100 men strong, was alarmed by the heavy artillery fire and immediately scurried into the cover of their motor vehicles. Now the Australians pushed into the line between the Italian 85th and 86th "Sabratha" Infantry Regiments and the 7th Infantry Regiment "Bersaglieri", and simultaneously cut off the batteries of the 3rd Mobile Regiment "Duca d'Aosta." After vigorous close combat, the Italians withdrew before superior forces.

Hauptmann Seebohm, the man to whom GFM Rommel owed much of his success.

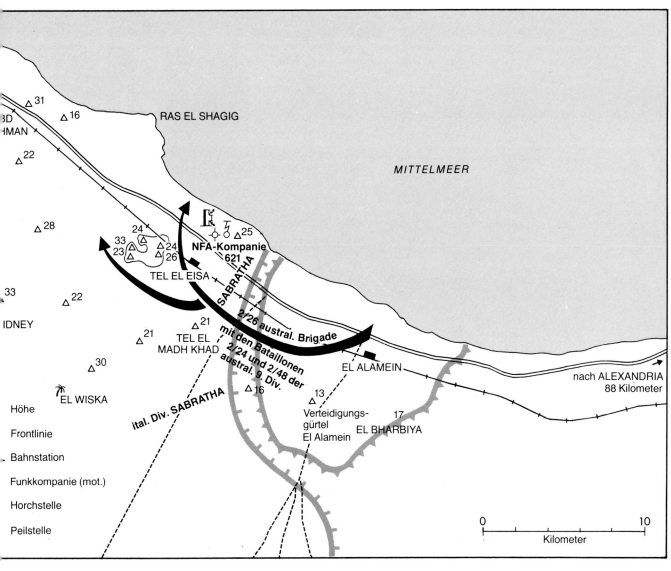

RAS EL SHAGIG

MITTELMEER

△ 31
△ 16
3D
HMAN
△ 22

△ 28

△ 24
33 △ 24
23 △ 26

NFA-Kompanie
621

TEL EL EISA

SABRATHA

2/26 austral. Brigade

mit den Bataillonen
2/24 und 2/48 der
austral. 9. Div.

ital. Div. SABRATHA

△ 33

△ 22
IDNEY

△ 21
△ 21
TEL EL
MADH KHAD

△ 30

EL WISKA

△ 16

EL ALAMEIN

nach ALEXANDRIA
88 Kilometer

△ 13
Verteidigungs-
gürtel
El Alamein

△ 17
EL BHARBIYA

Höhe

Frontlinie

Bahnstation

Funkkompanie (mot.)

Horchstelle

Peilstelle

0   10
Kilometer

∧

*On the night of
9/10 July 1942, a
surprise attack was
made against Tel el
Eisa by the
Australian 26th
Infantry Brigade.*

*Tel el Eisa on the
morning of 10 July
1942: A dead
radioman in his 3-
ton Opel Blitz "A"
radio truck of the
3rd Listening
Company.*

- 607674

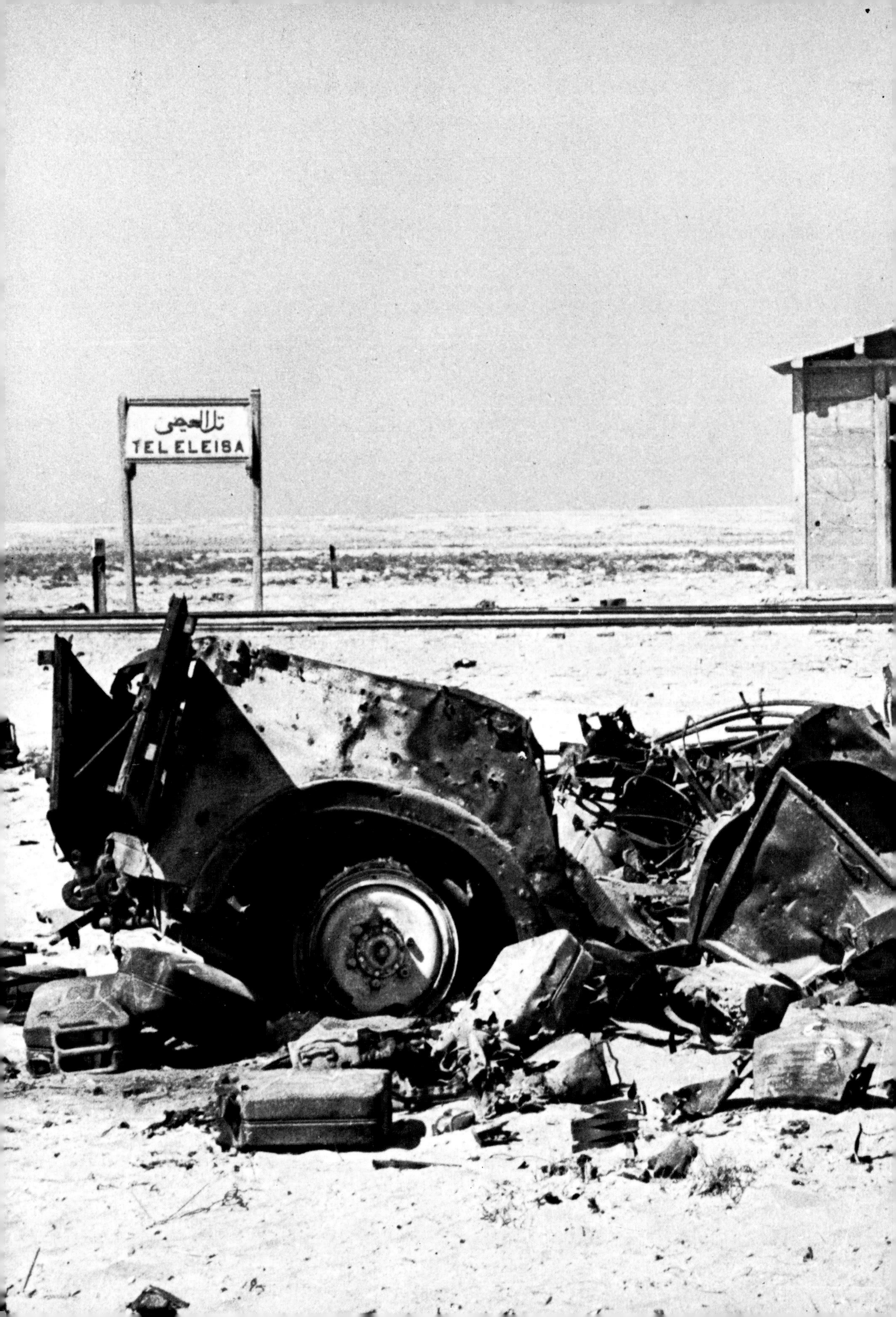
تلالعيص
TEL ELEISA

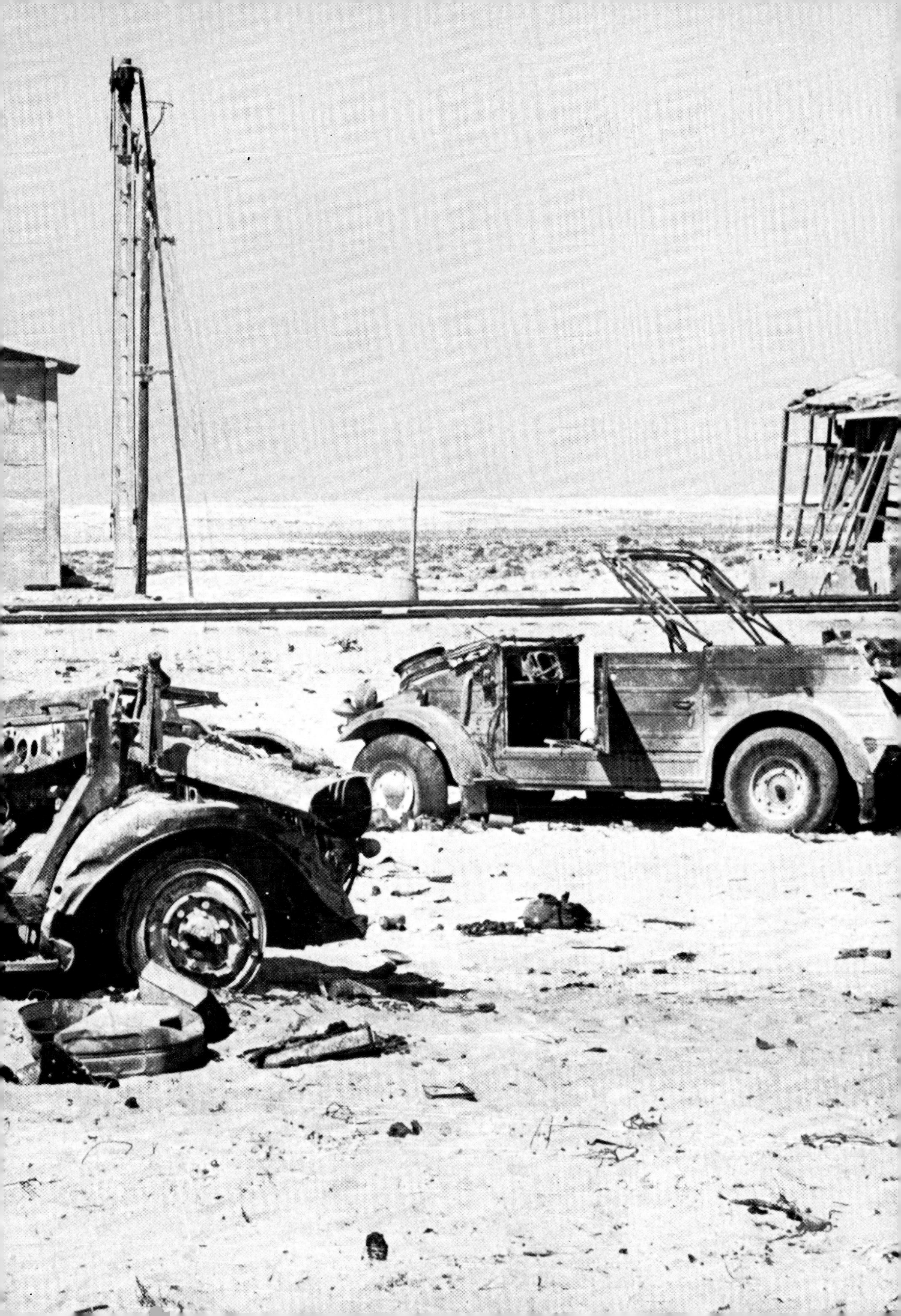

Tel el Eisa on the morning of 10 July 1942: Soldiers and radiomen of the 3rd Listening Company have been captured.

« *Before the desert station of Tel el Eisa on the morning of 10 July 1942 are the burned-out wrecks of the 3rd Listening Company's motor pool.*

Tel el Eisa on the morning of 10 July 1942: The men of the 3rd Listening Company are taken to their first interrogation.

SIS Headquarters, Cairo, summer 1942: An in-house display »
of Panzerarmee Afrika's radios and other intelligence-gathering equipment.

Meanwhile the Australians under Lieutenant Colonel Hammer stormed the built-up position of the *DAK*'s listening company. The Germans, rudely awakened and armed only with light infantry weapons, defended themselves bitterly. When the attackers had covered the company's entire position with grenade-launcher fire, a dozen British tanks appeared in the first light of day.

About 6:00 AM, after a fight lasting about 90 minutes, some Germans were able to escape in trucks from the company's supply train. *Hauptmann* Seebohm, who had visited the 2nd Echelon the previous evening, fought to his machine gun's last bullet and collapsed, his legs badly wounded.

The two officers, *Hauptmann* Seebohm and his deputy, Leutnant Herz, were taken prisoner along with 71 men of the 2nd Echelon with the 1st and 2nd Platoons, plus parts of the supply train. At the same time, the Australians approached Hill 33 and rolled over the German 52nd and 33rd Heavy Artillery Units.

In all, the Australians took 1556 men prisoner, including the 2nd Echelon of the Seebohm Company; with few exceptions, they were all Italians.

Panzerarmee Afrika's combat report for that day stated: "On 10 July, at 6:00 AM, the enemy attacked the "Sabratha" Division north of the coastal road, after an hour of very heavy artillery preparation and supported by tanks, with a reinforced brigade. The Italian troops situated here, whose artillery apparently consisted of one light artillery battery and one heavy artillery unit, surrendered, partly without offering resistance, or fled in retreat."

The booty, which was examined immediately on the spot by experienced intelligence officers, included the full equipment of NFA Company 621 with almost all its information that indicated the company's organization and methods, plus whole bundles of captured British radio codes, encoded lists of names, as well as intelligence material.

The members of the listening company were immediately loaded into trucks and transported to Heluan, where intelligence officers of the C-in-C Middle East and the 8th Army staff were waiting for them. The wounded men were taken

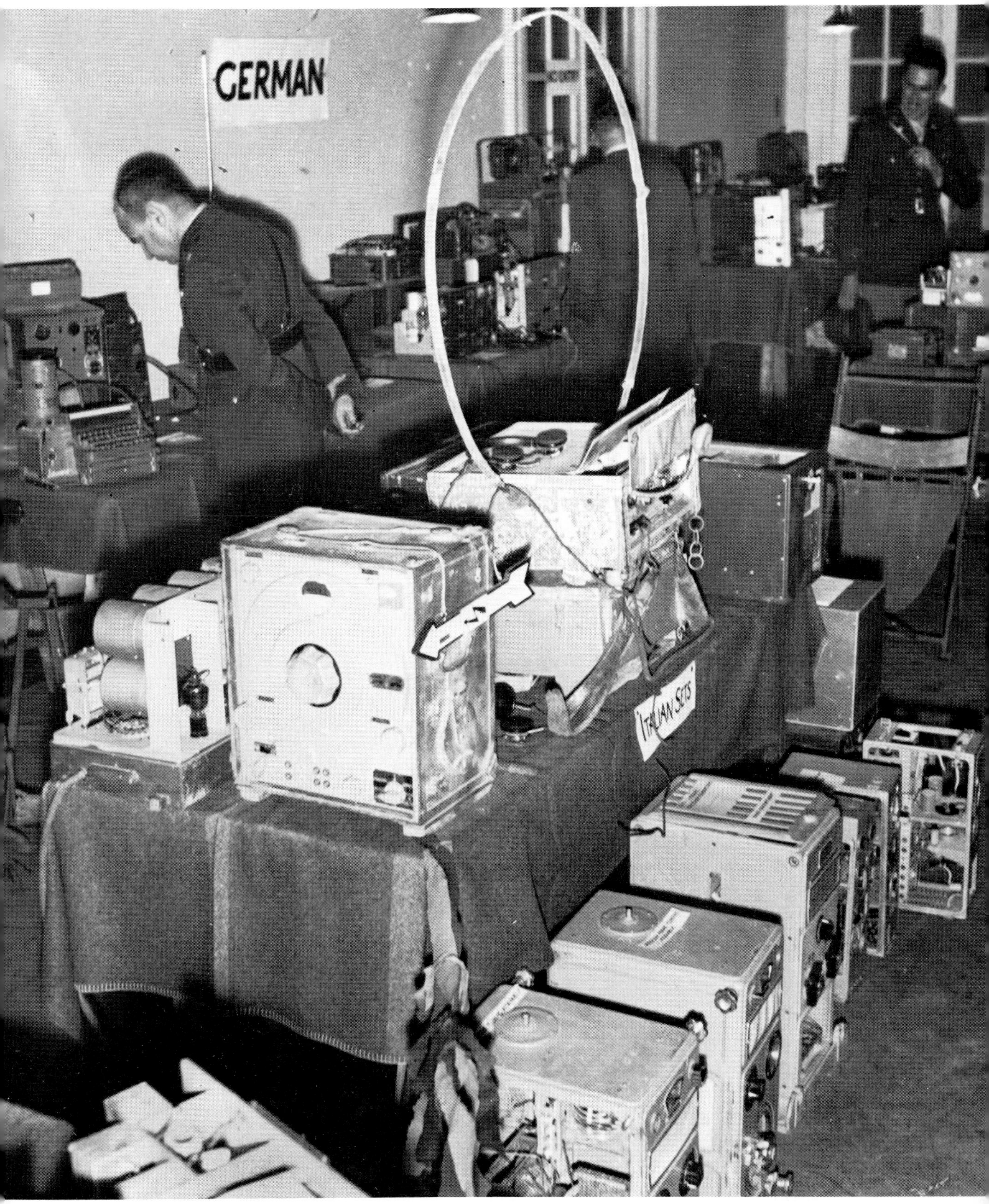
GERMAN
ITALIAN SETS

to the field hospital at Alexandria. *Hauptmann* Seebohm died there a few days later. The prisoners of war were taken, after their interrogation was finished, to the prisoner-of-war camp at Faid, on the Suez Canal.

In the opinion of the British intelligence specialists, this raid at Tel el Eisa was the most decisive intelligence action of the whole North African campaign. Brigadier Scott, who evaluated the captured material with his team of experts, commented: "This capture had far-reaching results, not only for further combat activity in North Africa, but also for the battles for Sicily, the Italian mainland, and even the invasion itself."

The captured documents proved that the many significant operations of the legendary "Desert Fox" were to a great degree attributable to the achievements of Seebohm's listening company. And hear at Tel el Eisa the battle of El Alamein was decided.

What made the greatest impression on the British intelligence experts was that the success of the German radio reconnaissance was made possible in the first place by the faulty British radio security.

Since the attack on the listening company, Rommel's luck had deserted him, and the *Feldmarschall* bore more and more resemblance to a man who had to find his way blindfolded through a dark room full of dangerous obstacles.

General Auchinleck immediately took steps to improve radio security in the field. A newly established special unit now made sure of strict adherence to all security measures.

The British intelligence service now twisted the knife. In possession of the materials captured from Tel el Eisa, it was now in a position to pull off a broad-based radio deception. It made sure that Rommel's listening service could hear only what would contribute to its confusion. The British had an easy time of it, for the new, just-established German radio reconnaissance company now consisted of relatively inexperienced radio experts who seldom could tell deception from truth.

Since 10 July the Enigma reports sent from B.P. to the C-in-C Middle East contained more and more references to the Luftwaffe's fuel shortage in North Africa. After a few days, this shortage increased to the extent that air transport in North Africa had to be halted so that the Luftwaffe could at least fly combat missions from time to time.

On Sunday, 12 July the SIS' battle against Rommel went into a new phase. On this day, independent of the GC & CS cryptologists' work, the deciphering of the Enigma "Scorpion" code began. It was used for radio traffic between the Luftwaffe communications officers and the *Panzerarmee*, the *DAK* and the individual Panzer divisions.

Mediterranean, July 1942: RAF bombers attack Italian supply ships.

On Monday, 13 July the C-in-C Middle East decided, on the basis of received Enigma and Y-service reports, to attack the Ruweisat Ridge in the night of 14-15 July. The decoded radio messages had confirmed that the 21st Panzer Division had been moved into the northernmost sector, near the British El Alamein position.

The C-in-C Middle East, General Auchinleck, radioed to the Chief of the Imperial General Staff (CIGS): "The German units seem to be very tense. Since the 21st Panzer Division is now located in the north, while the 15th Panzer Division is in the middle and the 90th Light Division is in the south, there is a good chance of advancing against the Italians in the middle of the front. My tactics foresee: If possible, I shall attack the Italians steadily. First because of their lower morale, and second because the Germans cannot hold their outspread front without them."

On the evening of 14 July Rommel decided to give up the attempt to break through to Alexandria until the *Panzerarmee* was again at full strength. The SIS learned nothing of this at the time, but on the very next day a report from aerial reconnaissance reached the C-in-C Middle East: "The *Panzerarmee* is beginning to mine their front field to an extent scarcely ever equaled before." That meant that Rommel had turned to defensive action.

From mid-July 1942 on, the supply problem, by now very critical, got worse and worse. The RAF bomb attacks on the harbors of Tobruk and Marsa Matruh, as well as on ship traffic between

El Alamein area, July 1942: German engineers laid minefields "to an extent scarcely seen before."

*In an office of the Italian Supermarina, July 1942, a »
radioman receives a message.*

This source of information was especially valuable; it provided not only exact details of the *Fliegerführer Afrika*'s intentions, but also indications of the German Panzer units' movements. The cracking of the "Scorpion" code was accomplished by the cryptologists serving with the CBME at Heliopolis, near Cairo.

In the afternoon, British bombers and Royal Navy units sighted a large Italian coastal steamer in the Marsa Matruh area. Several hours before, on account of a decoded Enigma radio message, they had been informed as to the ship's cargo, route and destination. Hit by bombs and torpedoes, the ship sank. This was already the second unit of this size that had been sunk within 24 hours. Both of these coastal ships, plying between Tobruk and Marsa Matruh, had supplied Rommel's army with vitally needed fuel.

—by Illingworth.

RAF bombers are like hornets, as a London cartoonist portrays Rommel's advance toward Alexandria.

transferred to North Africa, the first being parts of the 164th Division and their artillery.

At the beginning of the latter half of July 1942, *Generalfeldmarschall* Rommel realized that a further offensive was no longer possible, since the forces at his disposal were too weak. Meanwhile, defensive measures were taken on both sides of the front, beginning with the laying of extensive minefields.

Panzerarmee Afrika's vehicles were worn out for the most part, and could only be kept running by laborious work at the front-line workshops. Gradually the front became quiet, and until the end of August 1942 the quiet was broken only by the usual reconnaissance and artillery activity.

On Friday, 17 July the Y Service reported that the 21st Panzer Division had only ten tanks in working order. And in the information sent to General Auchinleck from B.P. it was said that parts of the German 164th Division would be transferred to North Africa before the end of July, but without the expected artillery.

Likewise on 17 July the C-in-C Middle East was able to learn from an Enigma report that the Italian "Folgore" Airborne Division and a German airborne unit, the *Ramcke Brigade,* were to reinforce the *Panzerarmee* within a week.

those two ports, plus the Royal Navy's activities, cut the supplying of Rommel's troops to a bare minimum. In addition, ground attacks threatened the coastal road and the very few railway lines on a daily basis. The supply trains of the *Panzerarmee* were decimated regularly.

The weakness of the Italian troops forced Rommel to take unusual measures. Particularly heavy minefields were laid out before their positions, and German units were moved closer to them.

On Thursday, 16 July several brigades of the British 8th Army (General Auchinleck) undertook individual attacks on the Italian front sector of *Panzerarmee Afrika* from their positions in the El Alamein line. The British were able to penetrate deeply into the front in several places and to smash the Italian X. Corps almost completely. On the same day, B.P. sent the C-in-C Middle East the last Enigma reports: Hitler had sent out a message that the 90th Light Division was to be brought up to fighting strength. This had priority; only then were the 15th and 21st Panzer Divisions likewise to be strengthened too. In addition, troops from the Balkans were to be

El Alamein area, late July 1942: A British radioman listens in on Panzerarmee Afrika's radio traffic.

Egypt, 21 August 1942: Churchill returns to Cairo after his visit to Moscow to inspect the British troops in the western desert. He made part of the trip in a captured Fieseler Storch Fi 156 C-3/Trop — ex TH+AC. From left to right: Churchill, Air Vice-Marshal Coningham, General Sir Alan Brooke and the pilot.

In July 1942 Rommel received, instead of the requested 30,000 tons, only about one-fifth of his supplies, some 7000 tons. The reason was probably the short, bright summer nights, in which a particularly large number of tankers and transport ships fell victim to the RAF and the Royal Navy. In all, the Italians lost 80 whips with some 163,000 tons (including the few ships outside the Mediterranean) from the beginning of January to the end of July 1942. In the same period, the Germans had lost ten ships with a total of 28,000 tons.

Saturday, 1 August was an important date for the intelligence service and the enemy situation expert of the 8th Army. On this day, General Staff Intelligence (GS Int) changed the form of its obligatory daily intelligence summary, hitherto one of the most important decision-making tools for the commanders of the individual units and their staffs.

Its most significant disadvantage, though, was the listing of facts with their evaluations and conclusions, which included a great many details and thus were never very clear. Effective immediately, all confusing details were to be put in the second part of the summary, which was issued to only the intelligence officers and a few chosen persons.

The first part, a kind of summary in clear, simple language without irritating specialized terminology, went to the staffs and the unit commanders. The advantage was that since both parts of the summary contained information from all sources, such as air and ground reconnaissance, statements of war prisoners, captured documents, Y Service and agents' information, as well as Enigma reports, the informational value of the Enigma reports could be judged better than before. This step taken by GS Int proved that the enemy's situation and intentions could be learned to a greater extent than ever before, and above all reliably, from the Enigma reports.

In the first week of August 1942 Rommel worked on the plans for his new offensive, with the goal of breaking through the El Alamein front to wipe out the 8th Army (now commanded by Lieutenant General Montgomery) and advancing to Cairo. The British defensive positions at the south end of the El Alamein line were only lightly occupied. Rommel intended, under the greatest

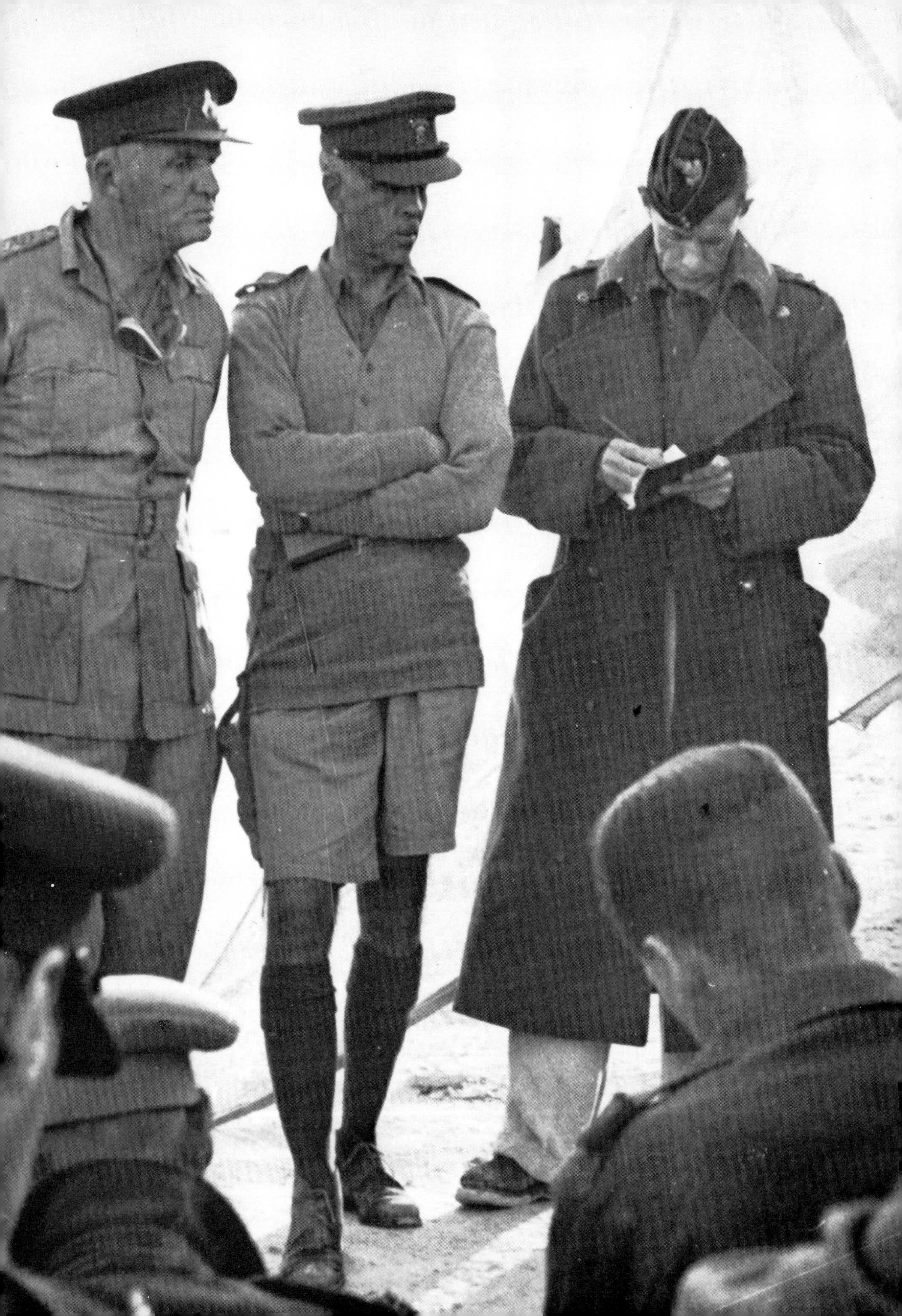

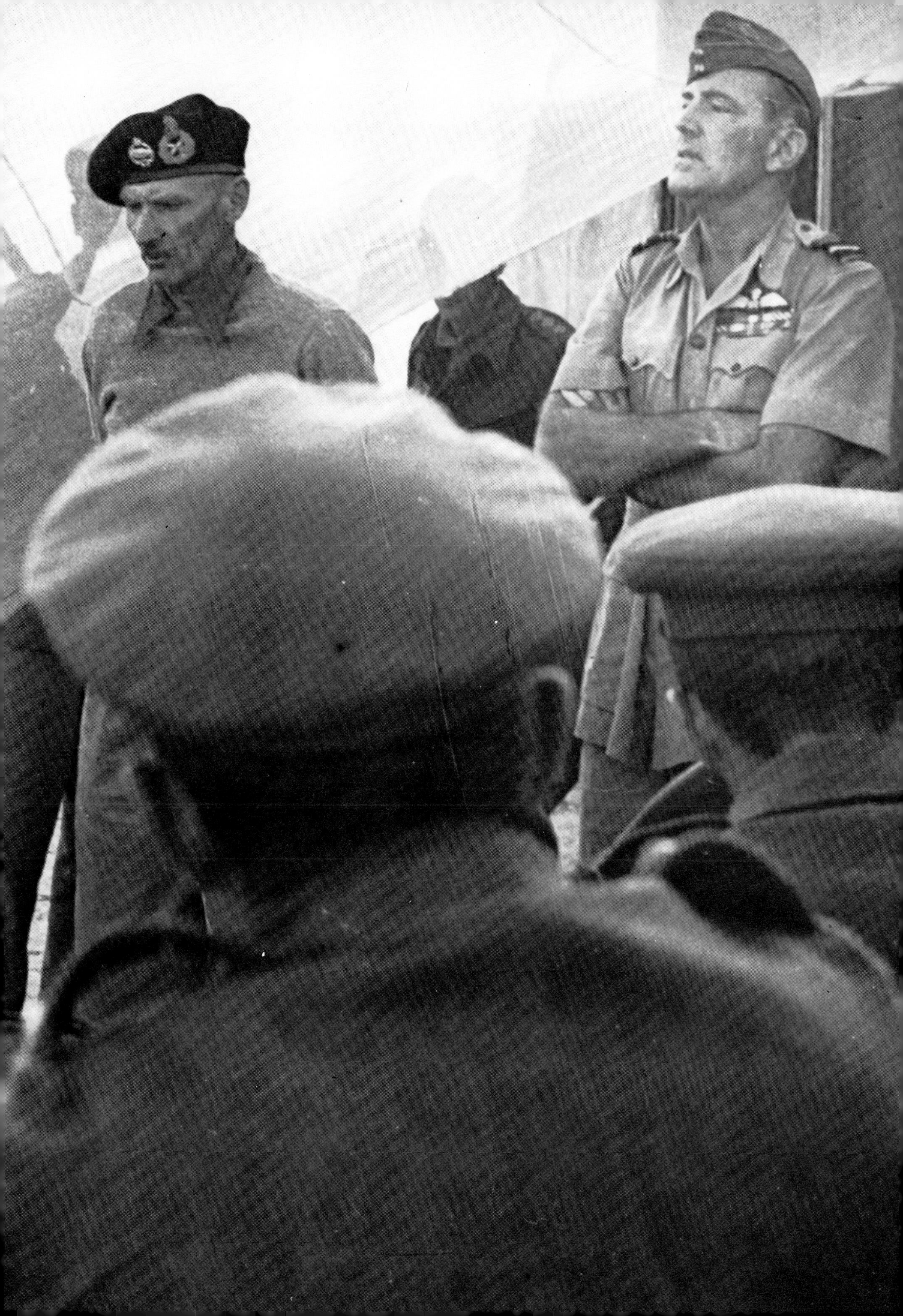

secrecy, to transfer parts of his Panzer army from the north to the south and into the Qattara Depression. After all the units had made their preparations, he wanted to break through the British defense lines and then push northward to the sea, smash the 8th Army in the "box" of El Alamein and immediately push forward to the Nile delta.

Time was of the essence; the nights with full-moon light had to be utilized for preparations, for the end of August was the latest date for a counteroffensive. As planned, Rommel moved his troops southward by night. He left dummy tanks and trucks behind in the northern sector, so that the troop transfer could be spotted neither by aerial reconnaissance nor by scout troops. Complete radio silence was also ordered, so as to give the British radio reconnaissance no indication. But Rommel informed *Generalfeldmarschall* Kesselring as well as the Italian and German High Command of his intentions, in order to obtain the greatest possible amount of air support and assure supplies.

On Friday, 7 August General Montgomery was named the commander of the British 8th Army. During a trip to inspect the front, the new commander said, filled with conviction, that he would defeat Rommel because he knew his intentions. He stressed this in a manner that alarmed SIS and caused fear that the enemy somehow would take this to be a reflection on Enigma.

On Monday, 10 August B.P. sent the C-in-C Middle East an Enigma report in which the commander of *Panzerarmee Afrika* requested the delivery of a quantity of guns and ammunition by 15 August. Now the General Headquarters Middle East suspected that Rommel intended to begin a new operation on that date.

El Alamein area, August 1942. On the high seat during a ground reconnaissance mission sits a British watcher in the desert . . .

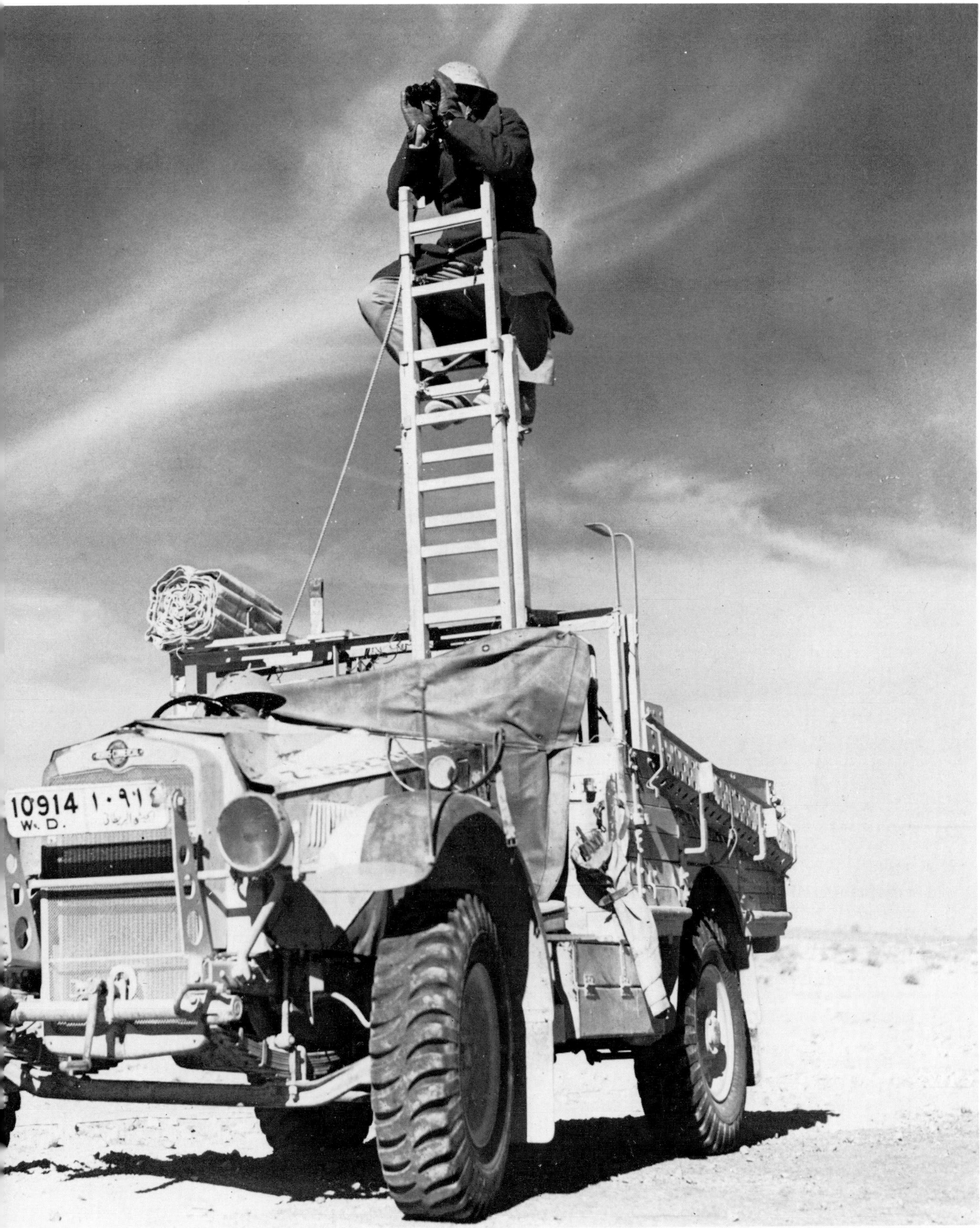
10914 ١٠٩١٤
W. D.

. . . and on the other side of the front sits a German eight-wheel armored scout car with a bow antenna, also during ground reconnaissance.

On Thursday, 13 August the enemy situation specialists of the 8th Army noted unusually lively Luftwaffe activity against the RAF's operational and tactical air reconnaissance. In the opinion of the General Staff Intelligence (GS Int), the quantity of supplies for *Panzerarmee Afrika* had reached a level as high as that of shortly before Rommel's Gazala offensive at the end of May 1942.

Likewise on 13 August General Auchinleck was relieved as C-in-C Middle East and replaced by General Alexander. In the Intelligence Office too, a number of personnel changes took place. Colonel de Guingand became Chief of the 8th Army's General Staff (General Montgomery), Brigadier Leiter became Chief of the Intelligence Service for General Alexander, Major Williams, who had taken part in the first combat against the *Afrika-Korps* in February 1941, took over the position of Chief of Intelligence for the 8th Army.

On Saturday, 15 August B.P. sent the new C-in-C Middle East an important Enigma report with the situation evaluation of the *Panzerarmee* for the same day. In addition to summing up his intentions for the forthcoming offensive, Rommel mentioned being happy that the supply situation was satisfactory.

It stated: "The Italian troops are refreshed and reinforced. An elastic back-line defense has been set up. Field fortifications and minefields are almost finished. Rommel believes that a British attack may well be possible before the end of August, but it is more likely not to occur until the middle of September . . . The supplying and equipping of the German and Italian troops for the forthcoming offensive will be completed, though, only after the arrival of the supplies already loaded aboard ships in Italy . . . In September, of course, the situation will change considerably, to the benefit of the 8th Army. The units of the Panzerarmee must, as always before an attack, be transferred to the preparation areas. Because of the British air superiority, this can only be done on moonlit nights. There will be a full moon on 26 August 1942, and thus the supply units of the Panzerarmee and the Luftwaffe could still do it by that date, as long as the convoys arrive at the right time. Only an attack on 26 August 1942 has a chance of succeeding. Any post-ponement, on the other hand, has to be a post-ponement for a whole month . . . *Generalfeld-marschall* Kesselring also saw 26 August as a favorable date 'provided the fuel for the Luftwaffe' arrives in the meantime."

On Monday, 17 August the latest Enigma report to reach the C-in-C Middle East, General Alexander, said that the *Panzerarmee* had strictly banned any air or ground reconnaissance in the Qattara Depression area, in order to avoid "that the enemy becomes suspicious." The decoded radio message also contained the date for Rommel's new offensive: 26 August 1942. This was probably one of the most important bits of information that SIS had received during the campaign in North Africa.

On the same day, the RAF sank the big Italian freighter "Pilo." which was underway to Africa with supplies for the *Panzerarmee.*

Mediterranean, August 1942: Alerted by Enigma reports, British bombers sink a big Italian freighter just off the North African coast.

Two days after the C-in-C Middle East had learned the date of Rommel's new offensive from the Enigma report, he initiated a major action in the eastern Mediterranean area: the RAF and Royal Navy, in around-the-clock missions, attempted to disturb Axis shipping lanes considerably until the end of the month.

On Friday, 21 August RAF torpedo planes attacked the fully loaded Italian tanker "Pozarica" and sank it.

In the night of 23-24 August the news reached the OKW that Rommel would not begin his offensive until a week later, in the night of 30-31 August. Just a few hours later, B.P. sent the contents of this radio message to the C-in-C Middle East.

At 1:17 PM on Monday, 24 August a radio message from the C-in-C Middle East reached the British XXX. Corps: "All units of the XXX. Corps are completely ready for action as of 11:59 PM tonight . . . ready for alarm every morning from 5:45 to 6:15 AM and evenings from 7:45 to 8:15 PM . . . No furloughs!" On the same day, 48 hours before the new German-Italian offensive was expected by the C-in-C Middle East, B.P. sent an Enigma report of 21 August. The C-in-C was astounded to learn from it that Rommel was notifying the OKH that he was not feeling well, would like to be replaced by Guderian and wanted a "rather long" furlough.

On Tuesday, 25 August British engineers laid a strong new minefield exactly where Rommel had intended to break through with his main fighting forces. Rommel said: "The attacking units would have been held up too much by the heavy, hitherto unknown barrages. The moment of surprise, on which the whole plan was ultimately based, was thereby lost."

Likewise on 25 August a newly decoded Enigma radio message arrived in Cairo: "*Generalfeldmarschall* Kesselring intends to go to his command post in the next few days." This text was given to Churchill, who had just arrived in the Egyptian capital, and he passed it on immediately to General Alexander.

At the edge of the El Qattara Depression, August 1942: An Italian reconnaissance unit on a mission.

*Mediterranean,
August 1942: An
Italian freighter
shortly before it
sank: "... decisi*
factor in the fuel
supply plans."

*El Alamein area,
August 1942: Un*
*camouflage nets
and guarded by t*
*Military Police
stands a radio tru*
*of the British 8th
Army
Headquarters.* »

Meanwhile, the British Y Service reports indicated that Rommel had withdrawn his tank units from the immediate front area and reinforced them with infantry regiments. Questioning of war prisoners confirmed that a large-scale regrouping had taken place. Aerial reconnaissance also provided proof of lively troop movements.

During the night 25-26 of August the C-in-C Middle East received a new Enigma message shortly after midnight: The answer from the OKW to Rommel's request to be relieved for

health reasons: "There is no general of the Panzer troops available to relieve him." After consultation with his doctor, Rommel remained at his post.

In the early hours of Wednesday, 26 August the C-in-C Middle East received a new Enigma radio message: The *Panzerarmee* complained that the sinking of the tanker "Pozarica" had delayed the departure of the tanker "San Andrea." Its cargo was regarded as a deciding factor in the *Panzerarmee*'s fuel-supply plans. A further Enigma message provided complete details and dates for a large-scale supplying program for the Axis troops in North Africa: Between 25 August and 5 September a total of 20 freighters and tankers were to bring supplies to Rommel's troops.

On Thursday, 27 August an Enigma message delivered to the C-in-C Middle East said that the disturbances to shipping caused by the RAF and Royal Navy had disorganized the *Panzerarmee*'s fuel-supply program. Worse yet, the Germans were now forced to give the fuel intended for them to the Italians. On the very same day, the ships "Istria" and "Dielpi" were sunk.

On Friday morning, 28 August the C-in-C Middle East learned from an Enigma report that the *Ramcke Brigade* would be transferred forward during the course of the day. The *Panzerarmee* turned to desperation measures to have fuel brought from Crete on transport planes.

On Saturday, 29 August B.P. sent a new Enigma report to the C-in-C Middle East: On 26 August Rommel had informed the OKH that after consultation with his doctor, he was able to take command of the coming operation. But after its

conclusion, he had to have a lengthy rest in Germany.

In the early morning hours of 29 August the C-in-C Middle East received further news from B.P. from an Enigma radio message: The *Panzerarmee* reported to the OKH on 27 August that it could not set an attack date before 29 August on account of its shortage of fuel and ammunition.

On Sunday, 30 August the C-in-C Middle East learned from a new Enigma report that Rommel had informed the OKH on 28 August that of the 24,000 tons of fuel that he had been promised by that day, only 100 tons had arrived. His supplies were sufficient for only six days of combat. He needed most urgently the particularly important ammunition for tanks and antitank guns. Several hours later, the neat Enigma message said that the tanker "San Andrea" had been torpedoed and sunk.

All of the transmission of information from Rommel's headquarters to the Comando Supremo in Rome as well as the OKW or OKH was sent from then on in Enigma-encoded radio messages. Thus thanks to Bletchley Park (B.P.), Mont-

A pack of Ju 52/3m transport planes flies low over the Mediterranean toward the North African coast.

Qattara Depression, August 1942: A German observer watches the foremost enemy lines.

gomery was able to have a clear picture of the forces, dispositions, supply situation, strength and combat readiness of the German Panzer units, plus details on Rommel's physical and psychological condition. With Churchill's permission, the actions ordered by Montgomery against German-Italian supply convoys were carried out to a previously unusual extent.

On the evening of 30 August Rommel undertook his last efforts to smash the 8th Army and break through to Cairo as well as Alexandria. He circumvented the British positions in the south along the edge of the Qattara Depression and attacked with tanks and motorized forces. The new offensive, though, came to a halt in the extensive minefields, and the intended encirclement turned into a frontal attack that lasted several days. Rommel's tanks and trucks were shot down by the British tanks and heavily bombed by the RAF for two days and nights.

On Monday, 31 August the C-in-C Middle East learned from a Luftwaffe Enigma report that

Generalfeldmarschall Kesselring had set up an emergency airlift on 29 August for the speedy transport of fuel by transport planes. The urgently needed gasoline was to be carried by plane from Italy to Crete, from Crete to Tobruk, and by truck from there to the front.

On Wednesday morning, 2 September an Enigma report from B.P. reached the C-in-C Middle East: At noon on 1 September Rommel had decided to go on the defensive on the line he had reached. This news was the first important information that SIS had been able to provide for the C-in-C since the beginning of Rommel's new offensive.

The supply situation developed into an ever-greater problem. After the tanker "Ficci Fassio" had been sunk during an RAF attack on 2 September the tanker "Abruzzi", which had been promised to Rommel by 30 August set out late. It was sighted, though, and damaged shortly afterward. This delayed the departure of the third tanker, "Bianchi", as well.

On the same day, the news reached the *Panzerarmee* that the expected tanker, with 8000 tons of fuel on board, had been sunk off Tobruk. Thereupon Rommel broke off the attack that had been begun 72 hours before from the southern part of the El Alamein front. He had already lost 2910 men, 55 field and antitank guns, and 395 vehicles of all kinds. Of his 145 tanks, fifty were left on the battlefield in the desert, wrecked. The *Generalfeldmarschall* ordered the retreat.

Rommel's last attempt to win back the strategic initiative in North Africa had come to grief. Probably for the first time in the events of this war, a decisive battle had been lost for lack of fuel. And the coming defeat could be foreseen already, for from now on the initiative passed into the hands of the British. Major Williams, chief of enemy situation assessment for the 8th Army, said of General Montgomery: "He won his first battle, the masterful defense of Alam Halfa, by accepting the enemy intelligence that was given to him that morning."

*El Alamein
area,
September
1942: In a
radio truck
of the British
8th Army.*

On Thursday morning, 3 September the RAF aerial reconnaissance reported that three great columns of Axis troops were moving westward and great numbers of damaged tanks were being left behind.

At the same time, the C-in-C Middle East received an Enigma message from B.P.: Because of the sinking of the "San Andrea" and absence of the "Abruzzi", Rommel had turned to defense on the afternoon of 1 September.

When seven supply ships, including three tankers, were sunk during this decisive week, Rommel suspected a traitor in Rome or a leak in Italian security.

In the first week of September 1942, rumors of Rommel's illness turned up in the world press. At the same time, decoded radio messages gave indications that the Germans — alarmed by the Axis ship losses in the Mediterranean — had already begun to raise questions about the security of their codes.

The awareness of Rommel's illness caused considerable alarm at SIS, especially as decoded diplomatic radio traffic of the Axis powers had indicated that the source of this news had to be in London.

In the morning hours of Friday, 4 September Rommel ordered a general retreat. Rommel said: "The enemy leadership was aware of our intention to attack around 25 August." For the most part, Montgomery had learned that Rommel had run into a trap and had to give up his advance toward the Suez Canal thanks to the successful work of his intelligence officers. They had learned not only to evaluate the actual text of the Enigma reports, but also, and more importantly, to include the personal and other conditions under which the radio messages had been sent.

On Tuesday, 8 September an Enigma report sent to the C-in-C Middle East said that the *Panzerarmee* had reported to the OKH that it had rations for 23 days and ammunition for only 14 days of combat. On the basis of the present consumption, there was only enough fuel for eight days, since their long supply trains from Benghazi and Tobruk to the front and back required tremendous amounts. The coastal roads were quite insufficient, and the railroad could carry only a small part of the cargo.

Rommel warned of a serious supply crisis. Because it had to be assumed that "the danger to sea traffic would continue", he requested that supplies be transported by plane.

On Wednesday, 9 September Churchill empowered Sir Edward Bridges to investigate the origin of the security leak in London through which the news of Rommel's condition had gotten out.

On Friday, 11 September B.P. sent the C-in-C

Middle East an Enigma report with the following contents: The staff of the *Panzerarmee* had learned from interrogating British prisoners of war that the enemy had learned the date and extent of the Alam Halfa attack from captured Italian soldiers. This information had been told to the British troops before the battle began.

This story had a sequel, though: Churchill suspected that Montgomery had used "the Italian prisoners of war" as a cover story for the information that B.P. had given him. In Churchill's opinion, this means of concealing an operation like "Ultra Secret" was quite insufficient.

Since this incident, the security measures involved in handling Enigma reports were strengthened considerably. No information that, in the opinion of the GC & CS, could lead to rumors, such as in the case of Rommel's illness, could be sent on to the War Office, the Admiralty

or the highest Army staffs without the Prime Minister's permission.

When Churchill gave such permission for a certain bit of information, then it could be given only to the Chief of the SIS ("C") and the directors of the Army, Air and Navy Intelligence personally. In Great Britain or overseas, this report would then be received personally by only a limited number of selected commanders or their senior intelligence officers.

On Monday, 21 September the C-in-C Middle East received a Supermarina radio message: The freighter "Apuania", with a large cargo of ammunition and provisions plus ten tanks, had arrived at Benghazi.

In the night of 22-23 September RAF bombers attacked the harbor of Benghazi. The freighter "Apuania" took a direct hit and blew up when its cargo of ammunition exploded. Other ships and

« *Over the Mediterranean, September 1942: Reinforcements for Rommel aboard a Ju 52/3m transport plane.*

A cartoonist portrays the activities of British desert commandos.

—*by Illingworth.*

harbor facilities were also badly damaged by this air attack.

On Wednesday, 23 September Rommel, whose state of health had worsened considerably, flew to Germany on medical leave. For the time being, *General der Panzetruppe* Stumme took command of the *Panzerarmee*. *General* Stumme received the most precise instructions for a further buildup of the defensive facilities at El Alamein. Since circumvention scarcely seemed possible for Montgomery, he appeared to be forced to make a frontal attack in an offensive.

On Friday, 25 September the C-in-C Middle East received from B.P. the contents of an Enigma report: The OKH advised the Panzerarmee that, in view of the general fuel shortage, it could not count on receiving any additional fuel in the near future.

On Thursday, 1 October the C-in-C Middle

East received a new Enigma message from the *Panzerarmee*: Despite the tense supply situation, it had been possible to limit the daily use of fuel to 10.5 On the other hand, in view of the difficulties of transporting supplies to the front line, considerable reductions were being made in rations of vegetables, fruit, flour and beverages.

On Friday, 2 October B.P. sent the C-in-C Middle East an Enigma report of 30 September: *Panzerarmee Afrika* reported the existence of 270 Italian and 224 German tanks ready for action.

On the same day, General Alexander learned from a Supermarina radio message the names, cargoes and routes of the two large Italian freighters "Nino Bixio" and "Unione." On Monday, 5 October these two ships were sunk by RAF bombers in Navarino Bay.

On Tuesday, 6 October the C-in-C Middle East received a new Enigma report from B.P. In it the

Panzerarmee reported that the troops were suffering from malnutrition, a great decrease in performance, and a high rate of illness. The fuel supplies had decreased to 8.5 per day. In fact, after the two big freighters had been sunk, no fuel reached Africa in the first week of October.

On Thursday, 8 October B.P. sent the C-in-C Middle East a new Enigma report, a radio message from General of *Panzerarmee Stumme*. The fuel situation was very tense and rations were so low as to be almost non-existent. Vehicles and spare parts gave cause for the greatest concern. The enemy was considerably superior and ready to attack.

On Friday, 9 October Montgomery's preparations for the decisive offensive had reached their last phase. This day began with introductory bomb attacks, which lasted until a few hours before the start of the offensive.

On Saturday, 10 October Kesselring opened an improvised German-Italian air offensive against Malta. Until 19 October some 200 to 270 missions against the island were flown from early morning to sunset. After seventy planes had been lost, the operation was halted.

While the British 8th Army moved into its preparation areas between 18-22 October, the RAF tried in every way to hamper the enemy air reconnaissance. Even more important for the outcome of the fighting in North Africa were the strategic missions of the Allied air forces and British submarines against the Axis supply routes in the Mediterranean Sea.

On Wednesday, 21 October the C-in-C Middle East received a new Enigma report with a message from the *Panzerarmee*, dated 19 October: Thanks to the supplies that arrived on U-boats and aircraft, the shortage of ammunition, and particularly of armor-piercing ammunition, had ended. The stocks of ammunition in the operational area had risen to 16 days' worth.

On Thursday, 22 October, according to the latest enigma report, the number of planes ready for action and available to the *Fliegerführer Afrika* (now *Generalmajor* Seidemann) totaled 90 planes, including 40 dive bombers, 40 fighters and 10 destroyers (fighter-bombers). The low level of readiness for action was also — according to the Enigma message — the reason for criticism from Kesselring.

On Friday, 23 October the C-in-C Middle East received a decoded radio message sent by the *Fliegerführer Afrika* the previous evening, ending with the words: "All quiet with the enemy, the British front line remains unchanged." About noon the next Enigma message reached the C-in-C; it was a radio message from the Panzerarmee, sent on 21 October: Although the next tanker, the "Proserpina", was scheduled to arrive on 25

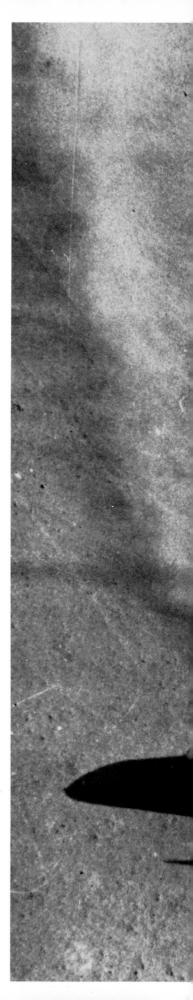

On an RAF desert airfield, a Baltimore bomber is about to take off.

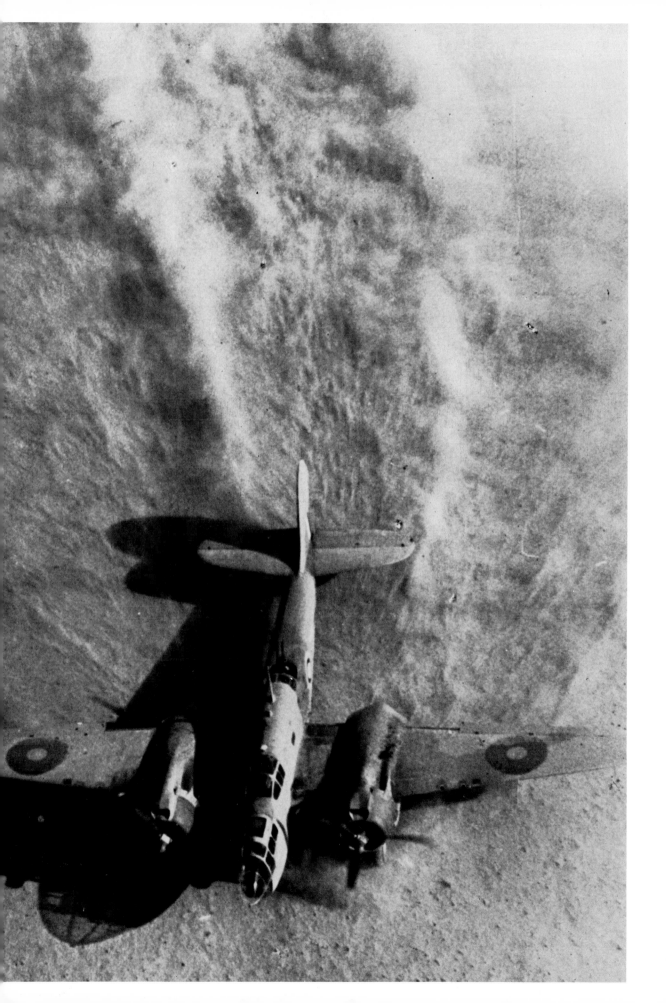

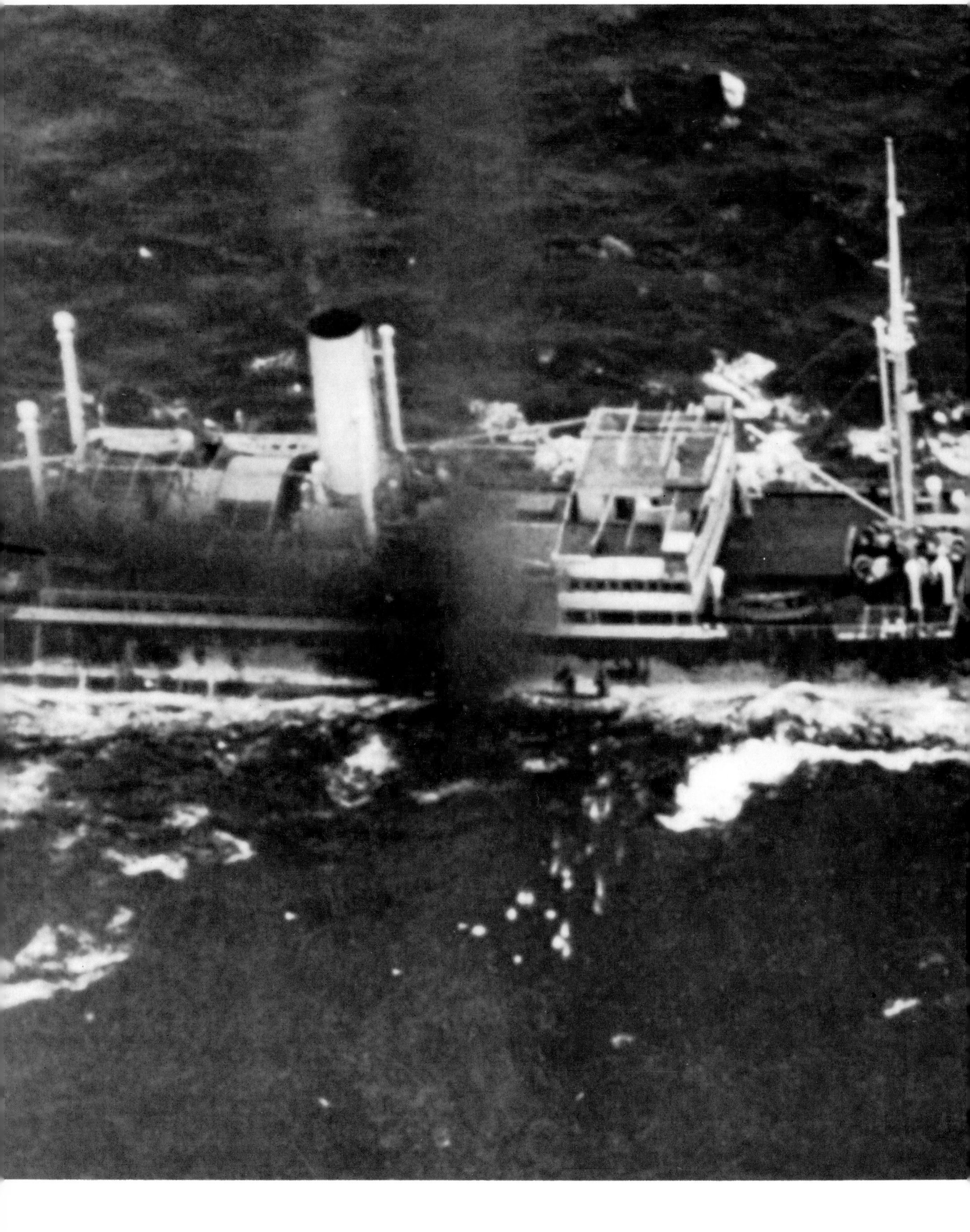

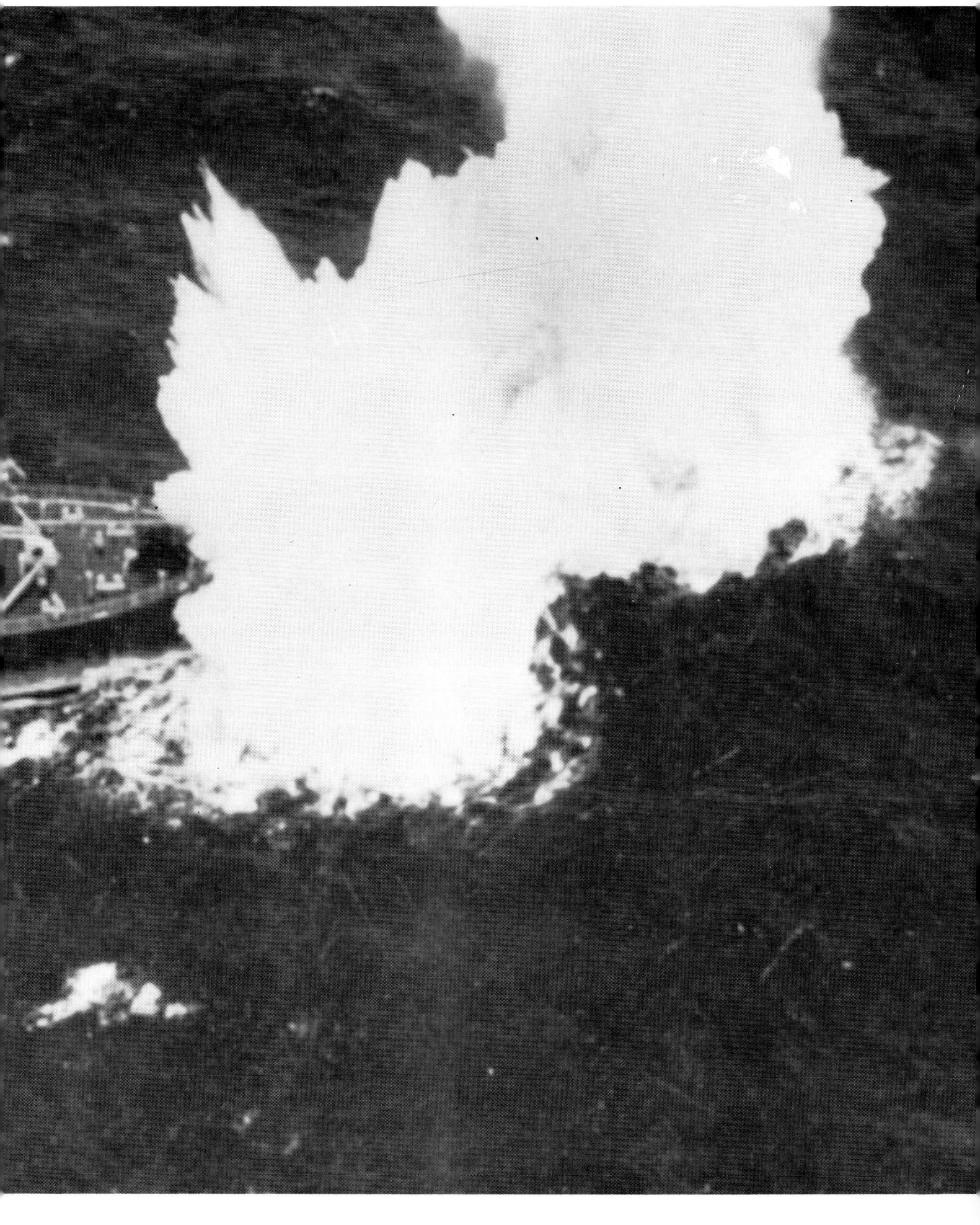

October, the fuel she delivered would not reach the front before 29 October. The Panzerarmee must therefore, effective immediately, receive fuel by air transport, because otherwise their supplies in Tobruk and east of there would be exhausted on that day just from normal use.

On this day, GS Int informed Montgomery after 6:00 PM: The enemy shows no sign that he expects our attack tonight.

At 9:40 PM, 1200 guns of the British 8th Army (General Montgomery) opened Operation "Lightfoot", the offensive on the El Alamein front. After the very first hours of the British attack, *General* Stumme died of a heart attack. *Generalmajor* Ritter von Thoma took command.

Despite all the reports that B.P. had sent the C-in-C Middle East, the information from Enigma radio messages at El Alamein were not decisive; the British owed their victory much more to their superiority in troops, tanks, artillery and aircraft, plus their immense supply capacity.

In the night of 23-24 October the telephone in Rommel's room at a sanitarium on the Semmering rang; on the line was *Generalfeldmarschall* Keitel. He was calling from the "Wolf's Den", the Führer's headquarters at Rasteburg, East Prussia. The enemy, he reported, had just begun a large-scale offensive at El Alamein, and *General* Stumme was missing and perhaps dead. At midnight Hitler called personally and wanted to know whether Rommel could return to North Africa at once.

On Saturday, 24 October a Heinkel He 111, coming from Wiener Neustadt with Rommel on board, landed at the Ciampino airfield near Rome about noon. *General* von Rintelen, the German General at the Comando Supremo, greeted Rommel at the airfield and reported to him on the progress of the British advance.

Since the Axis troops only had three days' supply of fuel for each vehicle, Rommel insisted that supply ships with fuel and ammunition set out for North Africa that same night. Kesselring immediately got in touch with Mussolini per-

« *Mediterranean, October 1942: An Italian supply freighter in a hail of bombs.*

sonally and arranged for the commander of the Supermarina to have all available transport ships loaded with the necessary supplies and sent out without delay.

Shortly after Rommel landed in Derna, a radio message from Kesselring arrived. He informed Rommel that five supply ships with fuel and ammunition would arrive in the North African ports in three days at most. At almost the same time as Rommel had this news in his hands, the C-in-C Middle East received the decoded radio message from B.P.

Rommel's overwhelming tactical ability and the operational ability of his chief of staff, *Oberst* Westphal, prevented a swift defeat of the Axis forces. Despite their massive superiority, Montgomery's units could not achieve the decisive breakthrough in the first days of the attack. To be sure, the Germans and Italians suffered heavy losses under the heavy British fire, but their front essentially held its ground.

Around 5:00 PM on the same day the first Enigma report involving the British offensive reached the C-in-C Middle East. It was a report from the *Fliegerführer Afrika*, dated 23 October

and saying that the *Panzerarmee* had expected the main enemy attack in the south.

On Sunday, 25 October General Alexander learned from an Enigma report that *General* Stumme was dead and *Generalfeldmarschall* Rommel was on his way to North Africa. On the same day, B.P. sent a decoded Enigma radio message to the C-in-C Middle East. It included detailed information on the routes and destinations of the supply ship "Proserpina" and its escort "Tergestea." The first ship carried 4500 tons of fuel, the second 1000 tons each of fuel and ammunition.

On Monday, 26 October, at about 5;00 in the morning, the C-in-C Middle East received from B.P. an Enigma report that was sent on to only a few British generals and staff officers. It said that Rommel had taken over his command on the previous evening. And on the same morning, the next Enigma report sent to General Alexander included a report from the *Panzerarmee:* On 24 October the fuel supplies had been reduced to three days' worth. One third of the total supply was stored in Benghazi. The Luftwaffe had set up an airlift to transport the fuel. Several hours later

El Alamein area, October 1942: An aerial photo evaluator at the headquarters of the British 8th Army.

the next report reached the C-in-C Middle East: The tanker "Tripolino", with a load "of decisive value for the situation on the front", and the steamer "Ostia", with a large quantity of ammunition on board, were ready to leave Benghazi for Tobruk.

In the early morning hours of 26 October, Wellington bombers spotted the tanker "Tripolino" northwest of Tobruk, dropped flare bombs, and sank her. Shortly after dawn, 20 RAF Beaufort bombers, which had taken off from the Luqa and Halfar airfields on Malta, spotted the first of the Italian supply ships, the "Proserpina", near Tobruk. After a series of daring attacks, in which six bombers were shot down by the escort fighters, the "Proserpina" burst into flames, and the "Tergestea" was sunk while running into the harbor of Tobruk.

During the evening hours, the C-in-C Middle East learned from a further Enigma report that the "Proserpina" was in flames after an air attack

and the "Tergestea" had exploded after taking a direct hit.

When Operation "Lightfoot" began, the flow of Enigma reports dwindled. A picture of the enemy's situation was gained by the intelligence staffs of the Middle East headquarters and the British 8th Army, mainly from the experiences of the Y Service's tactical radio surveillance, captured materials, statements of war prisoners and aerial reconnaissance.

There was one factor, though, that Montgomery could attribute exclusively to the Enigma reports, though he never admitted it: The certain knowledge of the extent of his success, and simultaneously Rommel's assessment of his own situation, his losses and supply difficulties. Remarkably, Montgomery never received from either the Y Service or Enigma a warning of Rommel's imminent counterattack on the evening of 27 October.

In the morning hours of Wednesday, 28 October

the escort ship "Ostia" was torpedoed. At the same time, Beaufort bombers torpedoed and sank the supply ship "Zara" some sixty nautical miles north of Tobruk. The escort ship "Boni" was able to reach Tobruk, but was sunk at its pier when a U.S. B-24 Liberator bomber hit it and set its cargo of fuel afire. The small tanker "Morandi" had more luck and made it through, reaching the harbor of Benghazi, but its cargo was only 300 tons of fuel. This fuel now had to be transported for a distance of more than 1300 kilometers (equal to the distance from Hamburg to Rome), over which RAF patrols constantly circled.

At 6:00 AM the C-in-C Middle East received a new Enigma report from B.P.: The *Panzerarmee* reported a critical fuel situation, resulting from the loss of the "Proserpina" and "Tergestea." Likewise on 28 October, the next shipload of supplies for the Axis troops left Navarino harbor at 4:00 PM; it was the freighter "Luisiano", with 2500 tons of fuel on board. At 10:00 PM the RAF was already reporting its sinking.

Half an hour later, at 10:30 PM, B.P. sent a new Enigma report to General Alexander. At 1:00 PM on that day, *Generalfeldmarschall* Rommel had requested that *Generalfeldmarschall* Kesselring send Luftwaffe reinforcements in view of the "extremely critical situation." Kesselring thereupon instructed his units to transport fuel to North Africa, "day and night, to the last crew and last airplane."

HELPING HAND   —by Illingworth

"Helping Hand" — as a London cartoonist saw the RAF attacks on ships carrying supplies to Rommel's troops.

El Alamein area, October 1942: A British radioman takes a radio message.

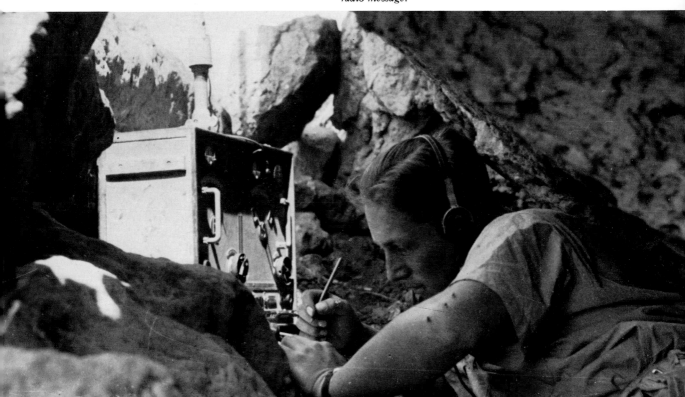

Meanwhile, the Allies were making preparations for their landing in North Africa under the strictest secrecy. Months before Operation "Torch" began, General Eisenhower and all the higher officers on his staff, plus Generals Bedell-Smith, Clark, Spaatz, Anderson and Air Marshal Welsh were informed as to "Ultra Secret." This was the first case in which Allied commanders were instructed before an operation as to the enemy information they could expect.

For a smooth transmission of Enigma reports from B.P., the staffs of the U.S. commanders were to be served at first by the "Ultra representatives" subordinated to them. They belonged to the G-2 unit, which was responsible for reporting on the enemy's situation. The task of the "Ultra representative" was "to evaluate the 'Ultra' intelligence and give it to the commander and the staff officers authorized as 'Ultra' receivers in usable form. In the analysis of ¢Ultra' intelligence, he was to integrate it with intelligence gained from other sources and evaluate the ways and means by which the staff made operational use of the Ultra intelligence, and was also to make sure that the secrecy of this source was never endangered."

The officers were rather young, and held the rank of Captain or Major. They were to intervene immediately if one of the G-2 officers, the chief of staff or the commander himself did not use the Ultra material according to instructions. For this purpose they were in direct contact with the U.S. General Marshall and with B.P.

The British and U.S. intelligence evaluators with the army and army group staffs did not have an easy task. They were completely on their own and were not allowed to work in teams. In addition, they were entrusted with making the final interpretation of the material and advising their superior officers. They also had to compare Ultra messages with information from other sources and judge their significance for the situation in various front sectors. Aside from this, they had to suggest to their commanders how the Enigma reports could be utilized practically without bringing the sources into danger.

On Thursday, 29 October Rommel received the news that the tanker "Luisiana" with its 1459 tons of fuel had just been sunk off Tobruk.

At 8:00 AM a new Enigma report reached the C-in-C Middle East. Rommel had instructed every available motor vehicle to bring fuel forward from Benghazi. In a daily command, he called for the greatest possible efforts for a "fight for life and death."

About 11:00 that evening, the C-in-C received from B.P. the *Panzerarmee*'s daily report for 28 October: The situation was "extraordinarily serious", the fuel supplies at the front were

In the Mediterranean, British fighter-bombers attack a German ship.

Aerial photo analysts of the British 8th Army check the latest aerial photos. The maps in the background have been erased by the censors.

reduced to 1.3 days' worth. The number of tanks ready for action had sunk to 81 German and 197 Italian. There were signs — the report noted — that strong enemy forces were preparing to break through in the north at Sidi el Rahman.

On Saturday, 31 October the C-in-C Middle East gained important information from a new Enigma report. The troop strength of the *Panzerarmee* had sunk even lower because of considerable losses. And about 6:00 PM a further Enigma report stated one of Rommel's most important decisions: He was transferring the battle-tested 21st Panzer Division, which until then had strengthened the front some 15 kilometers south of Sidi Abd el Rahman, to the north. The "Trieste" Division was now taking their place. This movement was also confirmed by the Y service.

Rommel did not suspect that Montgomery was preparing at that same hour to break through precisely in that sector of the front that the poorly equipped "Trieste" Division had taken over from the 21st Panzer Division.

The percentages of supplies and fuel for *Panzerarmee Afrika* that were lost on the way from Italy or Greece to North Africa were: August 1942: 30%, September 1942: 30%, October 1942: 44%.

On Sunday, 1 November B.P. decoded a long radio message from Kesselring to the OKW, in which he demanded an investigation on account of possible information leaks or carelessness in radio traffic, or possible treason by the Italians, or possibly the decoding of Enigma radio messages. The sinking of the five Italian supply ships within a short stretch of time seemed extremely suspicious to the *Generalfeldmarschall*, and could not be explained by normal means.

Likewise on 1 November the C-in-C Middle East received the newest Enigma report at 7:00

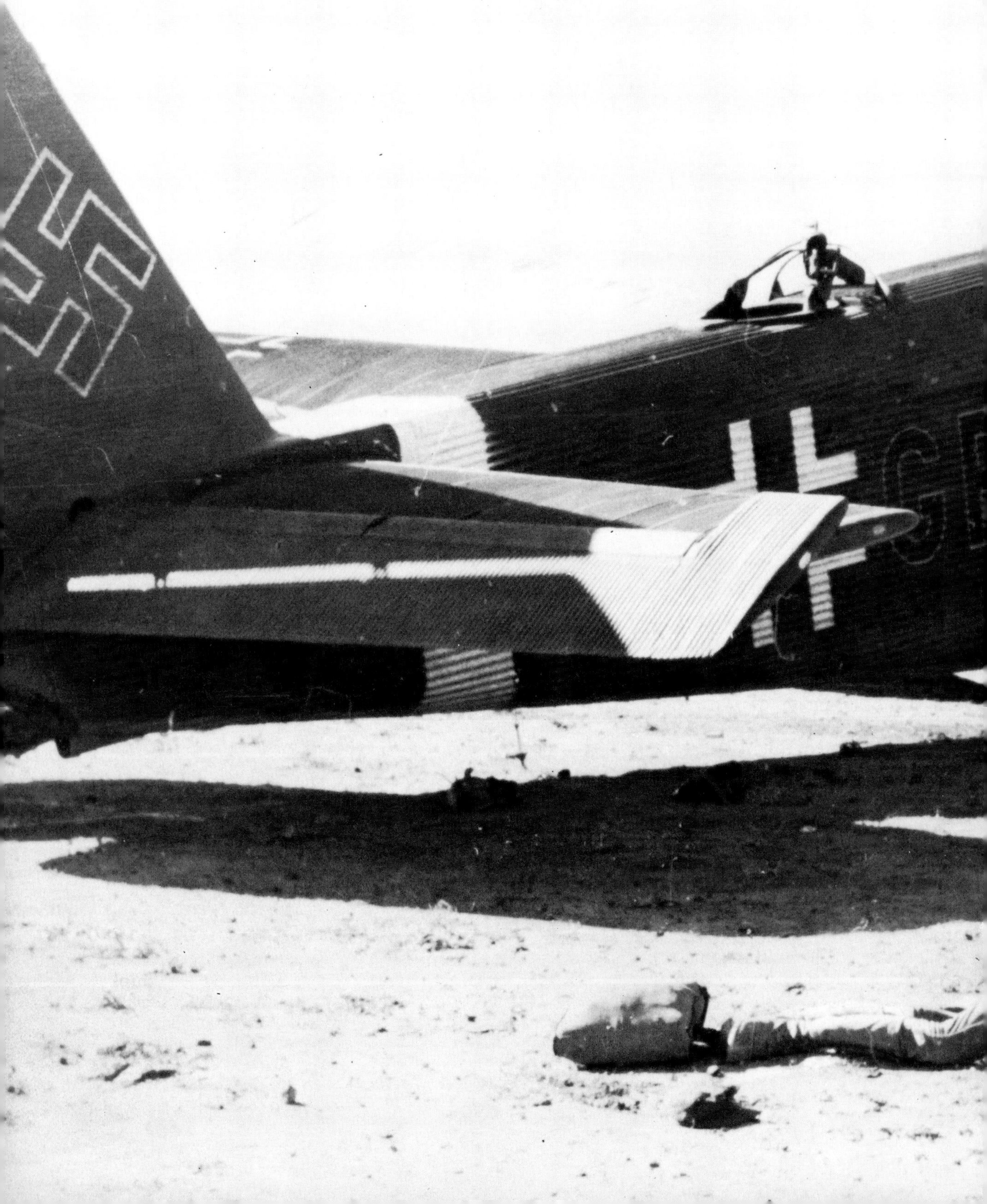

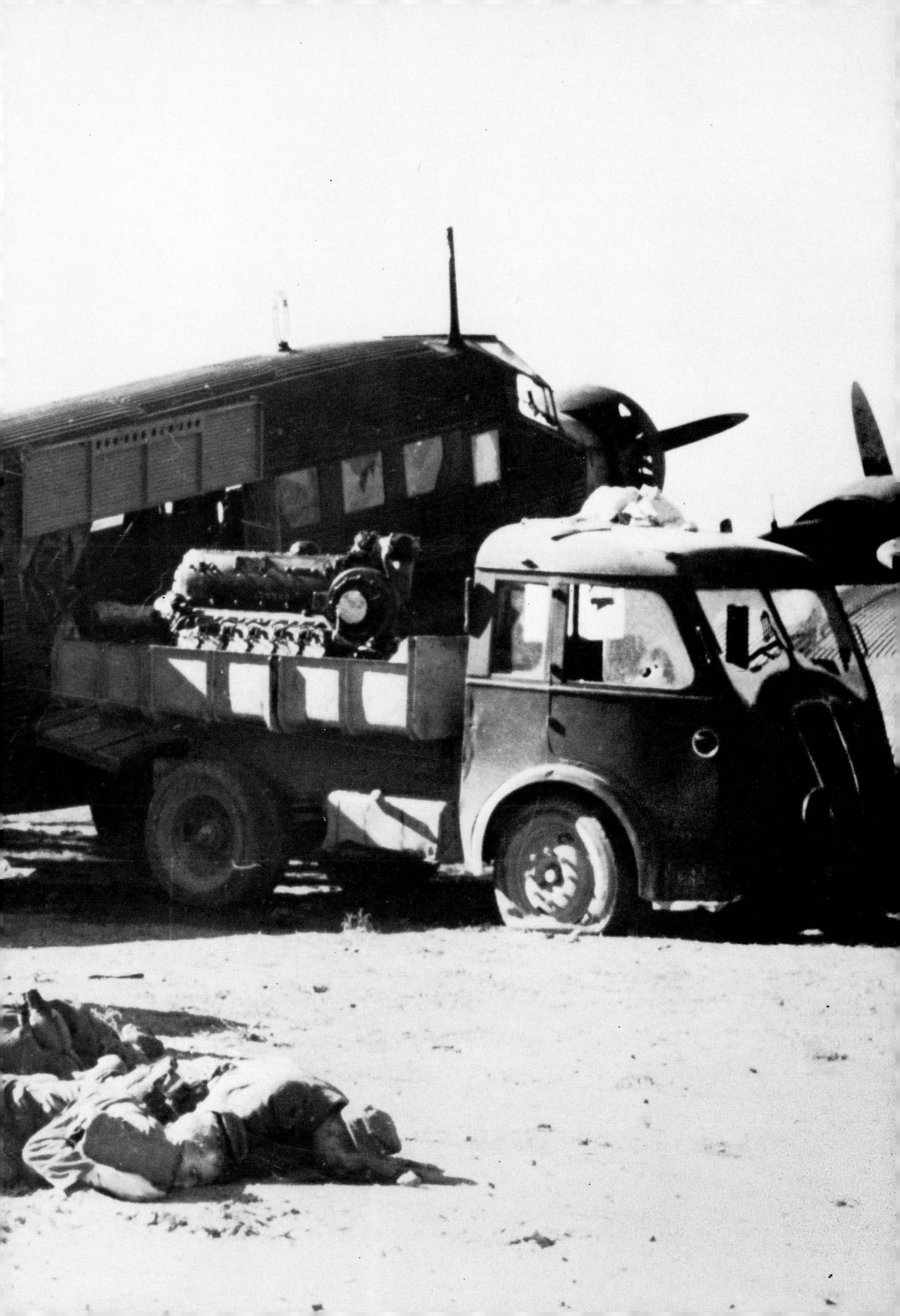

AM. It contained the daily report of the *Panzerarmee* on the evening of 31 October. Rommel had instructed his battle-ready troops of the 90th Light Division and the 21st Panzer Division to repeat the large-scale attacks (using all their forces) that they had undertaken in the north, in order to relieve Panzer Grenadier Regiment 125. There had been no previous indications of an intended attack from any other enemy forces on the rest of the front, the daily report assured. Now Montgomery knew the most important thing: Rommel's strongest units stood far away from the sector that he had chosen for the breakthrough — and suspected nothing.

On this day, B.P. sent the C-in-C Middle East another Enigma report. It was a strength report from *Fliegerführer Afrika:* Despite the reinforcements, he now had only 36 dive-bombers, 50 fighters, 8 fighter-bombers and 10 reconnaissance planes available. In the following Enigma report it was stated: The two Italian freighters "T" and "O", which were underway with fuel and ammunition for the troops fighting in North Africa, had been sunk by the RAF. Shortly afterward, two more units of the Italian Navy, likewise laden with fuel and ammunition, were also sunk by the RAF.

*Mediterranean, early November 1942: RAF bombers attack
an Italian supply convoy off the North African coast.*

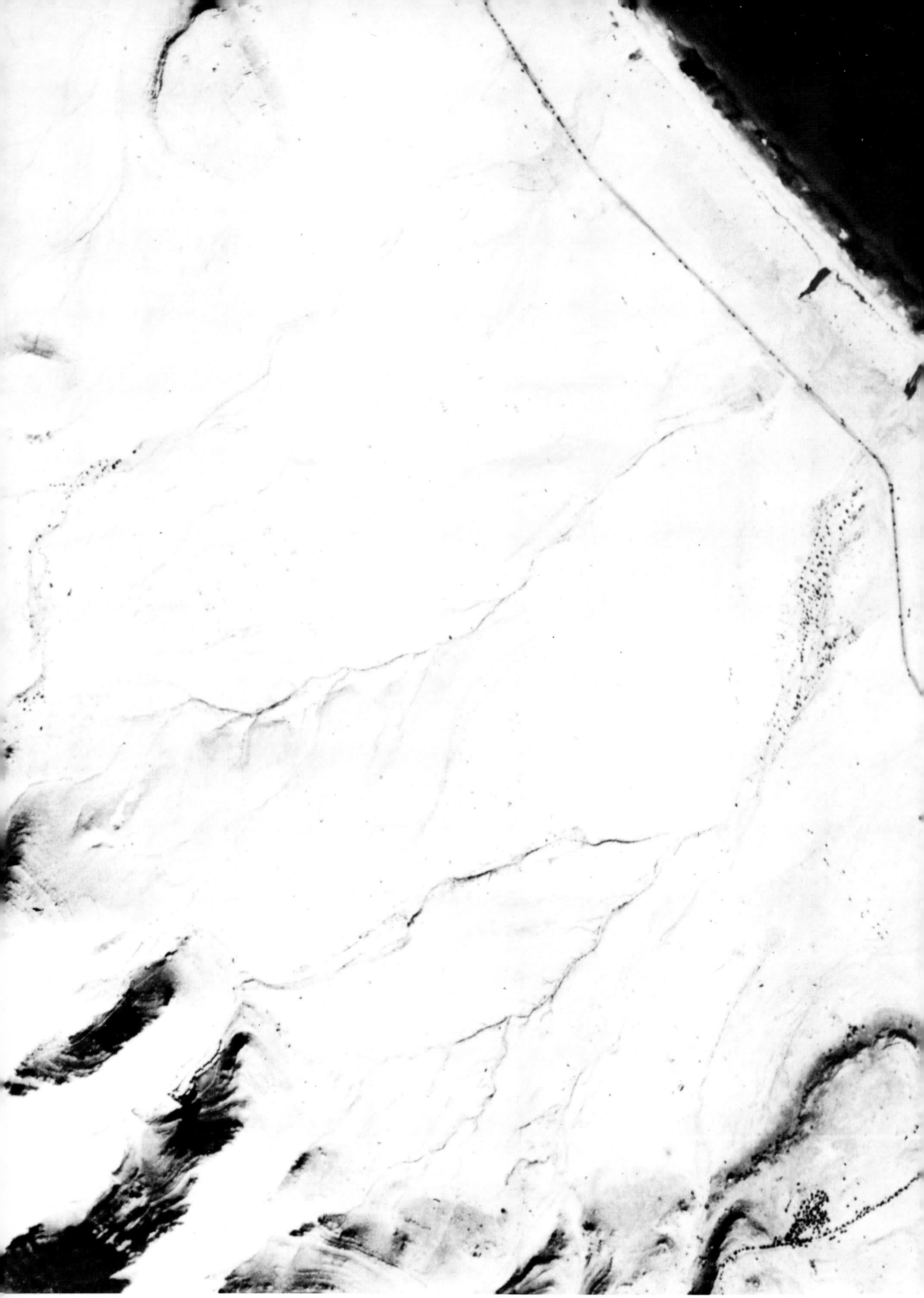

The El Alamein-Sollum coast road, early November 1942: As seen by an RAF reconnaissance plane, the vehicle columns of Panzerarmee Afrika retreat toward the Halfaya Pass.

On Monday, 2 November Operation "Super Charge", the British 8th Army's break through *Panzerarmee Afrika*'s positions at El Alamein, began. Because of the danger of encirclement, Rommel made the decision to draw his units back. On that evening he reported to the Führer's headquarters that the withdrawal was necessary, and at the same time he began to lead his troops out of the El Alamein area.

When Rommel ordered the withdrawal, the *Panzerarmee* still had a fuel supply of 1200 tons, but most of it was in the Tobruk and Benghazi areas. What was lacking, though, was trucks to transport it some 1500 kilometers to the front.

At 9:11 on that morning the Y service intercepted an Enigma message in the "Scorpion" code, sent to the liaison officer of the Luftwaffe, with Rommel's order for the 21st Panzer Division to attack; they had it decoded immediately. As early as 10:00 AM it reached the staffs of the XXX. Corps (Major General Leese) and the New Zealand 2nd Division (Lieutenant General Freyberg).

Only in the evening, hours before the 21st Panzer Division had begun the attack, was B.P. able to send this vitally important information to the C-in-C Middle East. This is a good example that under certain conditions in the tactical realm, the Y service could be more valuable than GC & CS.

About 6:00 PM B.P. intercepted an urgent Enigma message. Rommel informed the OKH that his troops were exhausted, "The army can therefore no longer prevent a possible breakthrough by strong enemy tank formations, which is expected either tonight or tomorrow morning. A withdrawal of the six Italian and two non-motorized German divisions is impossible for lack of transport vehicles . . . On account of this situation and despite the heroic resistance and the exemplary spirit of the troops, a gradual destruction of the army has to be expected."

Likewise on 2 November MI6 in Cairo — on instructions from the highest command in London — sent off a radio message to "its group of agents in Italy" in a code known to the Germans, thanking them for the information concerning the five supply ships that had left Naples on 26-27 October, and promising a pay raise.

At 5:55 AM on Tuesday, 3 November B.P. sent an Enigma report of 2 November to General Alexander personally. It said that Rommel was making preparations to withdraw his forces step by step, beginning on 3 November. His infantry units had already drawn back in the night of 2-3 November.

And in a further Enigma report it was said that the *Fliegerführer Afrika* was also to move the Luftwaffe units to the air bases further to the west

within the framework of this movement to the rear. The fuel supplies of the units on the front had sunk to 1.7 days' worth. The complete evacuation of the ammunition depots in El Daba appeared to be impossible. The supplies in Marsa Matruh and to the west, though, were very meager.

At 11:05 AM Hitler telephoned to Rome. At 11:30 his text was encoded by Enigma and sent on to Rommel by radio. To *GFM* Rommel: ". . . In this situation, there can be no other thought than to hold out . . . It would not be the first time in history that the stronger will triumphed over the stronger battalions. You can show your troops no other way than that to victory or death. Adolf Hitler."

As Hitler was personally answering Rommel's desperate radio message, his Enigma machine broke down because of a technical defect. Rommel requested a repetition of the Führer's message, which arrived at his headquarters two hours later. Meanwhile B.P. had decoded Hitler's first message and Montgomery held it in his hand an hour before Rommel received the repetition.

Now Rommel changed the plans for his operation and decided on a compromise: The 90th Light Division would be left in its position, as would the Italian infantry, and the Italian XX. Corps and the rest of the *Afrika-Korps* would withdraw to a position 50 kilometers west of Fuka and form a temporary line there.

Montgomery could now make use of the Axis forces' desperate plight by making a bold move to overhaul and catch Rommel, cut off his retreat to Tripolitania and smash his forces to pieces. The reason why he did not do it is a secret that Montgomery took to his grave. For example, the commander of the British 1st Panzer Division,

Enemy radio traffic is monitored in a radio station of the British Y Service.

In the aerial photo evaluating center of the British 8th Army, the retreat is watched.

General Briggs, wanted to make preparations for a lightning-fast move to catch *Panzerarmee Afrika* and block its retreat path. But Montgomery did not give him permission to do so. The Chief of his General Staff, Colonel de Guingand, also suggested setting up a motorized unit to encircle Rommel's troops, but "Monty" did not want to hear of it. Thus Rommel was able to save the nucleus of his fighting forces.

On Thursday, 4 November at 5:38 AM, the C-in-C Middle East received the newest Enigma report. It was the *Panzerarmee*'s radio message of 3 November, 7:00 PM. The motorized units of the *Panzerarmee* would remain in place and only withdraw after the enemy achieved a breakthrough with superior forces.

Several hours later, the next Enigma report reached the C-in-C Middle East, General Alexander. The Luftwaffe units were in the process of preparing to move their forces into the western Mediterranean area. The reason for this was a large convoy sighted off Gibraltar. The German leadership did not know that this was the last phase of the Allied landing in North Africa.

Rommel requested Hitler's permission to withdraw at about noon. At 5:30 PM, without waiting for an answer, he ordered the immediate withdrawal of all his fighting forces except the *DAK*, the 90th Light Division and what remained of the Italian tank units, which were to move back as soon as night fell. The SIS was not able to pick up Rommel's orders to retreat, but the 8th Army's Y service reported that preparations were underway for the 15th and 21st Panzer Divisions and other units to withdraw.

After the British 8th Army had broken through the German positions at El Alamein, there was no stopping them any more. The war in North

Africa was decided. The hopelessly inferior German and Italian forces retreated further and further to the west.

On Thursday, 5 November Rommel's troops were already in full retreat. Between El Alamein and Fuka, on a stretch of more than 100 kilometers, vehicles and troops pushed along the narrow coastal road to reach their new positions.

Only on Friday, 6 November was B.P. able to decode Hitler's permission for Rommel's retreat, which he had sent late in the evening of 4 November.

Meanwhile, the British 8th Army reported that since 23 October it had taken some 30,000 prisoners, captured or destroyed 400 guns and 350 tanks. Six Italian divisions had been eliminated, and after twelve days of heavy fighting, *Panzerarmee Afrika* had only 38 tanks ready for action.

On Saturday, 7 November Churchill sent a strictly secret message to Eisenhower to inform the commander of Operation "Torch" that "a radio message from Rommel to the German General Staff had been picked up, in which Rommel asked for immediate help, or else his troops would be wiped out."

In the night of 7-8 November Operation "Torch", the landing of Allied troops in Morocco and Algeria under the command of General Eisenhower, began. But these forces unexpectedly met with opposition from the French Vichy troops, especially in Algiers, Oran and Casablanca.

On Monday, 9 November German troops arrive in Tunisia, ordered to North Africa by the Commander South, Kesselring to prevent occupation by the Allies and cover Rommel's retreat. When these alarm units of the newly-named *Fliegerführer Tunesien* (*Oberst* M. Harlinghausen) landed at El Aouina airport near Tunis, numbering 284 men and supported by parts of *Fallschirmjägerregiment* (Paratroop Regiment) 5 and the 11th *Fallschirmjägerpionierbatallion* (Paratroop Engineer Battalion), they advanced to set up a defense line, and the French Tunisian Division, some 25,000 men strong, drew back. *General* Nehring was to form a bridgehead in Tunisia.

In fifteen days *Panzerarmee Afrika* retreated more than 1000 kilometers, from Fuka via Marsa Matruh to Sollum-Halfaya, where the British 8th

THE DAILY MAIL, Tuesday, November 10, 1942.

Daily Mail

LATE WAR
NEWS
SPECIAL

SIFTA SALT
Free Running
FOR COOKING SALT IS BEST

NO. 14,519   ONE PENNY   *   FOR KING AND EMPIRE   TUESDAY, NOVEMBER 10, 1942

AMERICANS DRIVING ON TO TUNISIA

2,000 Prisoners at Oran: Allied Losses Light

ROMMEL RUNS FASTER

8th Army Push on Into Libya

From **PAUL BEWSHER**, Daily Mail Special Correspondent

CAIRO, Monday.

THE Eighth Army to-day is operating in Libya. Advance units crossed the frontier near Halfaya Pass only a few hours behind the racing remnants of Rommel's shattered panzer army. The enemy were making for the devastated road through the pass, and it is not clear whether they succeeded in forcing a path.

The fleeing Germans, using Italian transport as well as their own, have, like the "vanishing lady," temporarily achieved the ultimate trick of disappearing altogether, despite the desperate efforts of our men to catch them.

But their numbers are small. Never has any army been picked off and thousands of its men scooped up so neatly as with this once-great force of Rommel's.

Rain, heavy, constant rain, is adding to Rommel's troubles. His fleeing columns have to plough their way through long stretches of low-lying desert road flooded by water pouring down from ridges and hills.

The road is often waterlogged for 50 yards at a time. The adjoining desert is a quagmire.

The effects on the retreating enemy are seen in the number of discarded vehicles, ranging from ten-ton lorries to "people's cars," abandoned axle-deep in water or desert mud.

And through it all the unhappy fugitives are suffering constant....

AMERICA BREAKS WITH VICHY

Passports Handed To Envoy

Ships Seized in U.S. Harbours

From **WALTER FARR**

WASHINGTON, Monday.

THE breaking of diplomatic relations between the United States and France was announced to-day by Mr. Cordell Hull, Secretary of State.

The breach of relations did not, for the time being, involve any question of war, he added.

The Vichy Ambassador, Gaston Henry-Haye, was handed his passports this afternoon.

President Roosevelt to-day expressed regret that Vichy had severed diplomatic relations with the United States. France, he said, was evidently still speaking the...

THIS special Daily Mail map shows the progress of the Anglo-United States occupation of Northern Africa as it appeared at an early hour this morning. Little is known yet of the progress of the new thrust in the direction of Tunisia, which is aimed eventually at Tripoli.

U.S. TANKS AT GATES OF CASABLANCA

AMERICAN troops were last night reported to be thrusting from two directions towards French Tunisia, which divides Algeria from Rommel's main supply base at Tripoli. Advanced motorised elements may already be across the frontier.

MAP above illustrates the terrifying prospect now facing Italy. Sicily, Germany's great air base, becomes vulnerable; the road to full invasion is left wide open; Malta threatens Italy.

LATEST

ALL QUIET ON THE RUSSIAN FRONT.
See Story in BACK PAGE.

JEAN BART IN

The Americans roll on toward Tunisia, the London press reports on 10 November 1942.

Army's strong forces overpowered the weak garrison.

On Tuesday, 10 November Montgomery learned from an Enigma report that the 21st Panzer Division had only eleven tanks ready for action, and the 15th Panzer Division had none left. The *Panzerarmee* had only a quarter of a day's supply of ammunition. The fuel would last at most four or five days. Montgomery ordered his main forces not to move further west than Capuzzo and, despite the Enigma report, would not change his plans.

On Wednesday, 11 November the *Panzerarmee* crossed the Egyptian-Libyan border on its retreat. At the same time, RAF aerial reconnaissance reported that the *Panzerarmee* was withdrawing from Bardia and Tobruk.

On the same day, the C-in-C Middle East learned from an Enigma report that Kesselring had ordered a paratroop battalion to capture the airfield at Bône before the enemy spearheads reached it. The C-in-C Middle East reacted immediately: In a lightning-fast action, British paratroopers in U.S. transport planes set out and

landed at the Bône airport before the German paratroops arrived. Thus the Allies had secured the best all-weather airport in North Africa for their air forces. This was one of the few cases in which a decoded Enigma report had decided a purely tactical situation.

On Thursday, 12 November Rommel evacuated Sollum, Fort Capuzzo and Bardia. Meanwhile in eastern Algeria, Allied troops landed at Bône and advanced across the Algerian-Tunisian border.

On the same day, B.P. decoded an Enigma report stating that the tanker was underway to Benghazi. Its load of fuel promised the *Panzerarmee* a certain improvement of its more than critical fuel situation.

In the night of 12-13 November Tobruk fell. Rommel had wanted to hold it until at least part of the 12,000 tons of supplies there could be taken away.

On Friday, 15 November *General der Panzertruppe* Nehring arrived in Tunisia and took command of the LXXXX. Army Corps, which included all the German troops in the Tunisian bridgehead. To meet the threatening military and political dangers, Hitler decided to send strong forces to Tunisia, even a complete battalion with new Tiger tanks.

On the same day, B.P. sent the C-in-C Middle East the latest enigma report: The German

« *One of the few British prisoners at that time is questioned by a Luftwaffe officer.*

Cairo, C-in-C Middle East, November 1942: Intelligence officers prepare the latest situation report.

leadership commanded not only the transfer to Tunisia of replacement battalions for *Panzerarmee Afrika*, but also of all the transport planes that had supplied Rommel's units with fuel up to this point.

On Monday, 16 November the C-in-C Middle East received the latest Enigma report at 5:00 in the morning. It was a special situation report from Rommel to Hitler, saying the fuel situation was catastrophic and the troops literally immobile. Rommel decided, partially for this reason, or perhaps because he had heard no reports on the enemy advance, not to withdraw from Benghazi before 19 November.

On Tuesday, 17 November the first combat between German and Allied troops in Tunisia took place some 50 kilometers west of Bizerte.

On Wednesday, 18 November the SIS reported to the C-in-C Middle East that Rommel had decided to evacuate Benghazi that very evening and leave his supply of ammunition there behind, because he had received reports of enemy tank forces south of Benghazi.

On Monday, 23 November the *Afrika-Korps* was again where it had begun its triumphal advance through Cyrenaica to Egypt. During the whole pursuit, the SIS — by decoding Enigma reports — plus the Y service and aerial reconnaissance had informed General Montgomery in detail as to the *Panzerarmee*'s situation. Even more important to Montgomery was the advance information about Rommel's intentions, also gained from Enigma reports.

THE BIG CLEAN-UP !

—by Illingworth.

"The Big Clean-Up" — *The advance of the 1st and 8th Armies as seen by a cartoonist.*

Marsa Matruh, 13 November 1942, a few minutes after it was taken by the British 8th Army. The radio truck is prepared for action.

Tunisia, December »
Tunisia, December 1942: A huge Messerschmitt Me 323 "Giant" transport plane has brought an intelligence truck for the 5th Panzerarmee.

Tripolitania, late November 1942: A native gives information to a German reconnaissance man.

On Friday, 4 December the German Panzer units in Tunisia scored their first major success. The LXXXX. Panzer Corps (*General der Panzertruppe* Nehring) was able to take the city of Tebourba, 30 kilometers west of Tunis, despite strong resistance from the U.S. 1st Armored Division and the British 11th Brigade.

On Tuesday, 8 December an Enigma report sent from B.P. to the C-in-C Middle East said that the Luftwaffe was crippled by lack of fuel throughout Libya. And the *Panzerarmee* had only enough fuel to move back from their advanced positions to their main defense line, but not enough to open a counterattack.

In the evening, the C-in-C received another Enigma radio message which included Rommel's intentions: The *Generalfeldmarschall* wanted to hold off the British attack, which he expected at any moment, as long as possible, and only retreat under strong pressure.

On Wednesday, 9 December the German 5th Panzer Army (*Generaloberst* von Arnim) was formed in Tunisia. This unit was an armored army in name only; in reality it had only the strength of a corps, and it was composed of two Panzer divisions, one motorized grenadier division and five infantry divisions, three of them Italian.

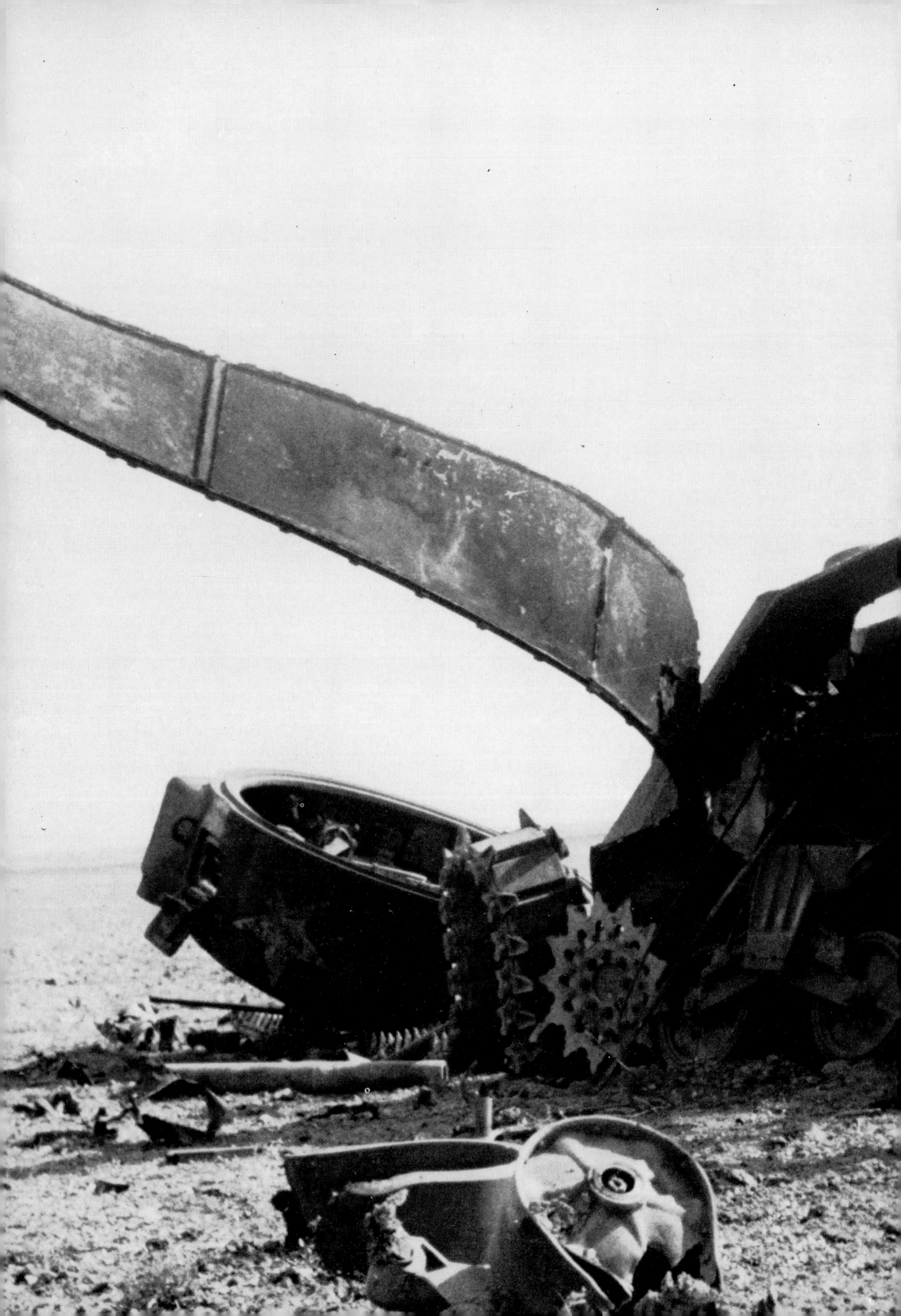

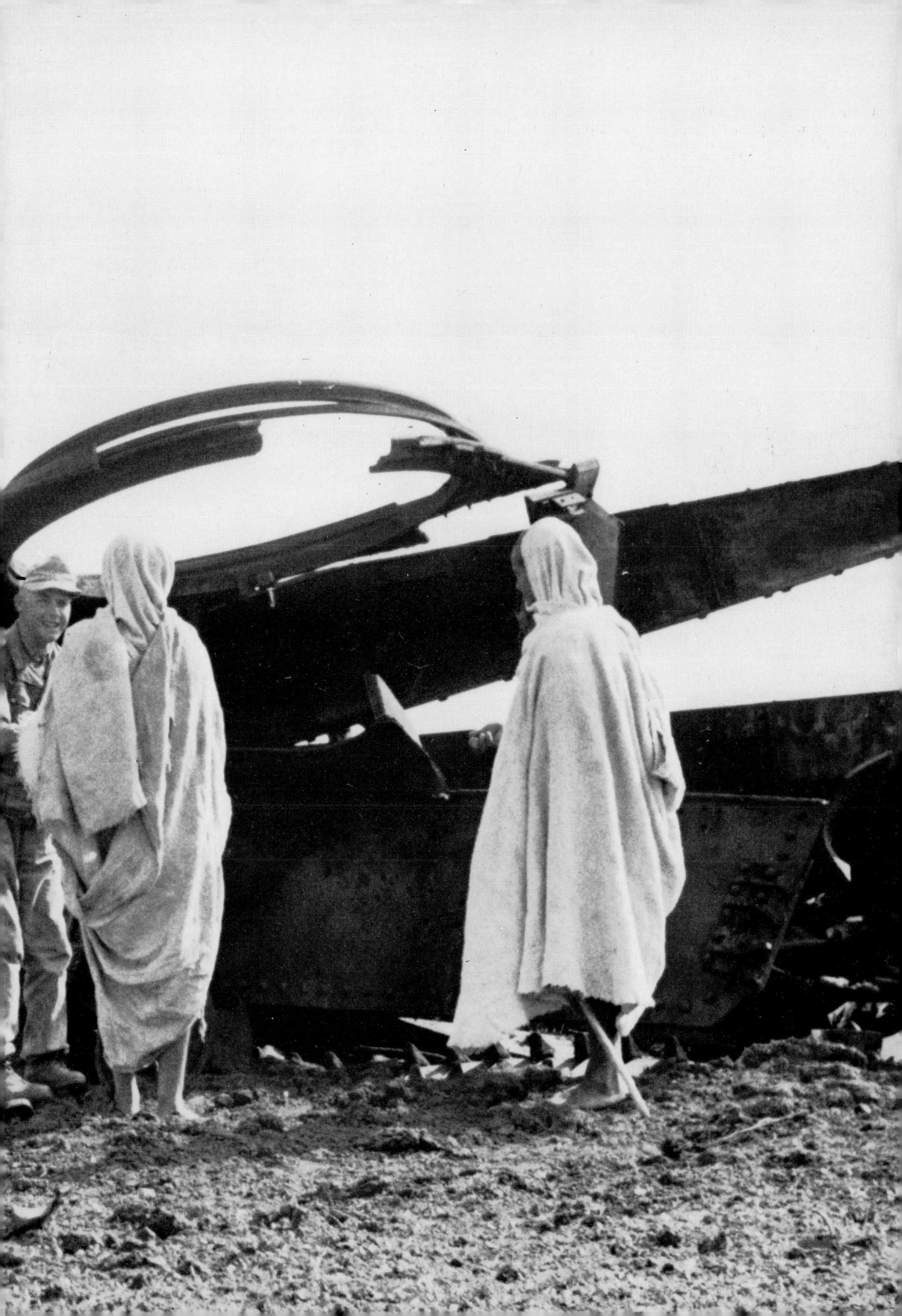

« *Somewhere in Tunisia, December 1942: A destroyed American tank.*

Syrte, late December 1942: The signs warn of concealed German mines and booby traps.

On Friday, 11 December the British 8th Army launched an attack on *Panzerarmee Afrika*, which now held the Marsa Brega positions. Under the pressure of the British forces, it had to move further west to the Buerat positions.

On Sunday, 27 December Churchill sent a highly confidential telegram to General Alexander: "Boniface (Author's note: Churchill's code name for Enigma) shows that the enemy in Buerat is in great want and disorder and lives under the constant fear of being cut off there by encirclement from the south, which he has expected since 26 December. After I had read 'Boniface' from the point of view that the enemy shows an understandable tendency to exaggerate his weaknesses in order to obtain more supplies, I can only hope you will be in a position to attack earlier than on the appointed date . . . In this way the 8th Army would have the great honor of capturing Tripoli." But even this intervention by the Prime Minister could not change General Montgomery's mind.

On Thursday, 31 December B.P. sent the C-in-C Middle East a new Enigma report which showed the results of the exchange of radio messages between Rommel and the OKH over the past several days. Rommel wanted to move his forces to Tunisia before his retreat and supply line west of Tripoli was broken. The high command of the Axis forces kept trying to cut the enemy's shipping lines through the Mediterranean Sea.

When the troops in Tunisia were reinforced, it was decided that Rommel was to delay the advance of the 8th Army under any conditions and move his non-motorized troops back to the Homs-Tarhuna line between Buerat and Tripoli. After his motorized divisions on the Buerat line had resisted the enemy as long as possible, they too were to be moved back to this line.

In the period from the beginning of August to the end of December 1942, the Axis shipping losses had increased extremely. The Italians had lost 150 ships with 276,000 tons of cargo, the Germans 24 ships with more than 44,000 tons.

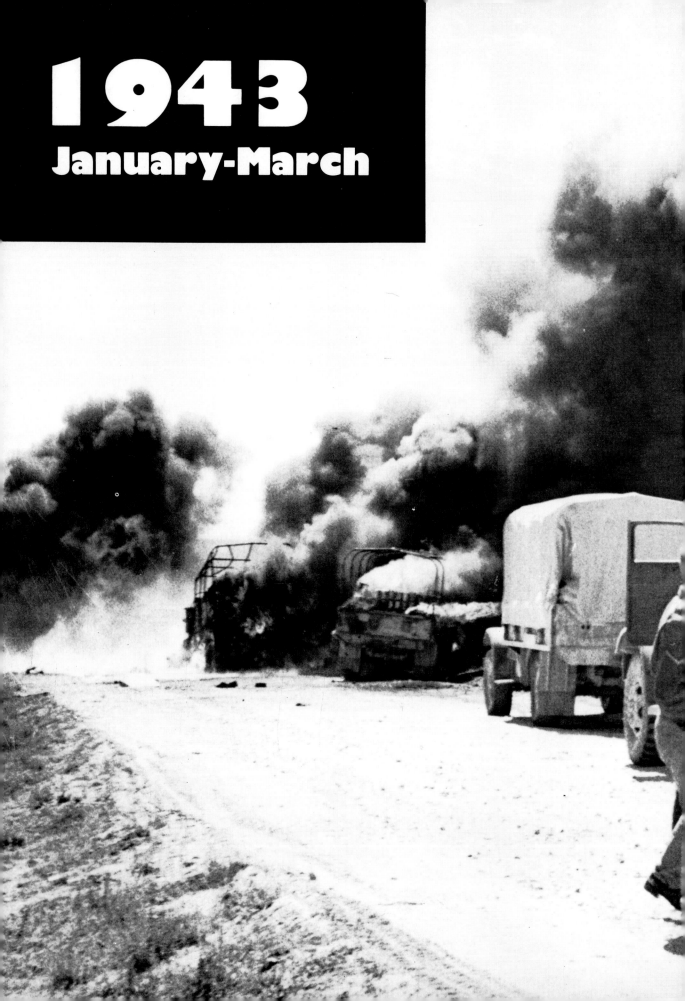

1943
January-March

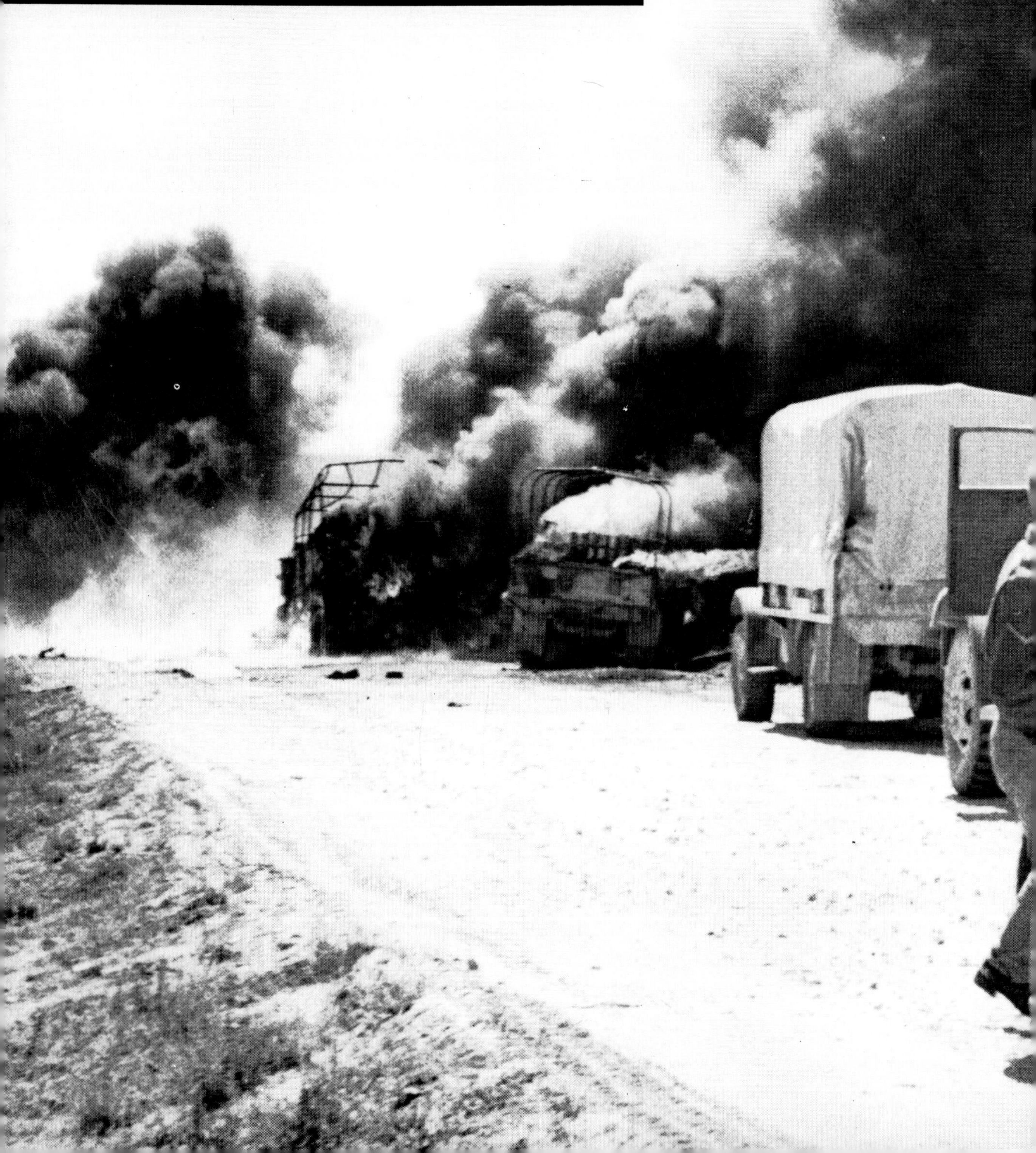

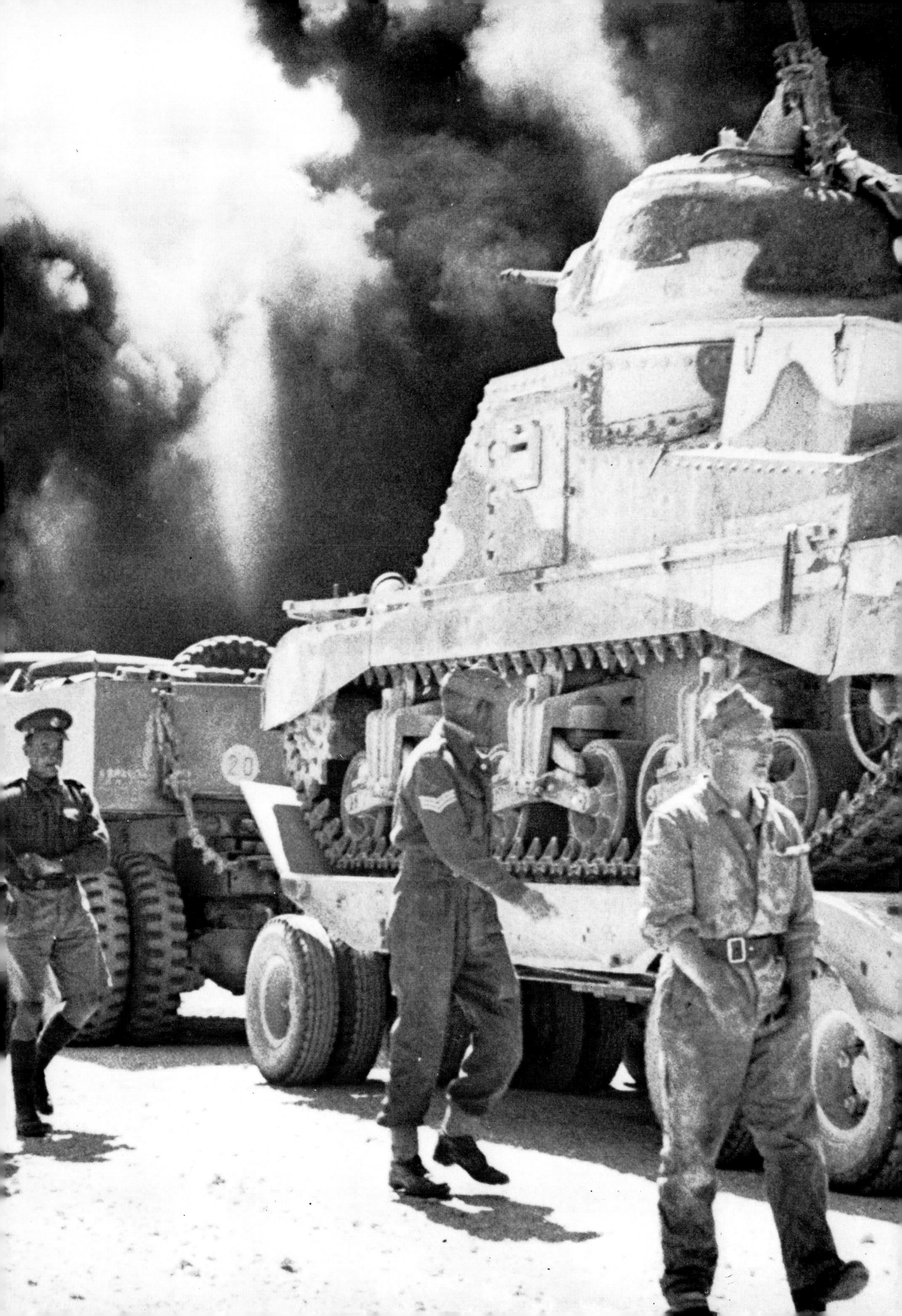
20

On Friday, 15 January 1943 Montgomery finally decided to make an attack at Buerat with his group of almost eight divisions and 700 tanks. He knew thanks to Enigma that he was opposed by only one and one-half German divisions with 34 tanks, plus six Italian divisions with 57 light tanks.

On Sunday, 17 January Rommel gave up the Buerat position because he expected Montgomery to make an encircling advance toward Tripoli.

On Monday, 18 January Allied fighter-bombers — in just one attack on the airfield at Tunis — destroyed 23 Junkers 52's on the ground. The Luftwaffe immediately withdrew some 400 aircraft from the eastern front and sent them to Tunisia.

On Tuesday, 19 January the C-in-C Middle East received the news from an Enigma report that the German 21st Panzer Division (*General-major* Hildebrandt) was to receive 34 tanks when it had reached Sfax.

On Saturday, 23 January *Panzerarmee Afrika* had to evacuate Tripoli under strong pressure from the British 8th Army and begin its retreat in the direction of the Libyan-Tunisian border. In pursuing Rommel's troops from El Alamein to Tripoli, the British 8th Army had covered more than 1500 kilometers within eighty days.

On Monday, 25 January the GC & CS decoded a directive from the Comando Supremo: *Armeegruppe Afrika* was established with Rommel at its command. The leadership of the German-Italian *Panzerarmee Afrika* went to *General* von Arnim. In addition to an offensive by the *Panzerarmee* in the north, it was planned that the new *Armeegruppe Afrika* would attack the advancing forces of the 8th Army at the beginning of March, after the conclusion of its retreat from Kasserine. For this operation, the 10th Panzer Division was to stay in Sfax and the rest of the motorized units in Gabes.

Tunis, January 1943: A German airfield after being attacked by low-flying Allied planes.

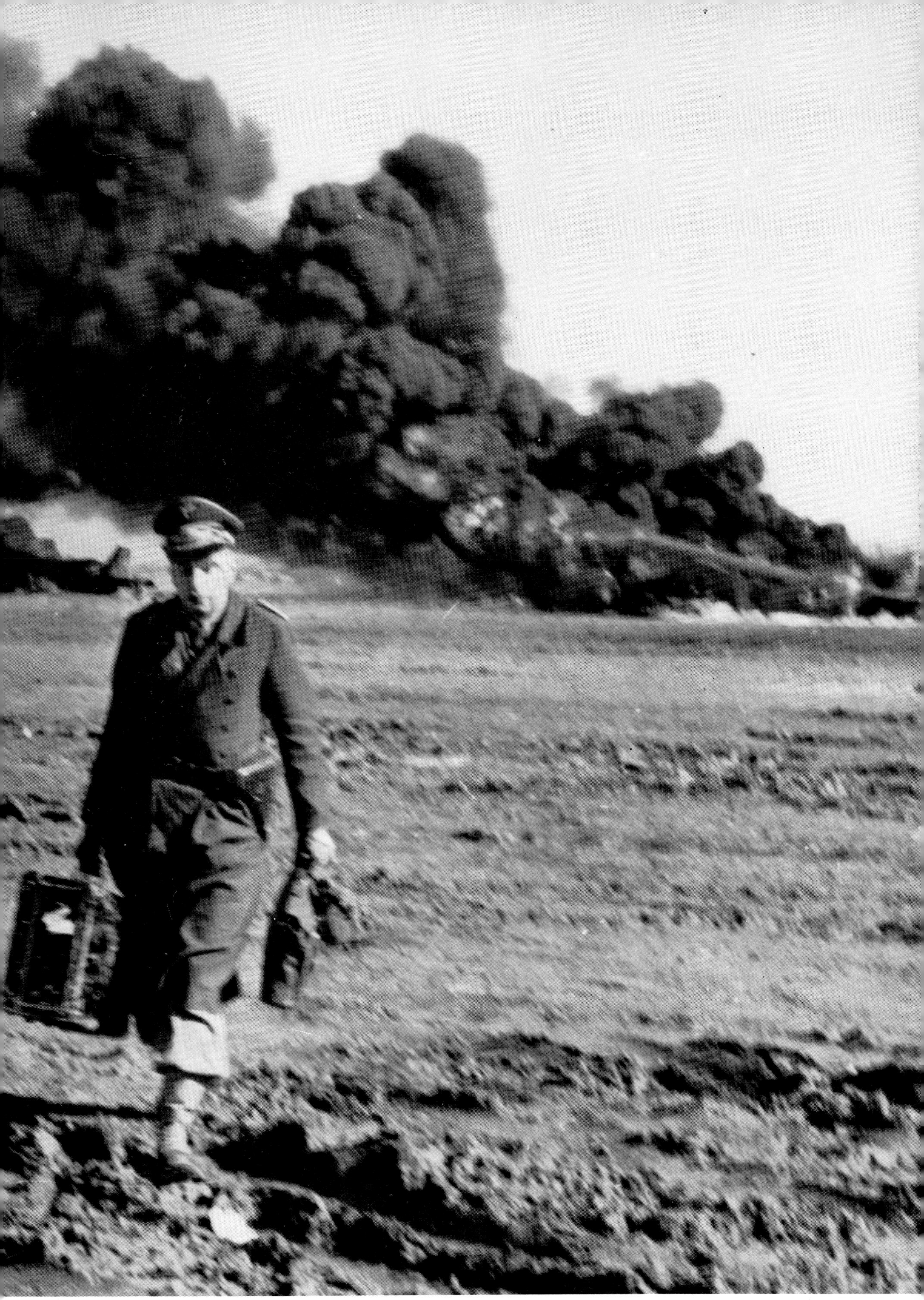

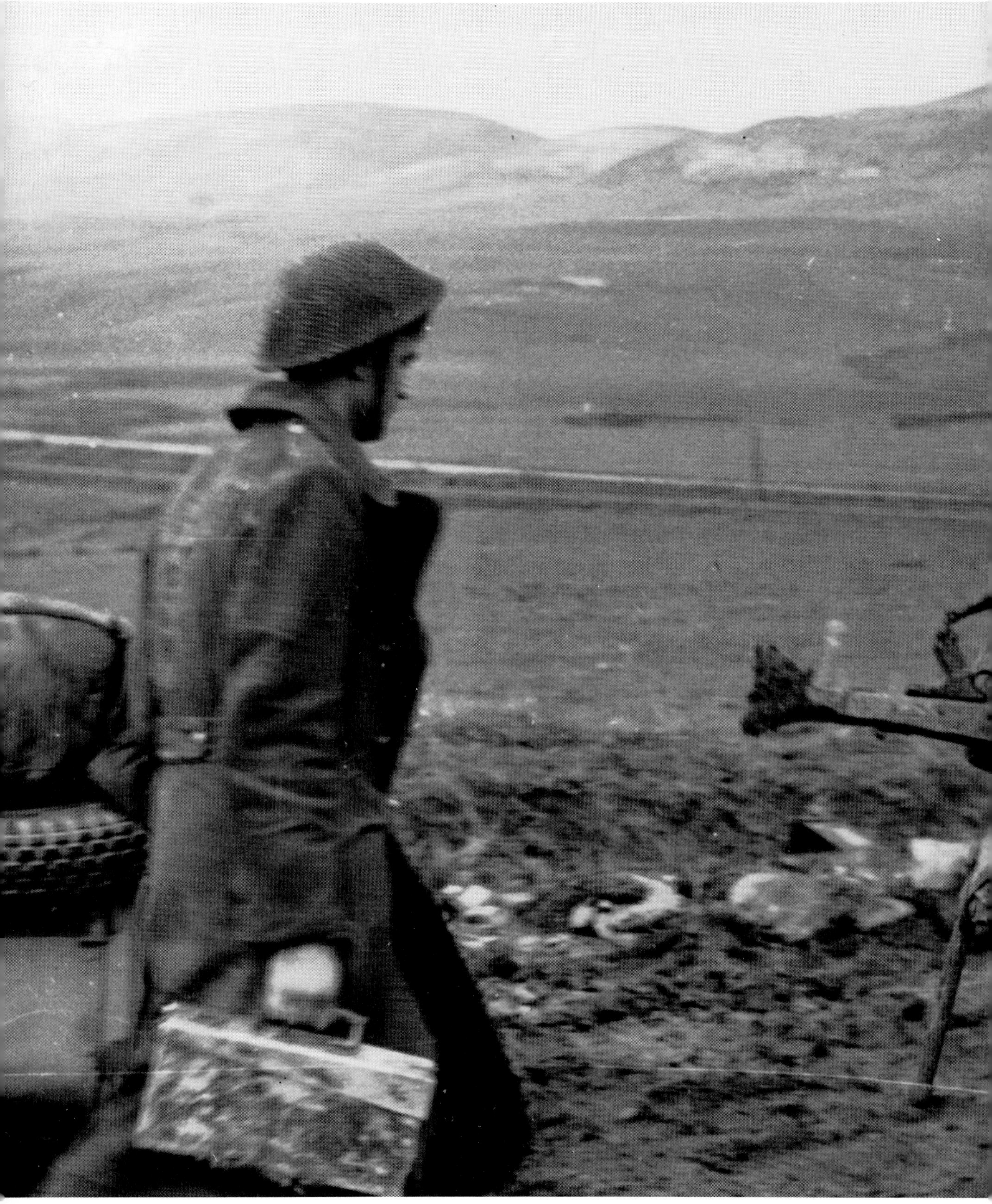

Tunisia, February 1943: German troops on the way to the Kasserine Pass.

On Tuesday, 26 January Rommel succeeded, despite British attempts to cut off *Panzerarmee Afrika*'s retreat route, in saving his troops and joining the 5th Panzer Army (*Generaloberst* von Arnim) in southern Tunisia.

On the same day, Rommel, at his new command post of the *Panzerarmee* on the Tunisian border, received a radio message from the Comando Supremo. At a time that he himself could choose, he would be relieved of his command.

On Thursday, 28 January *Panzerarmee Afrika* reached southern Tunisia and headed west on the offensive with their German and Italian forces. They tried in vain to capture Le Kef, but did take the Faid mountain pass and push toward Tebessa. They occupied Sbeitla and Gafsa, and slowly approached the Kasserine Pass.

But as Rommel's troops advance on Thala, they were thrown back by British tank forces, as also after their original success at Medjez-el-Bab.

Thanks to better supplying, Rommel could now fill his very weak 15th Panzer Division (*Generalmajor* von Vaerst) and 21st Panzer Division (*Generalmajor* Hildebrandt) for the first time in many months. He even gained the 10th Panzer Division (*Generalmajor* von Broich), just transferred from Europe to Tunisia and fully

Tunisia, Le Kef area, late January 1943: German infantrymen move forward; at left is a British prisoner carrying ammunition.

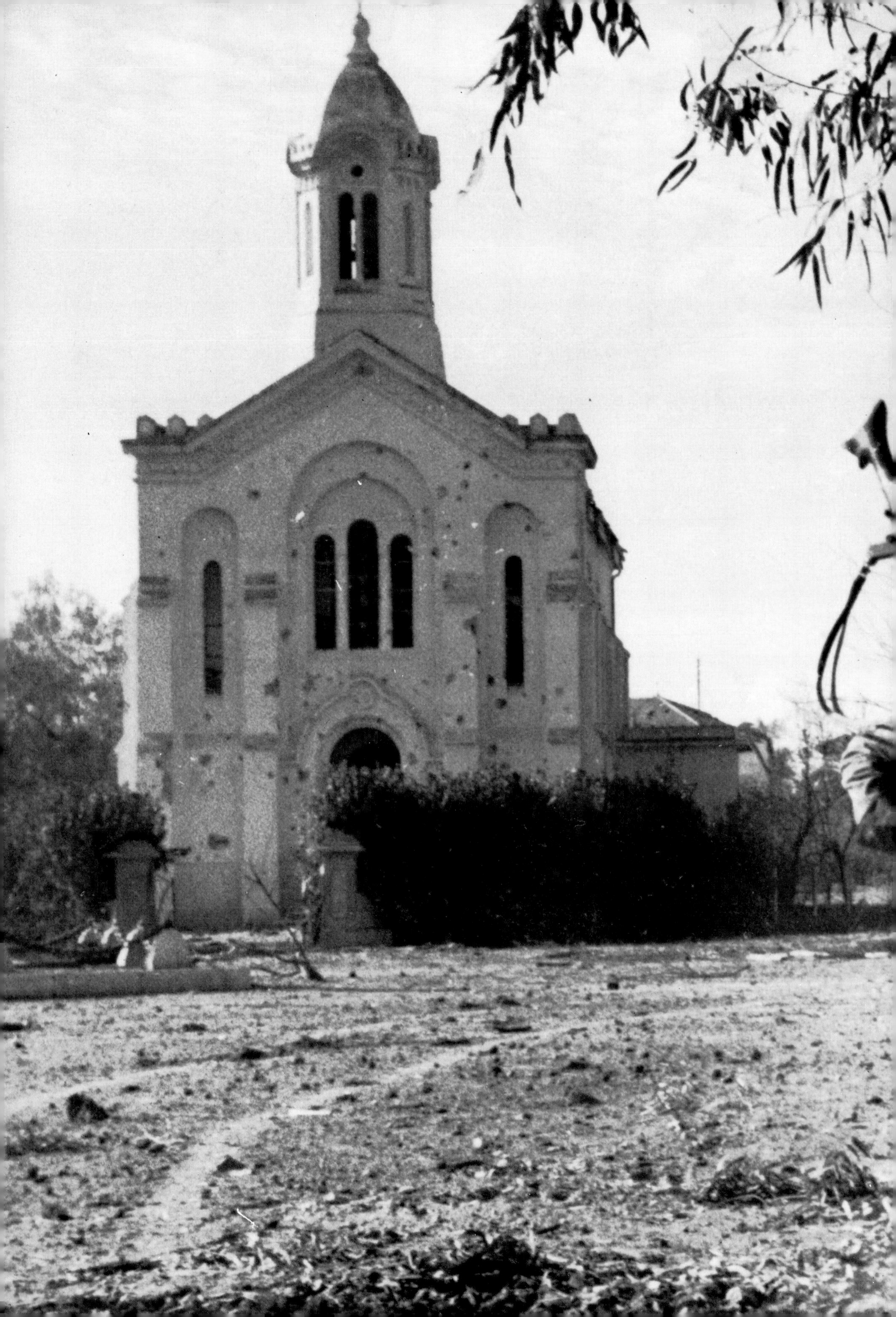

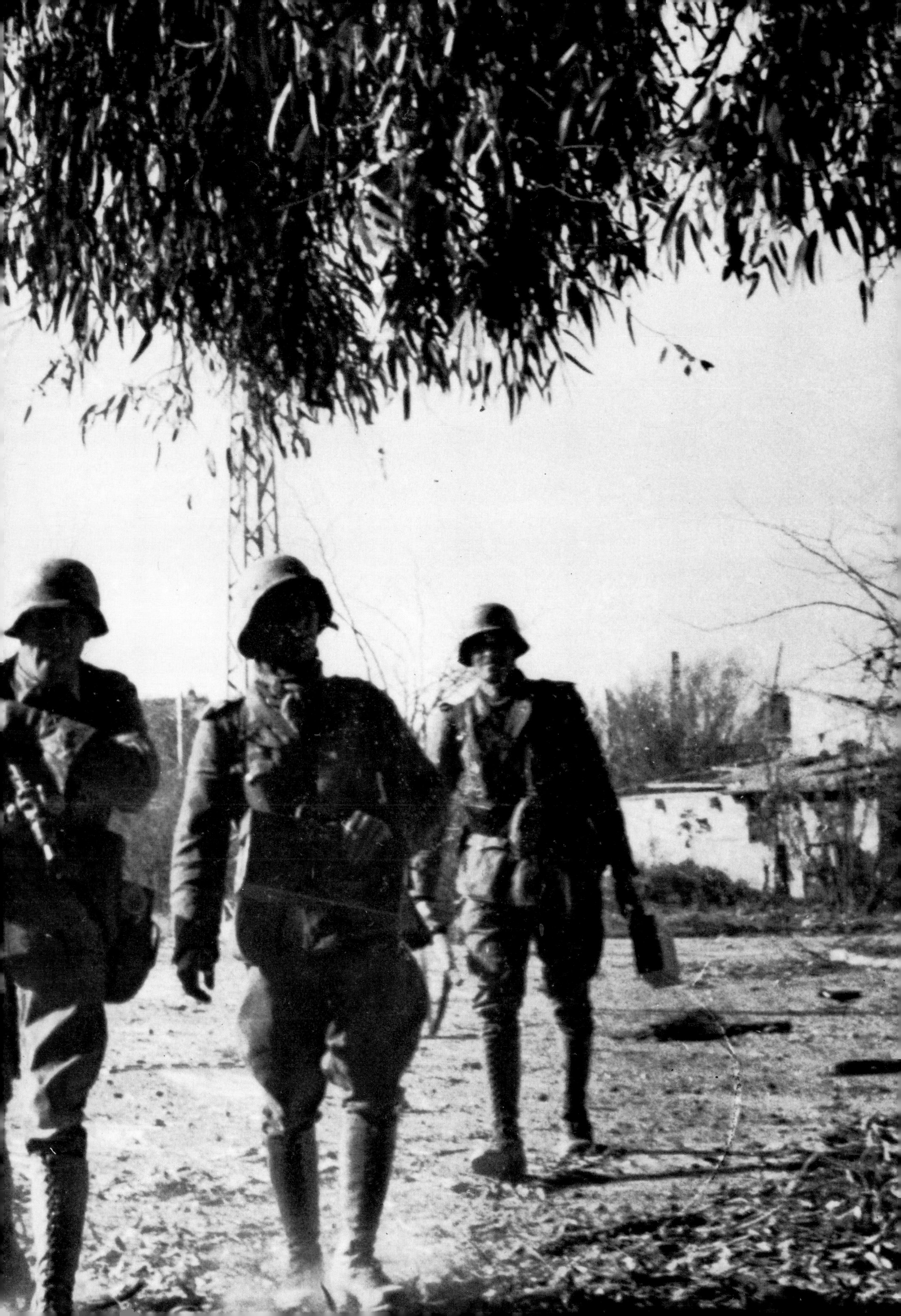

« *Tunisia, Gabes area, February 1943: German troops move forward.*

equipped. With the heavy Panzer VI Tiger tanks that were now in Tunisia and which the Allies could not oppose with anything of equal power, Rommel hoped to gain some success, especially in battle against the Americans, who were tactically inferior to the Germans on the battlefield.

On Thursday, 4 February B.P. sent the C-in-C Middle East a new Enigma report which included a memorandum from Rommel to the Comando Supremo. Rommel repeated his previous suggestion of carrying out a concentrated attack on Gafsa with both Panzer armies under a unified command, even before the 8th Army could begin its offensive.

In the second week of February 1943, *Panzerarmee Afrika*'s situation was worsened by the advance of the British 8th Army, which now held a position between Ben-Gardane, Médinine and Tathouine, facing the Mareth line, which was held by the Italian 1st Army.

On Saturday, 13 February B.P. sent the commander in Tunisia, General Eisenhower, an Enigma report: The headquarters of the 21st Panzer division was to be moved forward on that day. 14 February was planned as Day X for an operation of the 5th Panzer Army.

Eisenhower's intelligence chief, Brigadier Mockler-Ferryman, was firmly of the opinion that Rommel would not make an attack through Sidi bou Zid, but rather that the focal point of his attack would be further to the north. The reason for his assumption was that there were no corresponding Enigma reports at hand, and the Brigadier — accustomed for years to the reliability of Enigma — was convinced that he was right. What Mockler-Ferryman did not know was that there were no Enigma reports now because Rommel had ordered complete radio silence before the attack.

Tunisia, Sidi bou Zid area, February 1943: Units of the 5th Panzerarmee advancing in captured American vehicles.

Tunisia, near Gafsa, February 1943: Captured American soldiers wait for transport to a prisoner-of-war camp.

On Sunday, 14 February Rommel opened his last offensive, while Montgomery cautiously reconnoitered along the Mareth line in the south. This line of fortifications and bunkers in the Tunisian border area had been built by the French late in the thirties to guard against possible Italian attacks from the east.

Parallel to Rommel's offensive, *Generalleutnant* Ziegler's battle group, subordinate to *Generaloberst* von Arnim began Operation "Spring Wind", along with the 10th and 21st Panzer Divisions, but encountered the II. U.S. Corps (Major General Fredendall) west of the Faid Pass and scored heavy losses on the unsuspecting U.S. 1st Armored Division in the Sidi bou Zid area. Gafsa was thereupon evacuated by the Americans. Now Rommel, with several smaller units of the *DAK*, moved against their right flank.

About 10:00 PM, the commander in Tunisia received an important Enigma report, the directive from the Comando Supremo on 11 February. Immediately after the 5th Panzer Army's attack on Sidi bou Zid, the 1st Italian Army and a motorized battle group of the 5th Panzer Army were to carry out a pincer attack in the direction of Gafsa and — depending on how the tactical situation developed — continue their attack toward Tozeur after securing the Gafsa basin. Meanwhile, the 5th Panzer Army was to make a very strong advance concentrating on the right wing, in order to smash the enemy forces in the Sidi bou Zid area.

On Monday, 15 February the "Combat Command C" made a counterattack at Sidi bou Zid. It was beaten by the Ziegler Battle Group, losing many tanks, and left the battlefield in haste.

On Tuesday, 16 February B.P. sent the com-

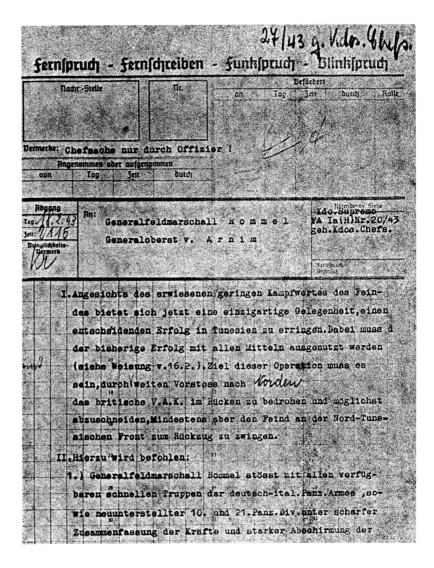

A radio message from the Duce (Comando Supremo) to Rommel and von Arnim, February 18, 1943, ". . . unique opportunity to score a decisive success in Tunisia."

mander in Tunisia the decoded daily report of the 5th Panzer Army for 15 February: 97 enemy tanks had been destroyed at Sidi bou Zid, many prisoners taken, secret documents including the complete U.S. battle plans captured. On receiving this news, the Allied commander gave the order to evacuate Feriana on 17 February.

In the night of 16-17 February *Generalleutnant* Ziegler's battle group had to break off Operation "Spring Wind", which they had begun on 14 February. The 21st Panzer Army had attained some success, to be sure, so that the U.S. 2nd Motorized Division could only hold its position at Sbeitla with difficulty, but *Generalleutnant* Ziegler's battle group was assigned to *Panzerarmee Afrika* for Rommel's planned advance through the Kasserine Pass to Tebessa.

By Wednesday, 17 February the Allied commanders had scarcely any intelligence reports

concerning the most important sector of the front, other than meager information from their fighting forces. The difficulty in making use of Enigma was mainly that the "Dodo" code used by the 5th *Panzerarmee* for their radio communications was harder to decode than the "Phoenix" code used by the Italian 1st Army for their radio connections with the Army high command.

On Friday afternoon, 19 February the Tunisian commander received a new Enigma report from B.P., a suggestion from Rommel to the Comando Supremo on 18 February for an advance of the 10th and 21st Panzer Divisions, under his command, on Le Kef.

On Saturday, 20 February Rommel's Panzer units occupied the Kasserine Pass. Several hours later, the 10th Panzer Division pushed northward toward Thala. Meanwhile, the 21st Panzer

The first men of the Allied 1st Army, advancing from Algeria to Tunisia, meet the British 8th Army advancing from Libya.

Division approached Sbiba. Rommel had chosen to march in this direction only under pressure from Mussolini, as there were said to be strong Allied troop concentrations near Tebessa. The operation, though, was brought to a stop when the supply lines were cut. On the same day, Eisenhower requested the replacement of Brigadier Mockler-Ferryman, his chief enemy situation advisor. He was succeeded by Brigadier W.D. Strong, the former military attache in Berlin. Eisenhower, who had not won a victory as the commander at the Kasserine Pass, also had the commander of the U.S. II. Corps, Major General Fredendall, and a division commander replaced.

The case of Brigadier Mockler-Ferryman, who had relied too much on the Enigma reports, clearly shows the dangers of too-great dependence on "Ultra Secret." This is also confirmed by the opinion held by the responsible higher officers that Enigma reports were only of any great use on the battlefield when they were confirmed by good local reconnaissance or information from the usual sources.

At 11:12 PM B.P. sent the U.S. commander the latest Enigma report. It was the acceptance by the Comando Supremo of Rommel's suggestion of 18 February that he lead an advance of the 10th and 21st Panzer Divisions to Le Kef. Since the enemy

troops showed a low combat value, this was a once-in-a-lifetime chance to achieve a decisive victory. The British V. Corps was to be cut off, or the enemy forces in the south were to be forced to retreat.

The 5th *Panzerarmee* now prepared to attack the front in northern Tunisia in order to hold the enemy there while Rommel advanced in the south. Because no major British attack on Mareth was expected in the coming week, only a few motorized reserves were to be left there.

On Sunday, 21 February the U.S. commander received a further Enigma report at 12:45 PM. It included orders from Rommel for his further advance. The 21th Panzer Divisionwas to attack through Sbiba in the direction of Ksour, while the 10th Panzer Division, at only half of its full strength because considerable parts of its forces were operating elsewhere, had the task of moving forward along the road to Thala. Meanwhile, the southern battle group was to push forward in the direction of El Hamma on the fork of the road to Tebessa.

On Monday, 22 February Rommel halted his advance and turned southward again to confront the 8th Army. Meanwhile, *Generaloberst* von Arnim was advised to begin Operation "Oxhead" on 26 February. This was to block the extremely

Daily Mail

NO. 14,606   ONE PENNY   FOR KING AND EMPIRE   MONDAY, FEBRUARY 22, 1943

AXIS CAPTURE KEY PASS IN TUNISIA

DNIEPER DRIVE SPEEDS UP
More Towns Fall in Donetz Bend

From HAROLD KING, Reuter's Special Correspondent   Moscow, Sunday.

THE RED ARMY has made rapid strides in the past 24 hours in its drive for the Dnieper. Forces advancing from Lozovaya down the Kharkov-Crimea railway stand to-night only 35 miles east of the river at Dnepropetrovsk.

Pushing swiftly south-

American Base Town in Algeria Threatened

THE KING'S SWORD OF HONOUR
For Stalingrad

STALINGRAD is to receive from the King a Sword of Honour.

Announcement of this last night came at the end of a day on which ceremonies in salute to the Red Army had been held through-

Doctors to Gandhi: 'End Fast or Die'

Appeal to PM

BOMBAY, Sunday.

FIRST ARMY'S TANKS ARE IN ACTION

From Daily Mail Special Correspondent   ALLIED H.Q., North Africa, Sunday.

GERMAN tanks and infantry in Central Tunisia have captured the vital Kasserine Pass, and have opened the way to Tebessa, in Algeria, in the rear of the Allied front, and presumably the American base. The town lies little more than 30 miles from the pass.

---

important supply route of the U.S. forces between Beja and Medjez-el-Bab and thus allow the Axis troops more freedom to operate.

About 9:00 that evening the Y service reported intercepting an order to retreat that was meant for one of the Panzer divisions. This was the first indication of a general retreat of the Axis troops through the Kasserine Pass, which had been discussed by Rommel and Kesselring that day.

At 1:45 AM on the night of 22-23 February B.P. sent the U.S. commander a new Enigma report,

an order from Comando Supremo at 9:30 on the previous evening. The attack was halted and the units subordinate to Rommel were to return to their original positions.

On Tuesday, 23 February a new organization of the Axis forces took place in the Tunisian bridgehead. The German-Italian *Panzerarmee Afrika* now became the Italian 1st Army (*Generaloberst* Messe) and, with other German and Italian troops, was included in the newly formed *Armeegruppe Afrika* (*Generalfeldmarschall* Rommel).

Tunisia, late February 1943: A German intelligence officer (enemy situation analyst) questions a non-commissioned officer of the British airborne troops.

Tunisia: Generaloberst H.J. von Arnim greets General von Vaerst (left).

On Thursday, 25 February the U.S. commander learned from a new Enigma message, the daily situation report for 22 February, of Rommel's sated reasons for the sudden halt of the offensive toward the west. The enemy's steady reinforcements, bad weather, rough country, low combat strength of his own troops, and above all the fact that the situation in Mareth required his motorized forces to be concentrated for a fast strike against the 8th Army before the latter had completed its preparations for an attack.

On Saturday, 27 February B.P. sent the latest Enigma report to the U.S. commander. It gave the news of *Generaloberst* von Arnim's attack on the northern front sector on 26 February, with the capture of Medjez-el-Bab and the spread of the 5th *Panzerarmee*'s attack front, in order to turn the enemy aside during the retreat of Rommel's troops from the Kasserine Pass.

On Sunday, 28 February the U.S. commander received a new Enigma radio message from B.P., including a report from Rommel dated 27 February. In it, Rommel sharply criticized the

intolerable waste of troops in *Generaloberst* von Arnim's initiative. Rommel himself planned to carry out an attack with the 10th, 15th and 21st Panzer Divisions no later than 4 March. To fool the enemy aerial reconnaissance, the 10th and 21st Panzer Divisions were to move southward from Gabes at first, deep into the inland area. These were the last two decoded Enigma reports that revealed Rommel's intentions in North Africa.

On Wednesday, 3 March a new Enigma report reached the U.S. commander. It included the fuel report of *Armeegruppe Afrika* as of 1 March. It was clear from this report that their fuel would only last for, at most, three more days — just enough to pull off a disturbing surprise attack, but not at all sufficient for an offensive like the Kasserine operation.

On Thursday, 4 March the Army's Y service reported that Rommel's troops were moving to the south. Aerial reconnaissance confirmed that Rommel was concentrating his troops on the western and southern flanks of the enemy lines. At that, Montgomery also moved his artillery.

On Friday evening, 5 March Montgomery's intelligence staff, after weighing the evidence from all available sources, was convinced that Rommel was going to begin his offensive the next morning.

On Saturday, 6 March the U.S. commander received a new Enigma report from B.P. at 5:36 AM. It said that Rommel had ordered the attack to begin at 6:00 AM on that day.

On this morning Rommel began Operation "Capri." the attack on the British 8th Army at the Mareth position in the Medinine area. Just short of Metamyr, though, the offensive came to a stop under concentrated defensive fire. On the basis of the Enigma report, Montgomery had strengthened the east-west line perpendicular to Rommel's expected direction of advance several days in advance by moving the artillery of the 2nd New Zealand Division (Lieutenant General Freyberg).

Montgomery said: "As expected, Rommel attacked in the early morning hours of the 6th with three Panzer divisions. The attack was beaten off.

In the afternoon he attacked again. Again he was beaten back . . . I was convinced that Rommel would attack and received him again in my way . . ."

The Operation "Capri" had to be broken off with high losses. Rommel left 55 of his remaining 141 tanks on the battlefield, plus 640 dead and wounded. The British losses numbered one Sherman tank and 130 men, mostly wounded.

General der Panzertruppe Cramer, Commanding General of the *Afrika-Korps,* said: "The enemy had obviously expected the attack. The terrain was heavily mined, and the artillery had formed a defensive front to the southwest."

Prisoners and captured documents proved to Rommel that Montgomery had known of the offensive to the last detail. "In this case the Italian Army commander, Marshal Messe, was worthy of joining the traitor from the navy, Admiral Maugeri." The failed Operation "Capri" was Rommel's last combat undertaking in North Africa.

Tunisia, March 1943: A radioman of a British listening unit (T service) with microphone in hand.

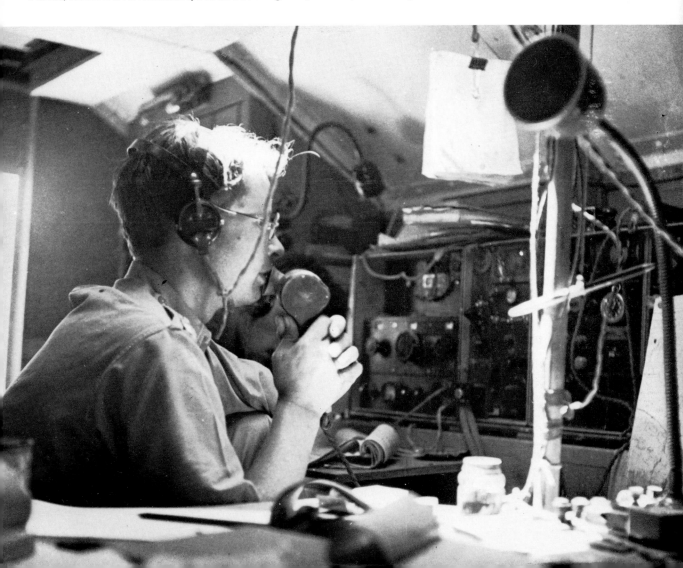

Tunisia, Medinine area, March 7, 1943, ". . . Operation 'Capri' broken off with heavy losses", destroyed German tanks on the battlefield.

In the early morning hours of Monday, 8 March B.P. sent the U.S. commander a new Enigma radio message. It was a situation report of *Armeegruppe Afrika* on 6 March. At 11:00 AM Rommel had decided, on the basis of the superior enemy artillery and the unexpected strength of the British defensive positions, to break off the action.

On Tuesday, 9 March a new Enigma report from B.P. reached the U.S. commander. According to statements from prisoners of war and captured documents, the Germans had concluded that the British 8th Army had not only known Rommel's intention to attack, but also the strength, the place and time of the attack. But it could not be ascertained from the message whether the Germans were of the opinion that Enigma was the source of the information.

This revelation set off an alarm at SIS. The CIGS tried to calm Churchill by stressing that the reference to statements by prisoners and captured

documents did not "necessarily" have to mean that the highest-priority secrets had been betrayed. But Churchill referred to "lacking security measures" that "could rule out intensified security measures among the German encoders, which would make any use of "Ultra Secret" by us impossible."

Likewise on 9 March Rommel turned the command of *Armeegruppe Afrika* over to *Generaloberst* von Arnim and, along with his ordnance officer, *Hauptmann* Berndt, and his doctor, Professor Horster, set off for Rome by plane. At first the German leadership kept this news a secret, and it did not appear in Enigma reports until the middle of March. There was only a message to Kesselring in Rome: "*Generalfeldmarschall* Rommel has presently been furloughed by the Führer. This fact is to be kept secret under all conditions, including from command posts and troops."

After his arrival in Rome, Rommel paid a visit

"He has bitten" — Rommel's defeat at Medinine as seen by a London cartoonist.

"Look out for his tail!"   —by *Illingworth.*

to the Duce at the Palazzo Viminale. Mussolini asked: "Did they (the British) know for sure about our attack in advance?" Rommel answered: "Yes."

The Reich Propaganda Minister, Dr. Goebbels, noted in his diary on 9 March 1943: "Rommel's last offensive has also been betrayed by Italian prisoners. We simply cannot play with the Italians. They are unreliable, both militarily and politically."

Before he began his convalescence, Rommel flew to the Führer's headquarters, which was at Winniza, Hungary, at that time. He wanted to speak in favor of an organized evacuation of the German troops from Tunisia. But Hitler refused and ordered him to begin his long-postponed medical furlough. Hitler said: "Get better, so that you will be back in form again soon. I guarantee that you will lead the operation against Casablanca."

Rommel never again returned to North Africa.

Tunis, Luftwaffe air support point, March 1943: The ruins »
of Rommel's air transport fleet.

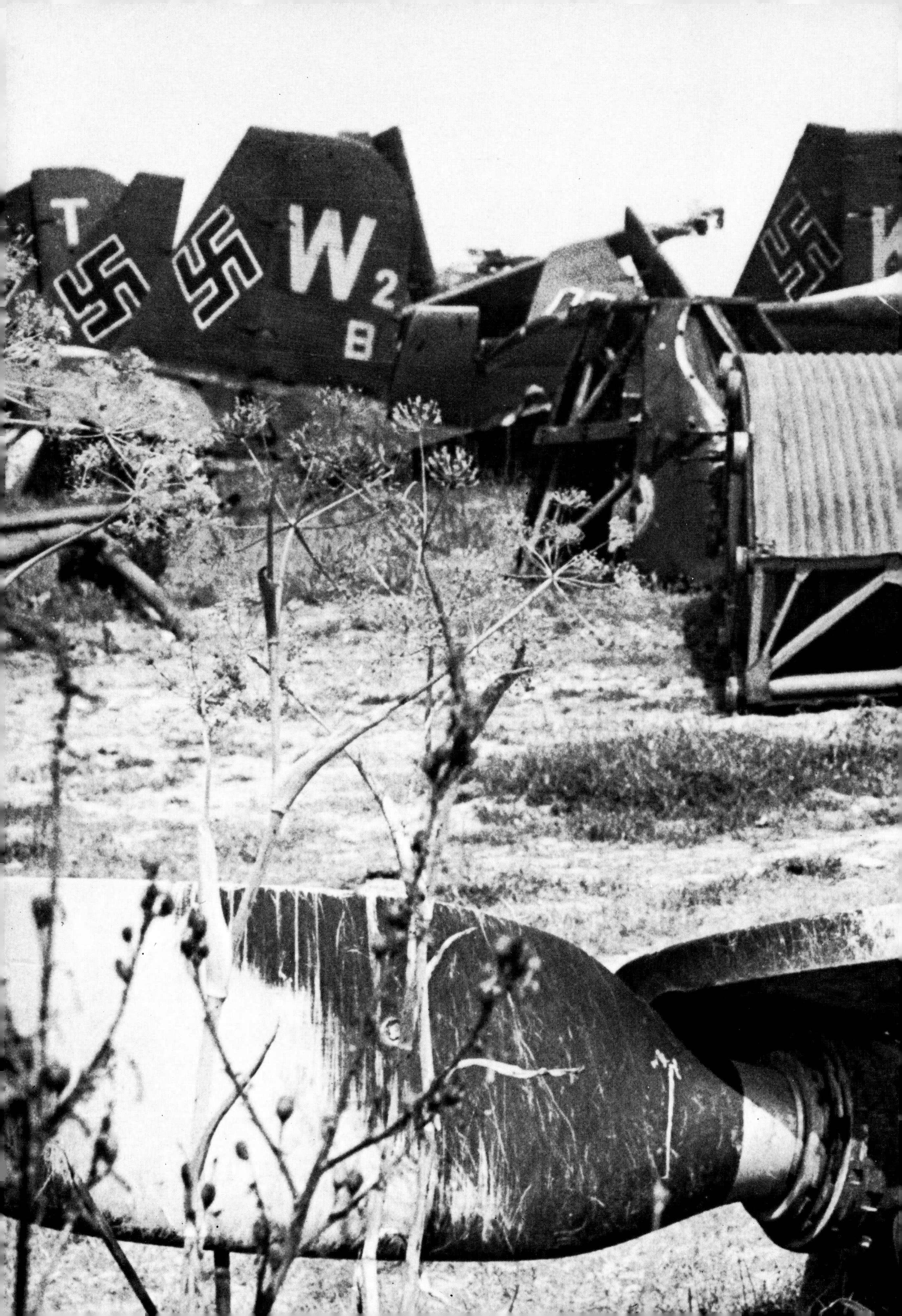
T
W2
B

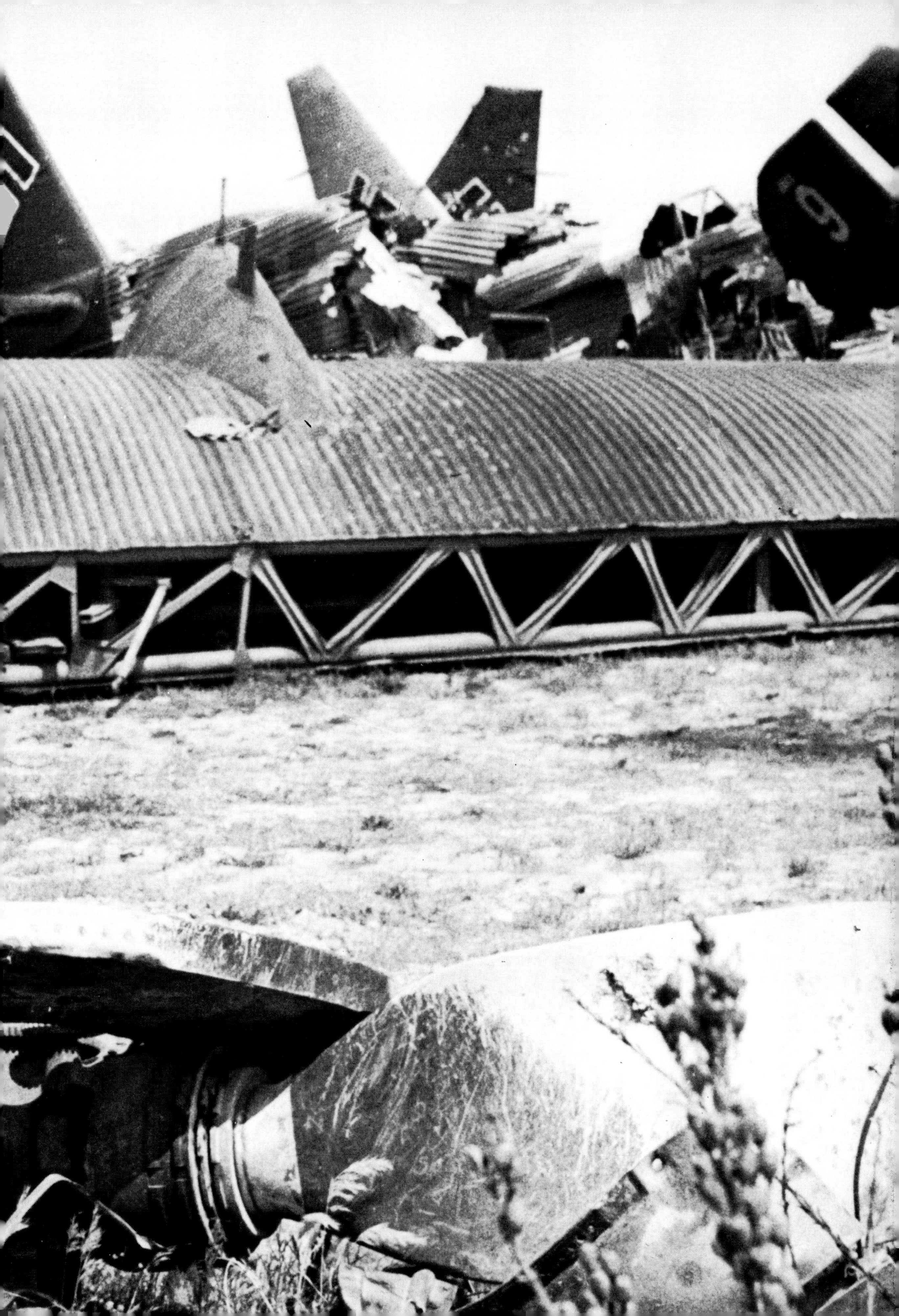

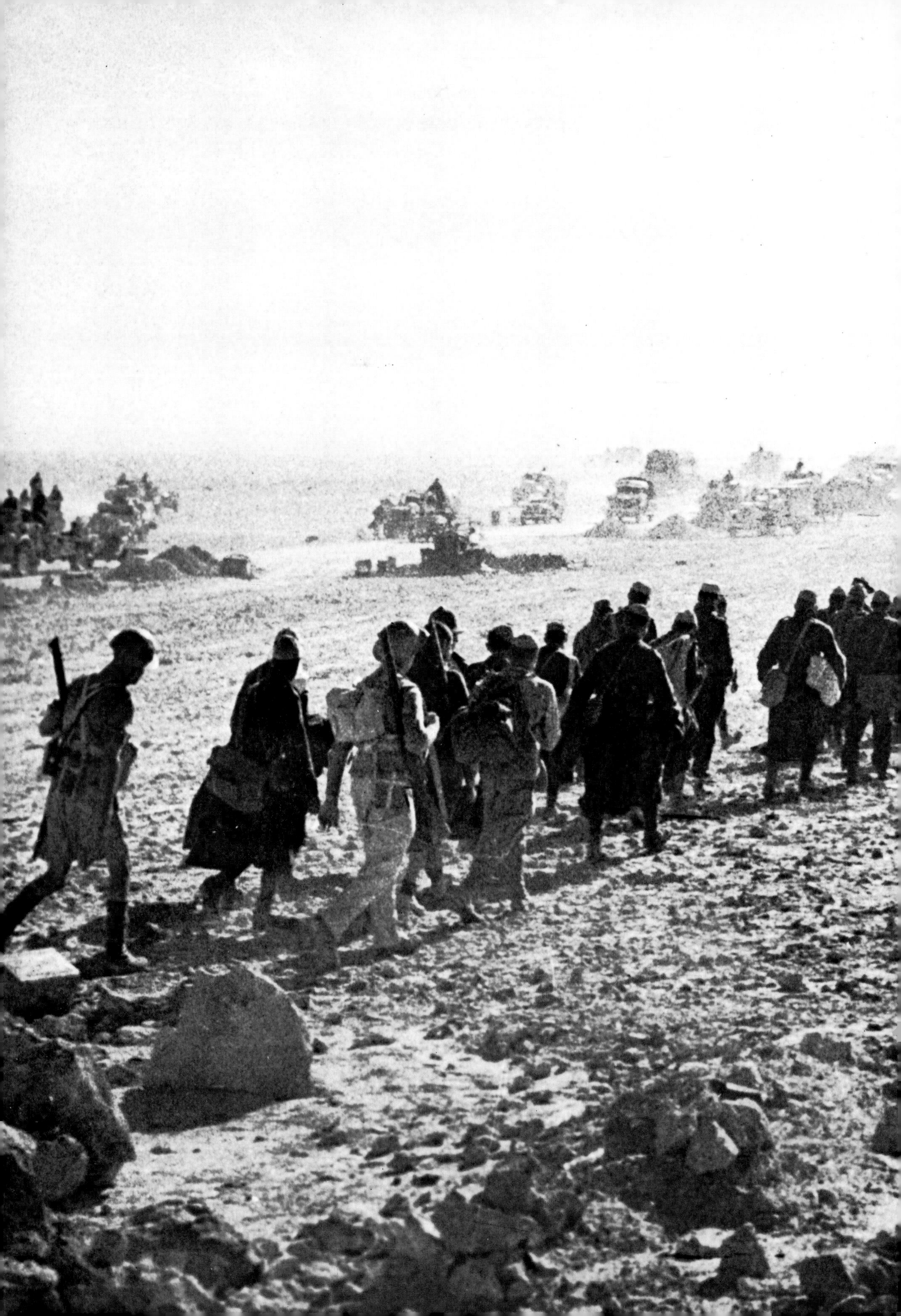

Epilogue

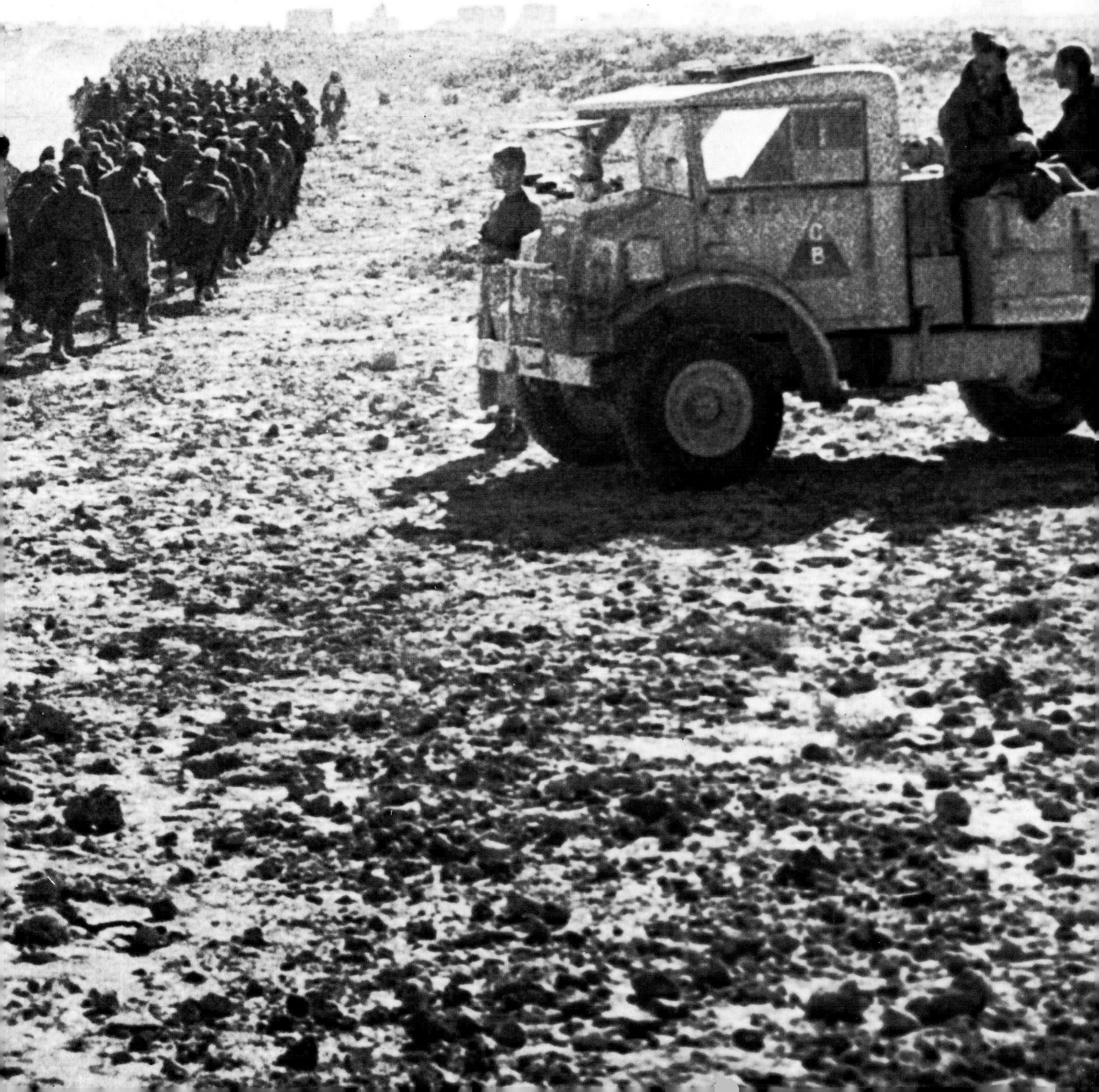
C
B

Tunisia, Kasserine area, March 1943, after the battle: Destroyed German 88mm Flak gun that was used as an antitank gun.

It still took more than two months after Rommel had left North Africa before the hopeless fight ended.

At the end of April 1943 the supplies for the Axis troops sank to some five to six per cent of their monthly minimum needs. The fuel supplies were now so minimal that they no longer allowed any operational action at all. For example, the 10th Panzer Division (*Generalmajor* Fischer),

that served as an army reserve behind the 5th Panzer Army (*Generaloberst* von Arnim), could no longer be transferred, so that it could only be utilized on the right or left wing.

When surrender in North Africa was very imminent, *Generaloberst* Guderian suggested that the many tank crews who no longer had tanks by brought home in the supply planes flying back to the homeland. But Hitler absolutely rejected this.

On Thursday, 13 May 1943 what remained of *Armeegruppe Afrika* (*Generaloberst* von Arnim) surrendered in Tunisia. The last German unit to lay down their arms was the 164th Light Division, and the Italian 1st Army (*Generaloberst* Messe) surrendered the next morning. A quarter of a million soldiers, including 130,000 Germans, were taken prisoner. The battle for North Africa was now over.

The Allies needed sox months to conquer French North Africa; in their operational plans they had planned on only six weeks.

Since 10 June 1940, when the Italians had begun their daring advance from Libya toward Egypt, the Axis powers lost 975,000 men, 7600 aircraft, 6200 guns, 2550 tanks, 70,000 motor vehicles and 624 ships.

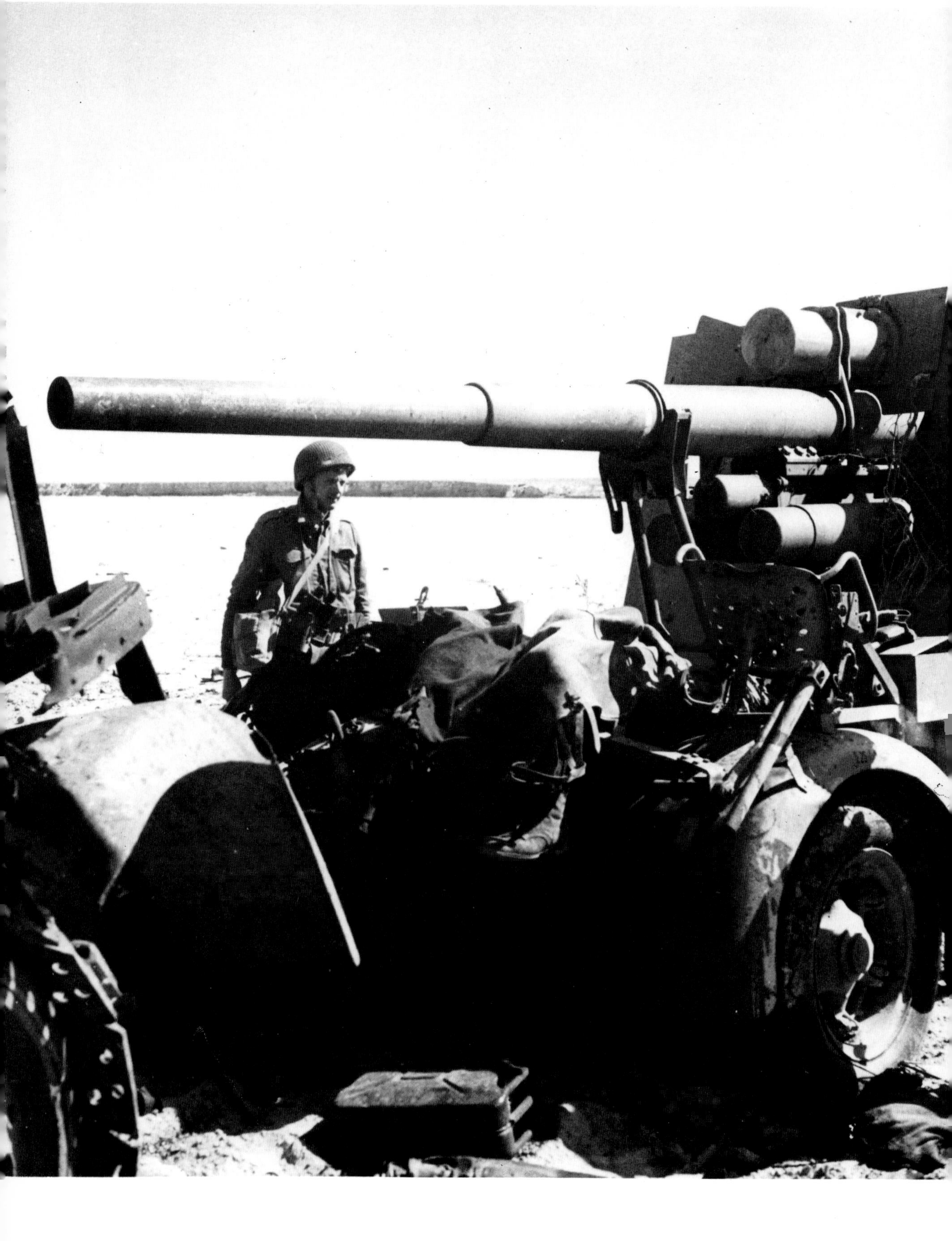

Tunisia, Tebaga area, March 1943, General Montgomery's command post: Intelligence officers at work.

Tunisia, El Guettar area, March 1943: A brand-new German 88mm Flak gun captured — and looked upon with awe — by American troops.

Structure of Axis Forces
As of 1 July 1942

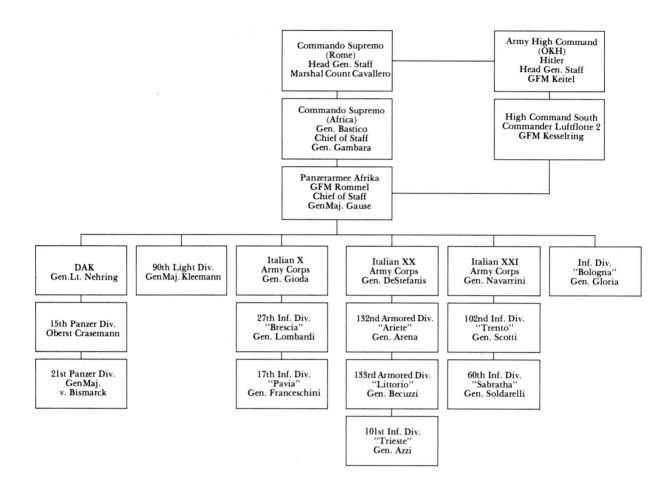

Commando Supremo (Rome) Head Gen. Staff Marshal Count Cavallero

Army High Command (OKH) Hitler Head Gen. Staff GFM Keitel

Commando Supremo (Africa) Gen. Bastico Chief of Staff Gen. Gambara

High Command South Commander Luftflotte 2 GFM Kesselring

Panzerarmee Afrika GFM Rommel Chief of Staff GenMaj. Gause

DAK Gen.Lt. Nehring

90th Light Div. GenMaj. Kleemann

Italian X Army Corps Gen. Gioda

Italian XX Army Corps Gen. DeStefanis

Italian XXI Army Corps Gen. Navarrini

Inf. Div. "Bologna" Gen. Gloria

15th Panzer Div. Oberst Crasemann

27th Inf. Div. "Brescia" Gen. Lombardi

132nd Armored Div. "Ariete" Gen. Arena

102nd Inf. Div. "Trento" Gen. Scotti

21st Panzer Div. GenMaj. v. Bismarck

17th Inf. Div. "Pavia" Gen. Franceschini

133rd Armored Div. "Littorio" Gen. Becuzzi

60th Inf. Div. "Sabratha" Gen. Soldarelli

101st Inf. Div. "Trieste" Gen. Azzi

Structure of British Forces
As of 1 July 1942

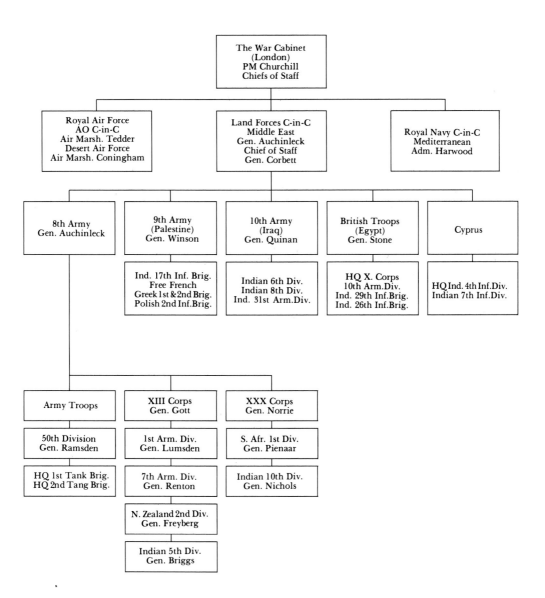

The War Cabinet
(London)
PM Churchill
Chiefs of Staff

Royal Air Force
AO C-in-C
Air Marsh. Tedder
Desert Air Force
Air Marsh. Coningham

Land Forces C-in-C
Middle East
Gen. Auchinleck
Chief of Staff
Gen. Corbett

Royal Navy C-in-C
Mediterranean
Adm. Harwood

8th Army
Gen. Auchinleck

9th Army
(Palestine)
Gen. Winson

10th Army
(Iraq)
Gen. Quinan

British Troops
(Egypt)
Gen. Stone

Cyprus

Ind. 17th Inf. Brig.
Free French
Greek 1st & 2nd Brig.
Polish 2nd Inf. Brig.

Indian 6th Div.
Indian 8th Div.
Ind. 31st Arm. Div.

HQ X. Corps
10th Arm. Div.
Ind. 29th Inf. Brig.
Ind. 26th Inf. Brig.

HQ Ind. 4th Inf. Div.
Indian 7th Inf. Div.

Army Troops

XIII Corps
Gen. Gott

XXX Corps
Gen. Norrie

50th Division
Gen. Ramsden

1st Arm. Div.
Gen. Lumsden

S. Afr. 1st Div.
Gen. Pienaar

HQ 1st Tank Brig.
HQ 2nd Tang Brig.

7th Arm. Div.
Gen. Renton

Indian 10th Div.
Gen. Nichols

N. Zealand 2nd Div.
Gen. Freyberg

Indian 5th Div.
Gen. Briggs

Notes

Thucydides, the 4th century **B.C.** Greek historian, and one of the best historians of ancient days, believed that "those who take part in a campaign know the least about it." That must be true; after all, Thucydides was also a field marshal, and he spoke from experience.

But ordering the highest-ranking commanders — to say nothing of other ranks — not to speak of their experiences for a generation was only possible in the Western World in Great Britain through the Official Secrets Act, which obligated all those in the service of the crown to keep the strictest silence in writing.

Almost until the end of the 1970s — which is how long the secret of Operation "Ultra Secret" was strictly kept — the most varied types of rumors, in which "treason" was spoken of, haunted the battlefields of North Africa. In Italy, for example, there were credible publications reporting, among other things, that the Italian Admiral Maugeri had been in the pay of the British and immediately reported every transport ship carrying supplies to Rommel to the SIS as soon as it left an Italian port. A whole series of legal actions on the subject took place in Rome, in which those under suspicion, or their relatives, sought to restore their tainted honor.

Even Field Marshal Sir Claude Auchinleck — duty-bound to silence on the "Ultra" story — invented the story of treason by an (Italian?) agent who supplied him with Rommel's own handwritten plans to attack Tobruk in November 1940. This sensational story could be read in the London "Picture Post" on April 25, 1953.

The first breakthrough was ventured in July 1974, presumably with permission from above, by the retired RAF Group Captain F.W. Winterbotham, former Chief of the Special Liaison Unit (SLU), in his book *The Ultra Secret*, in which, to be sure, the events leading up to the breaking of the "Enigma" code were recounted rather contradictorily.

The first official release of information on Operation "Ultra Secret" took place in October 1977. The British State Archives' Public Record Office (PRO), in the London suburb of Kew, Richmond, has made the texts of decoded "Enigma" messages available to the public since then. But a large portion of the released documents are still in the files of the Cabinet Office or the Ministry of Defence.

The decoded radio messages, though, came mainly from the medium range of command, since the highest Axis leadership generally communicated via unbreakable wire connections such as the teletype and telephone.

At this time, only a fraction of the files belonging to Operation "Ultra Secret" are available. First of all, the release of the documents has by no means been completed. Second, whole portions of the archives with countless pieces of information, in some cases not even precisely identified, were destroyed shortly after the war ended. Third, documents still labeled "secret" will be released only in the year 2015. And fourth, surely a great deal that would have been very interesting will never be made available. Nor is it possible to determine exactly where the borderline may be.

For example, it often happens that when one requests certain files at the Public Records Office, one is told that "it is not known just where the documents in question are at this time." As a rule, every copy of the released files, before leaving the Public Records Office, is checked carefully one more time and censored by a special office of the Ministry of Defence.

As is well known, the words "Ultra" and "Enigma" were not allowed to be used — or even hinted at — during World War II, and it was obligatory that the "Ultra" intelligence had to be supplied with a cover story, such as aerial reconnaissance, statements of war prisoners, or the like.

Since it often cannot be determined clearly enough from the files any more whether, for example, an aerial reconnaissance report actually came from that source or is in reality a bit of "Ultra" information in disguise, one can imagine the difficulties that will confront a historian doing research.

The secret documents involved in Operation "Ultra Secret" and the activities of the Secret Intelligence Service (SIS) during the North African campaign, from 1940-1943, are presently in the following archives:

1. Public Record Office, Kew, Richmond, Surrey TW9 4DU, England,
2. Cabinet Office, 70 Whitehall, London SW1A 2AS, England, and
3. Ministry of Defence, Savoy Hill House, Savoy Hill Strand, London WC2R 0BX, England.

The decoded "Enigma" radio messages have the file number DEFE/3 at the Public Record Office. The activities of the SIS cited in the text are taken from the following collections of files which are at the Cabinet Office and the Ministry of Defence:

AIR 40/2322, Minute of 4 February 1941
AIR 40/2323, p. 7
AIR 41/7, Photographic Reconnaissance, Vol. II, p. 105
AIR 41/44, pp. 82-83, 88
AIR 41/50, p. 141
ADM 223/75, Admry signals 1623/12 February 1941
ADM 223/102, Ultra signal 1803/22 July 1941
ADM 223/103, Ultra signal 0047/2 December 1941
ADM 223/103, Ultra Signal 1740/19 November 1941
CAB 44/94, p. 58
CAB 44/96, p. 105
CAB 44/100, pp. 19, 30, 33-38
CAB 44/104, p. 525
CAB 44/115, pp. 198-199
CAB 65/30 WM (42) 59 CA of 8 May 1942
CAB 80/20, COS (40) 820 (COS Resume, No.58)
CAB 80/26, COS (41) 124 (COS Resume, No.78)
CAB 105/3, No.28 of 2 April 1941
CAB 105/4, Hist (B), No.29 of 4 May 1941
CAB 105/16, No.81, January 1942
CAB 105/19, Hist (B) (Crusader) 5, No.31 of 17 September 1942
CAB 105/19, No.103 of 9 November 1942
CAB 105/33, No.343 of 11 May 1943
CAN 121/500, JIC (43) 3 (o) of 4 January 1943
CX/JQ 914
CX/MSS/1001/T 15
CX/MSS/1029/T 18
CX/MSS/1030/T 22
CX/MSS/1071/T 22
CX/MSS/1141/T 3
DEFE 3/573
MK 3641 of 22 May 1942
MK 7935 of 1 July 1942
ML 305 of 25 April 1943
QT 2091 of 24 September 1942
VM 8984 of 10 April 1943
WO 169/19, GS Int GHQ ME, Intelligence Summary of 23 October 1940
WO 169/19, WRMS of 13 January 1941

WO 169/19, WRMS of 17 February 1941
WO 169/19, WRMS of 17 March 1941
WO 169/53, HQ Western Desert Force, Intsums 83 of 24 September 1940
WO 169/1005 of 24 May 1942
WO 169/1010 of 28 November 1941
WO 169/1010 of 9 December 1941
WO 169/3936, 8 Army Intelligence Survey No.220 of 30 May 1942
WO 169/3936, No.231 of 10 June 1942
WO 169/3936, No.323 of 11 June 1942
WO 169/8519, 8 Army Intelligence Summary No.440 of 23 February 1943
WO 169/8519, No.445 of 3 March 1943
WO 169/8519, No.499 of 4 May 1943
WO 169/8519, No.503 of 8 May 1943
WO 190891, No.147 of 23 August 1940
WO 201/2150, GSI (S) GHO MEF, Captured Enemy Documents April 1942 — March 1943, German Wireless Intercept Organization, 30 July 1942
WO 201/2154. Nos. 251 to 255 of 6-10 July 1942
WO 201/2154, HQ Eight Army, Intelligence Summaries 255, 257, 258
WO 201/2154, No.288 of 12 August 1942
WO 201/2154, No.301 of 25 August 1942
WO 201/2155, No.330 of 2 October 1942
WO 201/2155, No.342 of 13 October 1942, Appendix A
WO 201/2155, No.343 of 19 October 1942
WO 201/2155, No.345 of 24 October (mistyped 25 October in original)
WO 204/978, AFHQ Daily Intelligence Summary No.102 of 17 February 1943
WO 208/2287, No.95 of 25 December 1942
WO 208/2914, War Office Periodical Notes on the German Army, No.30
WO 208/3573 of 20 April 1942
WO 208/3573 of 10 August 1942
WO 208/3581, No.I/215 of 29 March 1943
WO 208/3581, 18th Army Group Intelligence Summary I/309 of 21 April 1943

Abbreviations

B.P.	Bletchley Park
CBME	Combined Bureau Middle East
CIGS	Chief of the Imperial General Staff
C-in-C	Commander-in-Chief
CIU	Central Interpretation Unit
DDMI	Deputy Director Military Intelligence
GC & CS	Government Code and Cypher School
GOC	General Officer Commanding
GS Int	General Staff Intelligence
JIC	Joint Intelligence Sub-Committee (for the COS = Chiefs of Staff)
MI6	Military Intelligence 6 (Branch of the War Office)
MSOAFSO	Mobile Section of Army's Field Signal Organisation
OIC	Operational Intelligence Centre (Admiralty)
PR	Photographic Reconnaissance
PRU	Photographic Reconnaissance Unit
SCU/SLU	Special Communications Unit/Special Liaison Unit
SIM	Servizio Informazione Militari
SIS	Secret Intelligence Service
SLU	Special Liaison Unit
WRNS	Women's Royal Naval Service

Bibliography

Alexander of Tunis, *The Alexander Memoirs 1940-1945*, (Edited by John North), London 1961

Badoglio, P., *Italy in the Second World War*, London 1976

Bartimeus, *East of Malta, West of Suez*, New York 1944

Beesly, P., *Very Special Intelligence, Geheimdienstkrieg der britischen Admiralität 1939-1945*, Berlin 1978

Behrendt, H.O., *Rommels Kenntnis vom Feind im Afrikafeldzug*, Vol.25, Publ. by Militärgeschichtliches Forschungsamt, Freiburg 1980

Bell, E.L., *An Initial View of Ultra as an American Weapon*, New Hampshire 1977

Bertrand, G., *Enigma ou la plus grande énigme de la guerre 1939-1945*, Paris 1973

Blumenson, M., Will, "'Ultra' Rewrite History?", In: *Army*, August 1978, pp. 43-48

Burdick, Ch. B., *Unternehmen Sonnenblume, Der Entschluss zum Afrika-Feldzug*, Neckargemünd 1972 (= Die Wehrmacht im Kampf, Vol.48)

Butcher, H.C., *Three Years with Eisenhower*, London 1946

Bragadin, M., *The Italian Navy in World War II*, U.S. Naval Institute, 1957

Caccia-Dominioni, P., *Alamein, an Italian Story*, London 1969

Calvocoressi, P., "The Secrets of Enigma", In: *The Listener*, London 20-27/1/1977

Calvocoressi, P., *Top Secret Ultra*, London, 1980

Churchill, W.S., *Der Zweite Weltkrieg*, 5 Vol, Zürich 1949-1953

Clifford, A., *Three Against Rommel*, London 1943

Cocchia, A., *The Hunter and the Hunted*, London 1975

Clayton, A., *The Enemy is Listening - the Story of the Y Service*, London 1980

Connell, J., Auchinleck, *A Biography of Field Marshal Sir Claude Auchinleck*, London 1959

Connell, J., *Wavell*, London 1964

Cruickshank, Ch. G., *Deception in World War II*, London 1979

De Guingand, Major General Sir Francis, *Operation Victory*, London 1947

Deutsch, H.C., "The Historical Impact of Revealing the Ultra-Secret", In: *Parameters 8* (1978), No.4, pp. 2-15

Dixon, N.F., *On the Psychology of Military Incompetence*, London 1976

Gause, A., "Der Feldzug in Nordafrika im Jahre 1941/42/43", In: *Wehrwissenschaftliche Rundschau*, 1962, Vol.10, pp. 594-618, Vol.11, pp. 652-680, Vol.12, pp. 720-728

Goebbels, J., *Tagebücher 1942-1943*, Zürich, H.P. Lochner, 1948

Good, I.J., "Early Work on Computers at Bletchley", In: *National Physical Laboratory, Division of Computer Science, NPL Report Com Sci 82*, September 1976, 12 pp.

Halder, F., *Kriegstagebuch*, Vol.5, Stuttgart 1962-1964

Hart, B.H. Liddell, *The Rommel Papers*, London 1953

Haswell, J., *British Military Intelligence*, London 1973

Hinsley, F.H., Thomas, E.E., Ransom, C.F.G., Knight, R.C., *British Intelligence in the Second World War. Its Influence on Strategy and Operations*, Vol.1, London, H.M. Stationery Office 1979, Vol.II, London 1981

Howard, M., *The Mediterranean Strategy in the Second World War*, London 1968

Kesselring, A., *Soldat bis zur letzten Stunde*, Bonn 1953

"Kriegstagebuch des Oberkommandos der Wehrmacht (Wehrmachtführungsstab) 1940-1945", directed by Helmuth Greiner and Percy Ernst Schramm, for the Arbeitskreis für Wehrforschung, by Percy Ernst Schramm in collaboration with Hans-Adolf Jacobsen, Andreas Hillgruber & Walter Hubatsch, Vol.4, Frankfurt am Main 1961-1965

Lewin, R., *Entschied ULTRA den Krieg? Alliierte Funkaufklärung im 2. Weltkrieg*, Bonn 1981

Montagu, E., *Beyond Top Secret U.*, London 1977

Montgomery, B.L., *Memoiren*, München 1958

Nalder, R.F.H., *The History of British Army Signals in the Second World War*, London 1953

Norman, B., *Secret Warfare, The Battle of Codes and Ciphers*, Newton Abbot 1973

Paillole, P., *Services Speciaux 1935-1945*, Paris 1978

Potter, E.B., *Nimitz*, Annapolis, U.S. Naval Institite 1976

Piekalkiewicz, J., *Ju 52 im 2. Weltkrieg*, Stuttgart 1976

Piekalkiewicz, J., *8.8 Flak im Erdkampf-Einsatz*, Stuttgart 1976

Piekalkiewicz, J., *Luftkrieg 1939-1945*, München 1978

Piekalkiewicz, J., *Seekrieg 1939-1945*, München 1980

Piekalkiewicz, J., *Krieg der Panzer 1939 bis 1945*, München 1981

Playfair, Major-General I.S.O., *The Mediterranean and the Middle East*, Vol.III & IV, HMSO, London 1960

Praun, A., "Uber Klartext und Geheimschriften", In: *Wehrwissenschaftliche Rundschau 18* (1968), pp. 399-415

Randall, B., *The Colossus*, Paper presented at the International Research Conference on the History of Computing, Los Alamos Scientific Laboratory, Univ. of California, June 10-15, 1976

Rhoer, Edward von der, *Deadly Magic, A Personal Account of Communications Intelligence in World War II in the Pacific*, New York 1978

Rintelen, E. von, *Mussolini als Bundesgenosse, Erinnerungen des deutschen Militärattaches in Rom 1936-1943*, Tübingen 1951

Rohwer, J., "War 'Ultra' kriegsentscheidend?" In: *Marine-Rundschau 76* (1979), pp. 29-36

Rohwer, J., "Die alliierte Funkaufklärung und der Verlauf des Zweiten Weltkrieges", In: *Vierteljahreshefte für Zeitgeschichte 27* (1979), Vol.3, pp. 325-369

Rohwer, J. & Jäckel, E (ed.), *Die Funkaufklärung und ihre Rolle im 2. Weltkrieg*, Stuttgart 1979

Rommel, E., *Krieg ohne Hass,* Heidenheim 1950
Sambuy, V. di, "Un segreto svelato, In segreto 'Ultra'",
In: *Rivista Maritima 109* (1976), No.1, pp. 103-108
Santoni, A., *Il Vero Traditore,* Rome 1980
Spiller, R.J., "Some Implications of Ultra", In: *Military Affairs,* April 1976, pp. 49-54
Trenkle, F., *Die deutschen Funkpeil- und Horch-Verfahren bis 1945,* AEG-Telefunken AG, Ulm 1982
Ultra Secret, *The Ultra Documents,* 52,000 Messages, 104 reels of Microfilm, New York, Clearwater 1979
Walker, R., *Alam Halfa and Alamein, Historical Publications Branch,* New Zealand Department of Internal Affairs, 1967
Warlimont, W., "Die Entscheidung im Mittelmeer", In: *Entscheidungsschlachten des Weltkrieges,* ed. Hans Adolf Jacobsen & Jürgen Rohwer, Frankfurt am Main 1960
Welchmann, G., *The Hut Six Story,* London 1982
Winterbotham, F.W., *Secret and Personal,* London 1969
Winterbotham, F.W., *Aktion Ultra, Deutschlands Codemaschinen helfen den Alliierten siegen,* Berlin 1976
Woytak, R.A., "The Origins of the Ultra-Secret Code in Poland, 1937-1938", In: *The Polish Review,* New York, Vol.XXIII, 1978, No.3

Archives

Archivio Centrale dello Stato, Rome
Britannic Majesty's Stationery Office, London
Bundesarchiv, Koblenz
Cabinet Office, London
Institut für Zeitungsforschung, Dortmund
Ministry of Defence, London
National Archives, Washington D.C.
Public Record Office, London
State Maggiore dell'Aeronautica, Rome
Stato Maggiore della Marina, Rome
Weltkriegsbücherei, Stuttgart
Zentralbibliothek der Bundeswehr, Düsseldorf

Photo Sources

Bundesarchiv, Koblenz
E.C.P.A., Fort D'Ivry
Imperial War Museum, London
National Archives, Washington D.C.
U.S. Army, Washington D.C.
M.R. de Launay Archives, Paris
J.S. Middleton Archives, London
A. Stilles Archives, New York
K. Kirchner Archives, Erlangen
J.K. Piekalkiewicz Archives

A Word of Thanks

I would like to express my hearty thanks for their friendly assistance to:
Dr. A. Hofmann, Mr. Nilges, Mr. W. Held, Bundesarchiv, Koblenz
Oberstleutnant i.G. Dr. H. Rohde, Militärgeschichtliches Forschungsamt, Freiburg
Dr. M. Lindemann, Ms. H. Rajkovic, Institut für Zeitungsforschung, Dortmund
Prof. Dr. J. Rohwer, Mr. W. Haupt and their colleagues, Weltkriegsbücherei, Stuttgart
Dr. J. Sack and his colleagues, Zentralbibliothek der Bundeswehr, Düsseldorf
Mr. G. Weles, AEG-Telefunken, Ulm
Mr. H. Rehder, Berlin
Mr. K. Kirchner, Verlag D+C, Erlangen
Oberst (Bw) a.D. Dr. C.H. Hermann, Euskirchen
Mr. K. Lewitz, Rösrath
Lieutenant Colonel W.G.V. Kenney, British Embassy, Bonn
Mr. J.S. Lucas and his colleagues, Dept. of Photographs, Imperial War Museum, London
Mr. P.H. Reed, Dept. of Documents, Imperial War Museum, London
Mr. J. Westmancoat, The British Library Newspaper Library, London
Maj. R. Dembinski, Präses des Polski Institut im gen. Sikorskiego, London, and Capt. St. Zuarkowski
Mrs. J.C. North. Ministry of Defence, London
Mr. C. Smith, Cabinet Office, London
Mrs. J. Howard (GC&CS), London
Colonel W.D. Kasprowicz, London
Colonel Dr. M. Mlotek, London
Lt.Col. Dousset, Mr. G. Rolland (E.C.P.A.), Paris
Service Historique de l'Armee, Paris
Col. E. Ripamonti, Stato Maggiore dell'Aeronautica, Rome
Rear Admiral R. Fadda, Stato Maggiore della Marina, Rome
M.P. Mariana, Archivo Centrale dello Stato, Rome
Captain C.L. Blische, Dept. of the Army, U.S. Army Audio-Visual Activity, The Pentagon, Washington D.C.
Mr. W.H. Leary, National Archives, Washington D.C.
Colonel B.J. Morden, Center of Military History, Dept. of the Army, Washington D.C.
Mr. R. von Zabuesnig, Mr. F. Nellissen, Verlagsgruppe Langen-Müller/Herbig, München
Mr. H. Limmer, München

My special thanks to:

Dr. D. Bradley, Münster
Brigadier R.L. Walton, O.B.E., London
Colonel B.D. Samuelson, Washington D.C.

for their generous willingness to make their extensive knowledge available to me.

Schiffer Military History

Specializing in the German Military
of World War II

PANZERKORPS
Großdeutschland
•A PICTORIAL HISTORY•
HELMUTH SPAETER

Panzerkorps *Grossdeutschland* Helmuth Spaeter. The elite *GD* Panzerkorps and its divisions, *GD, Brandenburg, Führer Begleit,* and *Kurmark* are covered in this volume, including their formation and battle histories during World War II. An extensive listing of *Knight's Cross* winners rounds out this comprehensive pictorial.
Size: 7 3/4" x 10 1/2" 248 pp.
Over 500 photos, maps, documents, charts
ISBN: 0-88740-245-3 hard cover $24.95

Stuka-Pilot
HANS
ULRICH
RUDEL
HIS LIFE STORY
IN WORDS AND PHOTOGRAPHS

Stuka Pilot Hans-Ulrich Rudel Günther Just. Hans-Ulrich Rudel was the only soldier in World War II to receive the highest German decoration for bravery–the ***Golden Oak Leaves with Swords and Diamonds to the Knight's Cross.*** This book by one of his fellow officers covers his entire life's story in many never before published photographs and reminiscences by family members, friends, and those who flew with him.
Size: 8 1/2" x 11" Over 400 photos 280 pp.
ISBN: 0-88740-252-6 hard cover $29.95

THE HG
PANZER DIVISION
by
ALFRED OTTE
SCHIFFER MILITARY

The *HG* Panzer Division Alfred Otte. This panzer division was formed from the Luftwaffe and took the name of its commander-in-chief, Herman Göring. It was originally formed as a motorized police unit, however, it later became a panzer regiment and eventually expanded to divisional size. The *HG* Panzer Division fought in the African Campaign, the Italian Campaign, on the eastern and western fronts and in the final defense of Germany. This is their story.
Size: 7 3/4" x 10 1/2" 176 pp.
325 b/w photographs, maps, documents
ISBN: 0-88740-206-2 hard cover $24.95

GERMAN
MILITARY RIFLES
AND
MACHINE PISTOLS
1871-1945
Hans Dieter Götz

German Military Rifles and Machine Pistols 1871-1945 Hans Dieter Götz. This richly illustrated volume portrays the development of the modern German weapons and their ammunition, and includes many rare and experimental types. Among the weapons covered in this book are the Werder rifle, Mauser rifles, the various M/71 rifles and ammunition, the 88 cartridge, the Infantry Rifle 88, the 98 rifles, the Fallschirmjäger rifle, the 41 & 43 rifles, ERMA & Walther machine pistols and many more. Value guide included.
Size: 8 1/2" x 11" 248pp.
Many documents, drawings, and over 200 photos
ISBN: 0-88740-264-X hard cover $35.00

THE
WAFFEN-SS
A PICTORIAL DOCUMENTATION BY HERBERT WALTHER

The Waffen-SS Herbert Walther. This interesting pictorial and factual documentation presents the history of the Waffen-SS from their initial formation to the end of the war. Over 500 photographs, many taken in the heat of battle, show the Waffen-SS divisions on many fronts, in victory and in defeat. This book explains in words and pictures the development of the Waffen-SS and their place in modern history.
Size: 7 3/4" x 10 1/2" 240 pp.
500+ b/w photographs
ISBN: 0-88740-204-6 hard cover $24.95

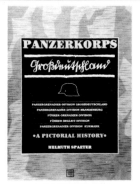